The Far Campaigning Soldier

GENERAL WILLIAM DYOTT

The Far Campaigning Soldier

A Personal Account of Military Service
from 1781-1813 in the West Indies, the
Egyptian Campaign and the Walcheren
Expedition During the Napoleonic Wars

William Dyott

LEONAUR

The Far Campaigning Soldier
A Personal Account of Military Service from 1781-1813 in the West Indies, the
Egyptian Campaign and the Walcheren Expedition During the Napoleonic Wars
by William Dyott

FIRST EDITION

Leonaur is an imprint
of Oakpast Ltd

ISBN: 978-1-78282-487-9 (hardcover)
ISBN: 978-1-78282-488-6 (softcover)

http://www.leonaur.com

Publisher's Notes

The views expressed in this book are not necessarily
those of the publisher.

Contents

Ye Diotts, in distress pledge not ye bowle.
For Favour, Fortune, Freeford fill the tankard full.'
Old Couplet.

Introduction

It has been said that the best form and method of historical representation is that which echoes the original voice. In the diary now for the first time made known to the world we almost hear, not the echo, but the original voice itself. History is a glass through which the past may be seen, but too often this is coloured by the bias of the historian, and the reader sees through the glass darkly. But contemporary writings are glasses of truth, and the reader may see things face to face. It is sometimes given to certain men of subordinate importance in their own day so to reveal themselves in their journals as to leave upon generations in after-years an impression of their personality, so vivid as to convince those who scan the page of the character and motives of the writers.

Of such was the immortal Samuel Pepys, whose remarkable diary of ten years extended from 1659 to 1669. Of such a character, too, was General William Dyott, who as a young man, in a probably thoughtless moment, began a journal, which he continued from 1781 to 1845, filling sixteen volumes of varying sizes, recording some thoughts, pleasures, accidents by flood and field, on almost every day for sixty-four of the most interesting years of English history.

The manor of Freeford, near Lichfield, Staffordshire, is of very considerable antiquity, being recorded in Domesday Book among the lands of the Bishop of Chester. The Dyott family have been connected with Freeford since 1553, and the family seat still remains in their hands. The main portion of the present house was built in 1734, and additions have been made in different directions during the last eighty years. In close connection with this estate were the adjoining lands of Fulfen, Fulfin, or Foofin, which are frequently mentioned in the general's diary, and passed into the possession of the Dyotts in the reign of Charles I.

It was during this reign that the Dyott family made themselves conspicuous owing to their loyalty to their sovereign. The Lord Paget of that day granted to them a commission to raise troops for Charles, which they did with the utmost zeal. Sir Richard Dyott, Knight, was one of the Privy Council to King Charles at York; and his sons all served the King. Anthony, a barrister by profession, was a major of foot in the royal army; the second son, Richard, was a captain of horse serving at Edgehill, and being obliged to fly from the country, only returned at the Restoration. Two other sons also served in the royalist cavalry, the youngest, Michael, being shot dead on the 16th March 1644. Above all, there was the famous Dumb Dyott, who killed Lord Brooke in his attack on Lichfield, and whose memory was kept fresh by annual dinners held to celebrate the famous resistance of that town to the parliamentary forces.

From the Restoration to the accession of George III. the Dyott family was not in any way distinguished. As far as can be ascertained they lived the usual lives of country squires and intermarried with the neighbouring county families.

William Dyott, afterwards general in the British Army, was born on the 17th April 1761. He was the second son of Richard Dyott of Freeford Hall, Staffordshire. When he was four years of age, together with his eldest brother and some of his sisters, he underwent the then very uncommon practice of inoculation for smallpox, in the house of Mr. Tom Levett at Lichfield. From the general's own account he must have been sent to school very young, for he could not have been much more than five years old when he first went to Clifford's school in Lichfield, where he remained for three years. At about the age of eight or nine he was moved to a school known as Price's, where he stayed until he was about twelve years old. For the next two years he was sent to the old Grammar School at Ashbourne, not far from the church, but he speaks of it in later life as 'such a school as fitted youth for no pursuit in life beyond a retail shop-board.' The last four years of his education were spent in Nottingham. From the time he was eighteen years of age he led an idle life, staying for the most part at Drakelow, the seat of an old family friend, Sir Nigel Gresley, and 'living upon the promises of great men.'

At last, however, the young man 'entered life,' as he called it, on the 20th February 1781, by which he meant that he went to London with the hope of getting a commission in the army. To assist him in this, he spent four months at Locke's Academy, near London, then a training-school for young officers. He was gazetted an ensign in the 4th regiment on the 14th March of that year, and in August went to Ireland to join his regiment. It was here that he had his first taste of military life, which seems to have been of a somewhat wild and idle character. There are frequent references to routs, dances, parties, dinners, and shooting expeditions with the colonel, but his military duties were nothing more than attending reviews or the flogging of deserters. And yet this was the period generally regarded as the darkest in English history. The War of American Independence was not yet concluded; the navies of the world were pitted against us, and Gibraltar had only just undergone its famous three years' siege.

On the 9th May 1782 William Dyott was promoted lieutenant, and was placed on half-pay in the following year. For sixteen months from October 1783, such was the curious military life of the period, Lieutenant Dyott spent his time between Freeford, Bath, and London. It was in the spring of 1784, as he afterwards recorded, that he 'saw the then Duchess of Devonshire, in a scarlet habit with a cap made of a fox's skin and the brush hanging down her Grace's back, canvassing for the celebrated Charles Fox' in the ever-famous Westminster election. In the following December he once more embarked for Ireland to rejoin the 4th regiment, for which he had the greatest affection. In the summer of 1785 he was moved to Cork, where he passed a gay and happy twelve months. His military duties were extremely light, though he was now adjutant of his regiment, and except for a few marches and the capture and trial of Whiteboys, he had nothing to do but, to use his own words, 'have a joyous time.'

Once again Dyott obtained leave of absence for three months, but on his return to Freeford he found his father lying senseless from a paralytic stroke. The old man passed away on the 2nd January 1787, much to the grief of his children. He was buried, according to the ancient rites of the Dyott family, at half-past nine at night, by torchlight, in St. Mary's Church, Lichfield. In the following April Dyott rejoined his regiment in Ireland, but his residence there was not to last for long.

Although England was at peace for the time being, troops were needed to garrison the outlying parts of the empire, and Dyott with his regiment was despatched in June 1787 to Nova Scotia, where he had his first experience of foreign service. It was when quartered here that he made the acquaintance of Prince William, afterwards King William IV., who was then commanding the *Andromeda* upon that

11

station. During the prince's visit the two young men became bosom friends and indulged in numerous practical jokes at the expense of their acquaintances. One of the most delightful records, as it is so unconsciously innocent, is the note at the end of the description of a dinner at which the prince had been. Dyott writes:

There were just 20 dined, and we drank 63 bottles of wine.

The description of Nova Scotia and the social life at that period is of considerable interest to all who wish to study the early story of that portion of the British Empire. Dyott has also sketched the military life of the day with a clear and impartial hand. He wrote, as he himself once said, either for his own amusement in his old age, or, should he ever have any, for the amusement of his children.

William Dyott was promoted captain on the 25th April 1793, and in the June of that year returned to England to take up the post of *aide-de-camp* to Major-General Hotham, commanding the Plymouth district. The news that had reached Nova Scotia had pointed to peace, so that Dyott was much surprised when he landed in England to find the whole country in a state of excitement and preparation for a war, which it was little thought would last, except for a brief period, for nearly twenty-two years. In anticipation of this colossal struggle, first against the mistaken principles of revolutionary France, and then to save Europe from the domination of the superhuman Napoleon, all Englishmen were training arms.

Dyott immediately went to Plymouth, where he drilled Lord Uxbridge's regiment, and his lordship obtained for him the position of major of brigade. These arduous military duties did not prevent him visiting Freeford and going with Lord Granville Leveson-Gower to the Lichfield races. In May 1794 he went to London to see about his majority in the 103rd regiment, and during his stay in the capital he attended the hearing of Lord Cornwallis's evidence for Warren Hastings, of whom, he says, 'surely never was a more persecuted man.' In this Dyott was perfectly correct, for Hastings had been impeached as early as 1788 and was not fully acquitted until 1795.

Dyott's promotion was now rapid, for in June 1795 he was appointed, by means of his friend Lord George Lennox, brigade major-general, and in the beginning of August he received his rank of lieutenant-colonel. In September he had to take leave of all his friends in Plymouth, and joined the 28th regiment to go on foreign service. He, however, effected his exchange into the 25th regiment and embarked at Portsmouth in November for the West Indies. The whole fleet, under the command of Admiral Christian, was driven back by what is known as Christian's storm. Many lives were lost off Portland, but Dyott's ship escaped. Having started again on the 9th December, Dyott writes that they were at sea four weeks, but owing to the south-west wind were really only four days' sail from England. On the 27th January 1796 they crossed the line, and Dyott records very vividly the old custom of the visit of Neptune. At last, on the 11th February, having been at sea for two months, they reached the island of Barbadoes, which is fully described in the diary.

A very serious negro rising had, about this time, taken place in Grenada. The negroes had been roused by the teaching of the French revolutionists, and Robespierre had sent Victor Hugues to circulate the doctrines of Liberty, Equality, and Fraternity. Sir Ralph Abercromby was at the head of an expedition to suppress the revolt, and Dyott with his regiment was sent to take part. He gives a very full account of the island, but, above all, of his first introduction to real fighting. He was in command of his regiment and saw some serious work, much of which was hand to hand. He paints a terrible picture of the sufferings of the British soldier at that time, and the carelessness of the government, he says:

> The army was suffering in a most shameful manner for the want of numerable articles in which it stood much in need. Neither wine nor medicine for the sick, and not a comfort of any one kind for the good duty soldier. Salt pork, without either peas or rice, for a considerable time, and for three days nothing but hard, dry, bad biscuit for the whole army, officers and men. Two days without (the soldiers' grand comfort) grog.

Dyott left Grenada in July, landed at Plymouth in October, and visited London, Freeford, and Keel. He returned to Plymouth in 1797, where he witnessed a naval mutiny similar to the more celebrated insurrections at Spithead and the Nore, he writes:

> The horrid business was only settled by means of great concessions on the part of the government.

The naval mutinies were but one of the many difficulties against which William Pitt had to contend. A large section of the Irish people had for some time been conspiring against England, and open rebellion devastated the country in the early part of the year 1798. In June

Dyott, with the Lancashire militia, was ordered to be ready to go to Ireland at a moment's notice. This duty, however, he was not called upon to fulfil, as the rebellion was crushed on the 21st June by the energy of General Lake at Vinegar Hill.

From July to December 1798 Dyott was quartered in Jersey, but just before Christmas he paid a visit to Sir Hew Dalrymple's regiments in Guernsey, and from there returned to Freeford. The spring of 1799 found Dyott once more actively employed, and in March, on the recommendation of the Duke of York, he was appointed assistant adjutant-general to the troops in the south-western district under the orders of Sir William Pitt. Dyott offered himself in June for service abroad, 'and received a very flattering answer' from the commander-in-chief. He was ordered to join Sir Ralph Abercromby, but did not do so in the end, and so escaped the disasters that happened to the 25th regiment in the famous expedition to the Helder.

The year 1800 opened with more honours for Dyott, for on the 4th January he was promoted full colonel. In June, at a review at Windsor, the old King George III. complimented him on the fine appearance of his regiment, and this probably led to his appointment as *aide-de-camp* to the king late in the following year. In February 1801 George III. showed symptoms of his old complaint, and Dyott records this, saying, as was the common talk of the day, that it was caused by Pitt's refusal to agree with the king. The disagreement on the question of Roman Catholic Emancipation led to Pitt's retirement on the 14th March.

Meantime, while the war continued unabated, and great matters of state were causing ministers to fall and a king to go mad, Dyott cared for none of these things, paying long visits to Sir Nigel Gresley 'for the sake of his dear daughter Maria.' But this love-passage was to be cut short, for on the 21st May, Dyott, with the 25th regiment, embarked at Portsmouth for Egypt. The troops were to reinforce the British army previously despatched under Sir Ralph Abercromby, to drive out the French left there by Napoleon. On the 21st March, the French Army was defeated at the Battle of Alexandria by Sir Ralph, who was mortally wounded on the field.

The force with which Dyott had sailed called at Gibraltar and Malta (of which he gives a full and interesting account), and reached Aboukir Bay on the 9th July. The regiments found that they were to be under the supreme command of General Hutchinson. Dyott records all that happened at Alexandria, and how he commanded his

14

troops in the action of the 22nd August, which led, first, to the capitulation of that city under Menou, and, finally, in September, to the French evacuation of Egypt. A month later Dyott reached Gibraltar, whence he toured about in the surrounding country and saw a great deal of Spain and the Spaniards.

The Treaty of Amiens having been signed on the 25th March 1802, there was no immediate evidence of a renewal of the great struggle. It was not likely, however, that peace would last for long, as Napoleon's restless ambition menaced the ascendency of Great Britain. Nevertheless many Englishmen took the opportunity of going abroad, and Dyott, therefore, left Gibraltar in June with the idea of seeing something of the Continent, and making his way home overland. He visited the Balearic Islands, Corsica, and landed at Leghorn. He then describes all that he saw on his journey through Italy and France, giving full information about the manufactures, theatres, *cafés*, etc., of Leghorn, Piza, Florence, Modena, Parma, Milan, Turin, Chambery, and Lyons. On the 25th July he landed in England and paid numerous visits. Between the 5th and 28th of August he was at Highfield, Richmond, London, Freeford, Seal, Ashbourne, Leicester, Nottingham, Sheffield, York, Leeds, Doncaster, and Scarborough. From this time until September 1803 he spent his time going backwards and forwards from Freeford to London and other places.

The war had now broken out again after Lord Whitworth's stormy interview with Napoleon on the 13th March, the rupture being finally completed on the 12th May. Dyott was therefore forced to take up his military duties once more, and on the 3rd September was appointed brigadier-general on the Irish staff, with headquarters in Dublin. He resided here for nearly eleven months, when he was suddenly recalled to take up his post as *aide-de-camp* to the king at Windsor in August 1804. His duties were of the very lightest kind. On one occasion he accompanied the royal family to Weymouth, and they all went sailing in the king's yacht, including, as he somewhat disrespectfully remarks, 'the queen and females.' The rest of his time was taken up by attending members of the royal party to the theatre, or playing cards with the queen and princesses.

It is astonishing to notice that when England was so full of the possible invasion by Napoleon from Boulogne, Dyott passes it over so briefly. Once and once only does he hint at this danger when he writes of 'a report of the enemy's fleet being off the coast,' but he notes later that 'it was a false alarm.' In just the same way the great battle of

Trafalgar, with all its important results, does not seem to have interested the diarist, for he does not write a single word concerning Nelson's magnificent victory. The diary records rather the writer's own marriage with Miss Eleanor Thompson, and between 1806 and 1808 he tells of his married life, the birth of his children, and his command of troops in Sussex.

The quiet life in Sussex, at Hollington Lodge, near Hastings, and the occasional happy visits to Windsor and Freeford, suddenly ceased, when orders came on the 6th December 1808 to join Sir John Moore in Spain, where the Peninsular War was now being waged. On the 8th January 1809 Dyott embarked for his new service, but before he could land in Spain news arrived that Sir John Moore had been killed in the hour of victory at Corunna. The general was therefore ordered to return to England, which he reached at the beginning of the next month.

Dyott's home was now broken up at Hollington Lodge, and he moved to Winchester, where he was no sooner settled than, in July, he was appointed to take command of a brigade, consisting of the 6th, 50th, and 91st regiments, in the ever-famous but disastrous Walcheren Expedition. The armament sailed from the Downs on the 28th July. The whole thing was an enormous blunder; there was an utter neglect of medical and sanitary precautions, when these ought to have been especially the care of the government, as Walcheren was notoriously unhealthy in the winter months. The fleet was under the command of Sir Richard Strachan, while the army was led by the incompetent second Earl of Chatham, who owed his position to royal favour.

Lord Castlereagh must also be blamed for the delays, and for the foolhardy choice of leaders. The objects of the expedition were to destroy the enemy's fleet and arsenals at Flushing, Antwerp, and Terneuze, to reduce the island of Walcheren, and, finally, to render the Scheldt no longer navigable for ships of war. Dyott's brigade was attached to the Marquis of Huntly's division, which occupied the island of South Beveland. In August Flushing surrendered to Chatham, but at the end of that month, having advanced his headquarters to Bath, he found that further advance was impossible, and recommended the Government to recall the expedition, leaving 15,000 men to defend Walcheren. Owing to the return of many of the senior officers, Dyott acted as second in command in South Beveland from September to October. The garrison suffered very severely, the general recording that nearly 9000 men were sick at one time. Eventually, on the 24th December, Walcheren was abandoned, the destruction of Flushing being the sole result of the expedition. Meantime, on the 1st November, General Dyott landed at Harwich, delivered his despatches, and never again went on active service.

The general's life now took upon itself a different character. Although he remained in the army, he became much more interested in agricultural pursuits and politics, and it is from this moment that he shows himself to have been a Tory of the old school. In July 1810 he was appointed on the home staff with headquarters at Lichfield, which post he held until his promotion to the rank of lieutenant-general three years later. In the autumn of 1810 the general was much disturbed by the calamity that fell upon the royal house. George III.'s intellect was finally upset by the death of his youngest and favourite child, Princess Amelia, and the result was that in the following year the chief business before Parliament was the Regency Bill by which the Prince of Wales became Prince Regent.

At the end of 1811 the general had very unpleasant work to do. By this time the effects of the war and of the industrial revolution were beginning to be apparent, and the lower classes launched upon those disastrous methods of making their existence known to a world that had up to then ignored them. The Luddite riots, named from a half-mad boy, Ned Lud, broke out in different parts of the country. The wrecking of machines became very common, and rick-burning and other excesses necessitated stern measures on the part of the government. It was natural at that period to connect all disorderly movements with revolutionary designs, and Lord Sidmouth increased the powers of the magistrates to punish rioters.

The organised conspiracy to break machines spread rapidly from Nottingham into the adjacent counties of Derby, Leicester, York, and Lancaster. General Dyott was ordered to check the riots at Nottingham, and he had with him the 15th dragoons and the Berkshire militia. The appearance of this strong military force quietened those districts for the time being, but the seed of discontent had been sown, and the General lived to witness other serious trouble of a similar kind.

From 1813 to 1817 Dyott's life was darkened by a domestic tragedy. His wife became an invalid, and while in a very delicate state of health fell in love with a man called Dunne, with whom she eloped. With all the difficulty of that period the general at last obtained an Act of Parliament divorcing his wife, and he never saw or heard of her again until she died in 1841. The book you are now holding, of course, excludes Dyott's later diary entries and focuses entirely on the period of his military career.

Colonel Dick Dyott has preserved a few notes that record the last years of his beloved father's life. On Sunday 6th April the old man was taken suddenly ill while sitting at breakfast. During the summer of 1845 his splendid constitution helped him, and he seemed to rally. He enjoyed a little exercise in a carriage, on foot, or even on his pony, and wherever he went it is recorded that his labourers welcomed him with delight. In March, June, September, and November 1846 the general had further seizures, but the plucky old soldier insisted on making sufficient effort to go to church. Christmas Day was a very happy one, as Colonel Dyott says, 'rendered so by the manner in which my dear father enjoyed himself.' In January 1847 the wonderful old man suffered a good deal from influenza, but shook it off with surprising constitutional strength.

On Friday 7th May, however, the end came. Colonel Dyott says:

> The two Morgans, his faithful attendant Florendine, and his three children whom he had loved, God only knows how dearly, were round his bed. There was no struggle, scarce an effort, and at ten minutes before one o'clock the spirit departed to the God who gave it.

It is perhaps worthy of record that the old general was buried in precise accordance with the ancient custom of the Dyott family. The funeral took place on the 14th May. The procession was formed at nine o'clock at night, so as to reach St. Mary's Church, Lichfield, at ten o'clock. First a carriage, then the hearse drawn by four horses; next followed a mourning-coach and pair, his own carriage closed the funeral *cortège*. Six of the eldest labourers bore the coffin of their beloved and honoured master; six other labourers carried the flaming torches together with two of the bearers.

A large concourse met the procession at the lodge and attended it to Lichfield, where the streets were densely crowded. St. Mary's Church, so it is recorded was:

> Filled with people of respectability, who manifested by their dress and demeanour the high respect and esteem in which they held the character of the departed.

So General Dyott passed to the tomb of his ancestors, leaving for future generations a journal of his doings, which from some aspects may be regarded as unique.

Dyott's Diary 1781–1813

The Diary of General William Dyott

Journal,—no, it is not a journal; well, what you please, Mr. William.

I entered life on the 20th day of February 1781, that is, I entered London in hopes of getting a commission in the army, after having been at home leading an idle life for the space of three years, and in truth living upon the promises of great men.

At last the Fates decreed me to be a soldier, for my worthy friend Lord Paget, (born 1744, created Earl of Uxbridge 1784; died 1812), as he has since proved, offered to my dear brother to get me a commission; accordingly when his Lordship got to London, and my dear brother having spoken to him. Master Billy was ordered to town.

A mighty fuss he made at setting out, and a terrible fright he was in going up; having taken a place in the stage, he got a most woeful overturn, which was rather an unlucky starting, but being arrived in town, and a very devil of a place I thought that said London, I waited on Lord Paget, who introduced me to Lord Jeffrey Amherst, (1717–97; knighted 1761; created Baron Amherst 1776; field-marshal 1796), and the latter recommended me to go to Locke's Academy near London, where I stayed four months, and spent my time very pleasantly, and though I should not boast of my character, I believe I left that place with as good a one as any member ever did.

When I left the academy I came into the country, and spent a month very agreeably at Freeford. On the 5th of August 1781 I left Lichfield about two o'clock in the afternoon in company with a Mrs. Cox, a person whom I knew at Chelsea. She, instead of being all that was entertaining, was in truth quite the reverse, for she did nothing but tire me with the gallant behaviour of her dear husband, showed me his picture, and said he was the handsomest man in Europe. So much for this most blushing of her sex; for I am quite in a fever when

I think of her.

We dined at Wolsey Bridge, from there to Newcastle. I wrote to Sir Nigel Gresley, (of Drakelow, co. Derby, succeeded his brother, Sir Thomas, in 1753; died 1787), where we waited some time for a chaise, and when it did arrive it was fit scarce to get into, for we only ventured ourselves in it as far as Folk-on-the Hill, where we beheld a spectacle much too horrible for me to relate, occasioned by a waggon of gunpowder blowing up, which killed the waggoner and set fire to five houses, which were burning when we left there.

From thence we went to Northwick, where, thanks to the commissioner of the roads, we parted, she to the right to Liverpool, I to Chester; this was about two o'clock in the morning.

When I had travelled about an hour I was awakened by the chaise stopping, when the post-boy did me the satisfaction of telling me he was lost, for which I made him a low bow and then kicked him.

It was in the middle of an immense forest, and not near light. We stood gazing about for an hour, and at last descried a house at a good distance from us, which we made for, but in our way there we were so unlucky as to get the chaise overturned, but by a little hard work we got it up again. When we got to the house the man told us we were about four miles from the road, but that he would take us a short cut through his grounds. I asked the man where we were lost, he said in the forest of Charnley.

I think if we had not seen his house there was not another within five miles of the place. I asked him what house it was, he said, 'Did you never hear of the Lawless House?' (a house very similar to this was in the Cotswolds, Rev. W. H. Hutton, *Burford Papers*), to which I replied in the negative. He said that house was not within any parish, did not pay any rates or levies, and that gentlemen that had the misfortune to have an intrigue with any lady, by which they became in an unlucky situation, always sent them there to rid themselves of their burden.

I asked him how many he had in the house, he said six, but would not tell me where they came from. He himself lived in a small house with his wife and daughters, and the ladies lived in a large house close to it. He said he did not keep any maid-servants, for fear they might tell; but that his daughters waited on the ladies that had not servants of their own. So that upon the whole I think I rather gained than lost by my mishap.

After I had parted from my lawless friend, I went on very well to Chester, where I arrived about five o'clock in the morning. Found that the coach to Holyhead set out at seven, but was full, so what to do I did not know, but the book-keeper informed me that if I got leave from the passengers he had no objection to carry five. Upon which I immediately applied to the passengers with my Meilleur address, and got leave. I wrote to Mrs. Lane and set forward about seven.

We landed at the Watch House on the quay about one o'clock on Thursday, the 9th of August.

When we got to Dublin, Mr. Tighe was so obliging to invite me to supper with him at some young lady's in Dublin, but I had promised to sup or at least to spend the evening with my brother-officer, so Mr. Tighe set me down at the hotel and we parted.

I don't recollect ever meeting with so much civility from anybody in my life, especially a stranger, as I did from this most agreeable man; and of which I hope I shall ever retain a grateful remembrance.

When I got to the hotel I found my messmate was gone to the Rotunda, as he mentioned in the morning. Accordingly I set out after him, found it a humble imitation of the London Ranelagh. There was a good deal of company of divers sorts. There is a large garden like the garden at Ranelagh, only I think larger, which is illuminated, and horns and clarinets. There is also a large and good band of music in the Rotunda, which is a good room, but not nearly so large as the English Ranelagh. I stayed there till about twelve, then went home and to bed.

Monday, Sept. 8.—At home. Received a letter from Sir William Montgomery to say I had a pair of breeches at his office. I find myself at a loss for want of a few more books, as there is not such a thing as a library in this place of Armagh. There is no believing the people of this nation, for they seldom or ever tell the truth, and never give you 1781 a direct answer. We get plenty of recruits, but they desert as fast almost as we get them, and they are never to be heard of afterwards. In short, I think them calculated merely to eat potatoes, or '*pratys*,' as they call them, though, by the bye, if they were totally abolished the country (the *pratys*, I mean), I think it would be of service, for it makes them so very idle.

A fellow perhaps gets a small piece of land for a mere trifle, which he sets with potatoes, that serves him all the year. He works at his loom by chance two days in the week, which is sufficient to pay for his ground and to buy a little milk to his potatoes. As for fuel, they burn nothing but peat, that they get for little or no money. Then they have another thing which they call whisky. It is distilled from malt, and is very cheap and devilish strong, so they get most beastly drunk for twopence. But I must not let the Irish know of my opinion of them, for the people I visit behave in the most polite way. I am only speaking of the 'musty' part of them, as Shakespeare in some of his plays calls the peasant or labourer.

Friday.—At home. Lord Charlemont, (James Caulfield, fourth Viscount and first Earl of Charlemont (1728-99), Irish statesman; created Earl of Charlemont 1763; associate of Henry Grattan and Henry Flood), arrived here, the reviewing general of the Irish volunteers. They made great rejoicings for him, bonfires, illuminations, etc. At night I received a letter from Daniel, with two letters enclosed, the one to Mr. Thornton of this place, the other to a Mr. Olpherts, but unluckily for me they are not either of them in town. I likewise received letters from Freeford.

Monday, June 9.—Marched from Armagh at five o'clock, of all the days I ever saw it was the worst. It rained the whole way from Armagh to Monaghan, as hard as I ever saw it. The road from Armagh to Monaghan very pretty; two or three gentlemen's houses as beautiful as anything I have seen in Ireland. We marched from Monaghan at five o'clock on Tuesday. There are some pretty houses between Armagh and Monaghan. First, Mr. Alexander's on the right five miles from Armagh, situated upon a most beautiful hill, with a very fine river running through some charming meadows below.

Next upon the left three miles further is a seat of a Mr. Leslie's, at a place called Glasslough. There is a very fine lake, and a fine hanging wood. From Monaghan we marched to Clones; rather a better day. A very fine country, but nothing remarkable to be seen.

Clones is situated upon a hill; there is a straight road of a mile long, before you come up to the town. The church is ancient; near it is an old fabrication or rather redoubt of earth; but it is not at all regular. From Clones we marched six o'clock on Wednesday; rain again, but the day proved pretty favourable. On our way we passed a pretty house belonging to a Mr. Roper (uncle to Major Roper). We breakfasted at a place called Red Hill; here is a good old house belonging to a Mr. White; nothing very particular.

We then came to a most beautiful place called Balleyhayes, belonging to a Mr. Newburgh. It is situated near a fine river with plenty of wood and a good verdure. From thence to Cavan; we saw at a distance as we came pretty near Cavan a fine-looking place belonging to a Lord Farnham, at Farnham,(Barry Maxwell, third Baron Farnham, and Earl Farnham 1785; died 1800). Captain Gouldney joined us at Cavan.

Sunday.—We all dined with Lord Granard, (George Forbes, sixth Earl of Granard in peerage of Ireland, and first Baron Granard in the United Kingdom (1760-1837); lieutenant-general 1813), at a place called Forbes Castle near Longford. He was lately a captain in the 68th regiment. His Lordship is very young, and I think not very wise. His house is very small, very bad, and very ill situated. He was vastly civil, gave us champagne, burgundy, etc., and a most excellent dinner.

From Longford we marched on Monday to Roscommon, which is fourteen miles, rather a barren country. Roscommon is but small, the only good building is the Town House; near the town is a very ancient and fine old ruin, reckoned one of the largest in Ireland; it belongs to the Ranelagh family. The castle (for so it is called) seems to have been a square with round towers at each angle.

On Tuesday morning we marched from Roscommon, as bad a morn it was as ever man beheld, to Moylough; on our way we breakfasted at a place called Mount Talbot. The village is very small; close to it is a very pretty house, etc., belonging to a Mr. Talbot, but the day was so bad and our stay was but short, so that I did not go to see it. From thence we went on to Moylough, which is eighteen miles from Roscommon, quite a village; our men were obliged to be quartered all round the country.

We left Moylough at three o'clock on Wednesday morn for Galway, where we arrived about two, after a march of twenty-four miles over a country that beggars all description.

The town of Galway is a pretty good size, very old, and the streets but narrow. There are three barracks, called the Shamble, the Lombard, and the Castle Barracks; there is a pleasant walk called the Quay, and close to a very fine river, which runs into the sea at the end of the Quay. I was Thursday and Friday settling myself, did not get into the barracks till Saturday.

Friday.—I was confined to my room all day with the damned influenza, better on Saturday. The colonel and corps received an address of thanks from the mayor and inhabitants of Galway for our great activity at the late fire.

Wednesday, Oct. 23.—The commander-in-chief arrived, (Sir John

Burgoyne—1722-92; capitulated at Saratoga 1777; commander-in-chief in Ireland 1782; wrote plays, including the *Heiress*).

He had a cap. guard from the regiment, and the two corps of volunteers lined the streets for him. We dined with him the day he arrived. His suite consisted of Adj.-General Major Bowyer, Quarter-Master Colonel Dundass, two *aides-de-camps*; Captain Stanley, and Captain Winford, and a Colonel something. After dinner we all went to the drum; the general and his suite did not stay long. The next morning he inspected the regiment at ten o'clock, and set forward for Cork immediately. He was invited by a corps of volunteers to dine with them the day he left town, but would not stay. We were likewise all invited, and all got pretty drunk.

Friday, Oct. 25.—At home. The commander-in-chief seems a very well-bred man, he was perfectly civil to us, and he is as fine an old soldier as ever I saw. He made a present of twenty guineas amongst the non-commissioned officers and privates.

Thursday, Dec. 26.—Went with Mrs. Tomlisson to Castlefane. Friday, Saturday, and Sunday there. Was sent for on Sunday evening by express, as the regiment was going to march to Cork to attend the execution of deserters. I left Castlefane about eleven o'clock on Sunday evening, got to Limerick about three in the morning. We marched about four; the first day twenty Irish miles to a small town called Charleville. I walked the whole way, and was completely tired.

Tuesday.—We marched fourteen miles to Mallow, a famous water-drinking place; the town is very small.

Wednesday.—Being New Year's Day, we marched fourteen miles to Cork. Got in about three o'clock, dined all together at Scott's Tavern, which by the bye is the best I have met with in Ireland. Cork is a very large and populous city; the merchants carry on an amazing victualling trade, and the stores in the place are most wonderful.

Friday.—We all dined with the 32nd regiment, who were in Cork. Got very drunk.

Saturday.—We dined with the 11th regiment, who were also in the garrison of Cork; and also got very drunk.

Monday.—Was the execution, which was the most melancholy piece of business I ever was a spectator of. There was only one out of the four that were sentenced, that suffered. After the poor unfortunate wretch had suffered death, the other three were brought forth, and to describe their countenances is not in the power of a pen to give the smallest idea: they were pardoned on condition of their serving abroad during life, and receiving five hundred lashes, which they gladly embraced.

Tuesday, Jan. 4.—The two prisoners received a part of their punishment, but were not able to stand the whole.

Wednesday.—We marched from Cork, and arrived at Limerick on Friday. I walked the whole way. I was very happy to come again to my old quarters.

Sunday, Feb. 23.—Morning packing up, paid visits and dined with T. Grady, S. Grady, and mess at Knight's. In the evening went to take my last leave of my dear Susey. The parting was as dismal as I ever experienced, but true lovers must part sometimes. I stayed at Mrs. Ross's till two o'clock; and on Monday the 24th February we marched about eleven o'clock from that dear place Limerick, a town that I shall ever hold in my highest esteem, and where I received more civility than ever I experienced.

It is without doubt the best quarter in the world. I was told by several people that there never was more real grief shown by the inhabitants of Limerick to a regiment leaving it than to ours. The concourse of people in the streets as we marched through was immense. We arrived about three o'clock at a small town called Newport, nine miles from Limerick. Tom and Hardy Grady accompanied us to that place, but we were not at all in spirits.

Tuesday.—We parted with my friends the Gradys; we marched to Nenagh, a small neat town, the 16th Dragoons were quartered there.

From thence we marched through the finest country I had seen in Ireland to a very pretty town called Birr; at the upper end of the great street is a very handsome pedestrian statue of the Duke of Cumberland. We halted at Birr on Thursday.

Friday.—We marched from Birr to a small town called Cloghan; there is a horse barracks with one troop of the 2nd horse; and Brown a cornet who was at Locke's. We left one company there, and proceeded two miles on to a little dirty place called Ferbane. We marched on Saturday morning through a nasty boggy country to Athlone, through which the Shannon runs, but has a most excellent horse barracks. Four troops of the 2nd horse were there. There are some pretty walks near the town, which was a place of some strength in the Rebellion. The Royal army forded the Shannon here, and took possession of the town.

Sunday.—We halted, and dined with the 2nd Horse, who have a very genteel mess; we all got very drunk.

Monday.—Morning, we marched ten miles to a dirty town called Ballymahon, a most wretched inn.

Thence we marched on Tuesday sixteen miles to Granard, which place we passed on our march from Armagh to Galway. From Granard the same road to Cavan, where we halted on Thursday.

Friday.—Thirteen miles to a place called M'Guire's Bridge, at which place there is the best inn we have met with from the time we left Limerick. We marched the next morning only seven miles to our quarters, which was Saturday, March 8th.

The town gives title to Lord Viscount Enniskillen, (William Willoughby, second baron; who was created Viscount Enniskillen 1776, and Earl of Enniskillen 1789; died 1803), who has a house not far from it. I believe there never was such a place to be headquarters of a regiment. The town is situated in an island in Loch Erne. It is very ill built, scarce a house but what is thatched; there is the remains of an old castle, but nothing worth notice.

Sunday.—We dined with Lieutenant-General Earl Ross (?). He lives at a place called Belle Isle. It is one of the islands in the Lake Erne. A most beautiful place, and his Lordship lives in a very elegant style. We have had more fine weather, (April), since the regiment arrived at Enniskillen than I have seen in Ireland.

Sunday, Oct. 26.—I left the King's Own, a corps I ever shall revere. Got to Dublin on Tuesday, did not sail till Friday. Arrived at the Head, Sunday evening, after a tedious passage of forty hours. Came in the coach to Chester, and from that in another coach to the 'Welsh Harp.' Took a chaise there and got to Freeford on Wednesday evening the 5th of November. November The next morning my brother Richard was married to Miss Mary Astley, daughter to my uncle Christopher Astley of Tamhorne, parish of Whittington.

March 1784.—Remained at Freeford and about that country till March, when I went with Swinfen to London; stayed there only two nights, and went down to Bath and stayed there two months. I spent my time as pleasantly as I ever did in my life; my good fellow-traveller Swinfen made me a present of £50, which kept me in a great style.

We returned to London, and I had the misfortune to have my portmanteau cut off from behind Swinfen's chaise. Remained in London two nights and returned into the country the latter end of May.

Found my father had left Freeford. I got into the King's Own regiment again the 26th December 1784, and embarked at Liverpool to join the regiment the 30th March.

Was two days at sea in the most filthy packet possible. Had the pleasure to join the old 4th once more on the 3rd day of April as Lieutenant and Adjutant in the barracks of Dublin, which are most magnificent. Found the regiment greatly improved. The regiments in garrison, the 4th, 6th, 15th, 26th, 48th, and 65th. Some very pleasant men. Colonel Ogilvie commanded the garrison. I had the honour of being admitted a member of the Blue and Orange Society.

May.—I remained in Dublin till the 23rd May. The May regiment was reviewed on the 9th May by Major-General Henry Lawes Luttrell, (second Earl of Carhampton—1743-1821; entered the army 1757; major-general 1782; succeeded his father 1787).

On the 18th the whole garrison by Lieutenant-General Pitt, commander-in-chief, (Sir William Augustus Pitt—1728-1809; entered the army 1744; commander-in-chief in Ireland 1784; governor of Portsmouth 1794-1809), and on the 20th by his Grace the Lord-Lieutenant, (Charles Manners, fourth Duke of Rutland (1754-87); succeeded to the dukedom 1779; lord-lieutenant of Ireland 1784).

Dublin is a very pleasant quarter, but as adjutant a good deal of duty. The parade of the Guards is very fine, they mount near two hundred men a day. A captain and fifty-six men, two subs, and colours at the castle for the Lord-Lieutenant. The regiment left Dublin on Monday the 23rd May for Cork. Marched by the way of Rathcoole, Kilcullen, Carlow, Kilkenny, Callan, Cloghan, Kilworth, and arrived in Cork on Monday the 23rd. We passed through a fine country in general, but found the accommodation in some places very bad.

The 20th regiment were in garrison with us in Cork. Our chief business, I think, when first we went to Cork, was eating strawberries. I never saw greater quantities, and very fine. Fish very good; nothing to drink, no water in the town, the men in the barracks were obliged to pay for the water they drank and used for washing after; the rate of a penny a man per week. The beer, the very worst I ever tasted.

We had remarkable hot weather for some time after our arrival in Cork. There are some very beautiful rides about town, and some pretty places on each side the river that runs from town to Cove, which is eight miles. Cove is an island of about seven miles in circumference. You cross at a ferry, at a place called Passage. The ferry is about a quarter of a mile over. The village of Cove lies upon the coast on the opposite side the island from Passage, The whole navy of Great Britain may all lie in safety at Cove; in time of war they generally come to Cove to be victualled from Cork. The victualling business in time of peace is nothing when compared to the vast trade they carry on in time of war.

July 2.—I went with colonel and a party to see Kinsale, situated about eleven miles from Cork. The town itself is very indifferent, no manufactory, indeed no trade of any kind, although there is as fine a harbour as in His Majesty's dominion. The only thing the town is famous for, is its having a very fine shore, which causes a great number of people to resort there in summer for the purpose of bathing. They are very gay during that season; they have concerts, balls, public breakfasts, etc.

The 10th regiment were quartered there. The barracks very indifferent. The town itself lies under a hill and at the very end of the harbour. His Majesty's frigate the *Calypso* was lying there as a guard ship; and what I was astonished to see, astonished and at the same time struck with a certain degree of pleasure, the ship *Discovery*, the very same vessel that the ever-memorable Captain James Cook, (1728-79, circumnavigator), sailed round the world in; that he was on board her. Alas! poor fellow, he was not suffered to reach his native shore to receive the rewards he deserved.

There is a work called Charles Fort about a mile from town, meant to guard the harbour; it is very irregular, and what is very extraordinary, situated at the bottom of a hill, so that it is commanded on all sides except from the water.

August 18.—We founded a club at the halfway house August between Cork and Kinsale, from the two regiments at Cork and the regiment at Kinsale and Charles Fort. I flatter myself I was principal in bringing it about, as I first proposed it. Our first meeting was very jolly, we gave it the name of the 'All Four Social Club.' Sir Andrew Cathcart was our first president, and a fine good-humoured man he is, as I have met for some time.

Sept. 2.—The assizes began for the county of Cork. On September the 26th October his Grace the Lord-Lieutenant and the Duchess of Rutland arrived in this city. A captain's guard from our regiment immediately mounted over them on their arrival. The next day there was a *levée* at which all the officers in garrison attended, and in the evening a most splendid ball. I did not dance. The next day they took an airing and examined the beauties of the city of Cork and environs. On the following day they went to Kinsale. That day I dined at Mrs. Beecher's and returned the next; and on the proceeding day their Graces reviewed the two regiments in garrison. Our regiment looked vastly well when first they went out; but his Grace was so very long before he came that we were nearly wet through e'er he arrived. In the evening an assembly, the duchess did not dance at the first. She danced with a Mr. Hutchison and with Johnston of our regiment.

The next day they left town. In the evening I was at a fine ball at Mrs. Armstead's.

Nov. 4.—Our great Blue and Orange day. In the morning the regiment fired three rounds, and the duke promised to return to dine with the Society, as he was chose Superior of the Order; but he was delayed by unavoidable business; notwithstanding the disappointment we had a most joyous day, and sat till after five o'clock in the morning.

Sunday, Dec. 11.—Went to Killarney to pay a visit to my friend Major Coote of the 47th, and also to see the famous lake. I shall not attempt a description of it, as it is not in the power of my pen to give the most faint idea of its perfections. We had the greatest sport cock shooting I ever saw. Surprise. The last two days we did not see less than one hundred couple each day. Coote's civility was beyond anything I ever met with; gave me a bed in the barrack and my horse in his stable.

I stayed there a fortnight, and I may say I never spent two pleasanter weeks in my life. We kept Christmas Day very merrily, and in the evening went round the different barrack rooms and drank a merry Christmas to all the men. We had to repeat our toast so often that we all got very drunk at last, both officers and men. Returned to Cork on the last day of 1785; found the roads very slippy and bad. Indeed in the finest weather, the road from Cork to Killarney is but very dreary, over mountains the whole way. The frost set in the 27th December and broke up the 3rd January.

January 13, 1786,—Dined at a Mr. Gray's, a fine jolly old sportsman, and one thing in particular I must mention of him, that is a custom he has after dinner, and before the cloth is taken away, he has a bottle of liquor set on, and a silver fox's head. He fills the head a bumper and drinks fox-hunting; then passes it round, you drink as little of it or as much as you like.

February.—This month I have been a good deal engaged February out at parties and balls; one at Mrs. Beecher's; one at Connor's; at Mr. Piercy's; at Mrs. Wood's; all very pleasant. The Grenadier company of the 46th regiment marched through here on the way to Inchigeelagh to keep the white boys, in order, as they are become almost as outrageous as ever. (The Secret Society of White Boys was organised in 1761 in Munster and parts of Leinster to resist the enclosure of commons, unjust rents or tithes).

On the 21st March the 10th and 45th regiments sailed from Cove. The 6th and 26th regiments marched through, the former to Charles Fort, the latter to Kinsale.

On the 3rd of April the assizes commenced for this county. There were to have been between twenty and thirty white boys (a set of people who commit depredations of every kind, and pretend to say on account of being overburthened with tithes), were to have been tried, but the government thought proper to try what effect lenity would have, and the judge allowed them to give bail for their appearance at the next assizes, the meaning of which is that if they are none of them discovered committing murders they will not be taken any further notice of.

August.—The white boys began to get to great lengths, having risen in large bodies in many parts of the country and committed many shameful depredations. I went over once or twice to Cork to see Miss Brunton, who I think a most promising actress.

I left the regiment at Charles Fort on Saturday the 16th December, having with much difficulty obtained three months' leave of absence from Colonel Ogilvie, who, on account of my not being a favourite, thwarted me in my leave in every particular.

I got to Cork, and found on Sunday morning a collier was to sail that day for Workington. I accordingly took my passage on board (having called on most of my friends) about five o'clock in the afternoon, but on account of low tide and want of wind the vessel could not get down the river and went aground. Finding myself pretty near my friend Bousfield's I got the boat and went ashore, stayed supper, very pleasant, and got on board again by twelve o'clock, at which time we again got under weigh and cleared the harbour of Cork with a tolerably good breeze by ten o'clock on Monday, which continued till the evening, when it changed and blew so hard against us we were obliged to put about, and after being a good deal tossed on the coast between Cork and Youghall, we were drove back into Cork harbour on Tuesday evening. I went on shore to Passage, slept there. I had been very sick on board, as in addition to our misfortunes the captain of the vessel was drunk the whole time and not able to give the least assistance, and we were very indifferently manned.

On Wednesday morning I went again to Cork, and finding a vessel to sail to Minehead on the Thursday night, I took my passage on board her.

On Wednesday I met with Dickson, Ormsby, and Spicer; we agreed to dine together at the Bush Tavern. Barber of the Artillery, Wood of the 45th, was our party. Had a very pleasant day; we all supped at Barber's, and I went on board the *Britannia* about three o'clock.

We were as unfortunate as in the collier, for having no wind the brig went aground before we had got a mile down the river. I again returned to Cork to breakfast, as the captain told me she would not float till next tide. I remained in Cork till about two o'clock in the afternoon, when I returned on board. We got under weigh, but could not proceed on account of wind. At length, however, we got clear of the harbour of Cork on Friday morning the 22nd with a fair wind, which continued for twelve or fourteen hours till we made the island of Lundy at the mouth of the Bristol Channel, when the wind changed and we were beating about till Sunday morning, at which time it began to blow very hard and continued blowing almost a gale of wind till Monday morning, when we endeavoured to get into the Bay of Tenby in the Bristol Channel, but could not make it. At length we were obliged to put into Milford Haven, where we landed on Monday evening, being Christmas Day, at a small fishing place called Angle.

The passage would have been much more unpleasant had I been alone. But fortunately there was a very agreeable man on board. Major Thompson of the 57th. On our landing we enjoyed ourselves very much over Welsh eggs and bacon, cleanliness (which one is not much accustomed to on board ship), and some superb ale. I left the major the next morning, he having so much baggage that it obliged him to wait till the wind changed and proceed up the Bristol Channel, as there was no conveyance by land.

I got a one-horse chaise from Pembroke, fourteen miles, in which I put my baggage and servant, mounted a little Welsh pony, and so proceeded to Pembroke; changed my horse and got to a place called Noah's Ark, where I and my servant got into a chaise and proceeded to Caermarthen, where I slept.

Next morning breakfasted at Llandilo, from thence to Trecastle, and through a very pretty country to Brecknock, then to the Hay and slept at Kinnersley; and morning to Leominster. Breakfasted at Tenbury, to the Hundred House, Kidderminster, Birmingham, and got to Freeford by eight o'clock on Thursday the 28th.

Unfortunately my brother and sister had set out to Leicester that very morning. However, I got a mutton chop and a good night's rest, and the next morning, after breakfasting with Swinfen, I went to Leicester, and there found my poor father had been taken that very morning with a paralytic stroke, and was lying quite senseless; a most melancholy welcome for me after an absence of near two years.

My father had been unwell some time previous to the attack, which was very sudden indeed; for he was remarkably well the night before, and my mother had left him in bed about nine o'clock. They had scarce got downstairs when he rang his bell, and on the maid going into the room he asked her if she saw any alteration in him; on her replying in the negative, he, poor man, desired her to call her mistress, but not to alarm her. On my mother entering 1786 the room, she found his senses almost gone; all he could say was 'brush, brush,' meaning the flesh brush, took his right hand up with his left, shook his head and said it was all over. He was deprived entirely of the use of his right side. He continued exactly in that situation till Tuesday morning the 2nd of January about half-past one, when he expired without a groan. (Death?)

Derwin and Dr. Bue assured us he had never suffered the least pain from his first seizure, which was some consolation. He was a most kind and indulgent parent, and was himself his only enemy. He would have been sixty-five had he lived till the following April. He was interred at St. Mary's, Lichfield, the Friday following, when at his particular request the same ceremony was observed as at the funeral of his father; that is, that the bells should chime him to church, and be carried from the hearse by six labourers, and the ceremony be at night, which it was, as near nine o'clock as possible. There was a most astonishing concourse of people assembled at the church, as I believe he was most universally beloved in Lichfield.

The mourners were Mr. Dennis, Mr. Hill (my brother's bailiff), my brother's butler, and his own man. My brother, Mrs. Dyott, and I went to Freeford the day after he died. I forgot to mention one circumstance, which was that the bells of St. Mary's rung three peals the day before he was buried with the bells buffed.

On the 4th March I went up in the mail coach to March London. Got there the next morning; when in town I waited on a Mr. Hey, a friend of my brother, who was so kind as to introduce me to a Mr. Dunn, one of the Canadian judges. And Mr. Hey also gave me a letter to Lord Dorchester. (Guy Carleton, first Baron Dorchester—1724-1808; commander-in-chief in America 1782-3; created Baron Dorchester 1786; governor of Quebec 1786-91 and 1793-6).

I was also fortunate in meeting my friend Major Thompson, who very kindly gave me a letter to Major Beckwith, the commander-in-chief's *aide-de-camp* in America.

I spent a week only in town and returned to Freeford on the 13th. The spring in that part of England had not been remembered so fine or so forward by the oldest men.

I left Lichfield about three o'clock, but here I must indulge myself in paying some tribute of gratitude to the best of brothers. Never did one brother experience more kindness from another than I did from my dear brother Richard. To enumerate all his acts of friendship would be more than I am able; but all I can say is, he could not do more to serve me than he did. He anticipated every wish.

I got to Chester about twelve, ate a sandwich and went to bed. Found there was no packet sailed till Monday morning. We had a very good passage, and after being April very sick, landed in Dublin. Next day about one o'clock, I was fortunate in meeting with the commander-in-chief's *aide-de-camp* that day to make my excuses for not being with the regiment by the 1st of April, the day my leave expired. I was at a good deal of trouble to get my luggage out of the custom-house, which made it late before I had finished. I got a beefsteak at five o'clock and went to bed by nine.

I left Dublin the next morning, travelled in a chaise with Kane and his brother, which we took the whole way; paid six guineas for it. I got to the regiment on the 10th April, 1787 found the whole corps joined and preparing for the embarkation. I forgot to mention having heard from Major West in Dublin that our foreign quarters were changed, and instead of going to Canada we were to relieve a battalion of the

60th in Nova Scotia and Newfoundland. This coincides with my usual ill-luck, as I had through the kindness of my Aunt Herrick got letters of recommendation from the Duke of Richmond, (Charles Lennox, third Duke of Richmond and Lennox—1735-1806; succeeded to the title 1750; master-general of the ordnance 1782-95), to Lord Dorchester, the Commander-in-chief in North America, who resides at Quebec. So that I may conclude it very unfortunate our being ordered to Nova Scotia instead of Canada, as in all probability I may not have an opportunity of presenting my letter to his Lordship. On the 16th April we had a very joyous meeting of the Blue and Orange, dined upwards of forty, and of course got a good deal inebriated.

I never saw such hard living at the mess as during our stay at the Fort; we were literally drunk almost every day, and wishing for the arrival of the transports, as we were almost ruined both in purse and constitution. At last the looked-for day arrived; we marched from Charles Fort at two o'clock in the morning of Thursday the 24th May after supping together, and without bed, embarked on board the transport about nine, a most pleasing though at the same time rather a pathetic sight. Our regiment embarked in three boats; immediately on their rowing off they gave three cheers, which were answered by the regiments (5th and 26th) drawn up on the beach. Three companies of the regiment went to Newfoundland, and their parting with their comrades was rather affecting.

After all the regiments were embarked, I went to Cork, where I remained for some days enjoying myself with my friends. The day before we sailed I dined with my friend Johnston and Colonel Gordon and two other of our regiment at the Bush Tavern. We intended to have had a 'cool' day, as Gordon and Johnston were to proceed that evening to Dublin, but parting had such an effect that we all got most wondrous drunk. We put Gordon and Johnston into their chaise, then I got on the box of our carriage and set off through the town as hard as I could gallop.

After driving two miles on our way to the transports, on a sudden it struck us as a good thing to drive back, and parade through the Mall, where all the ladies and gentlemen were walking. I was driving away in great pomp amidst all the *belles* of Cork, when on a sudden I was stopped by the owner of the carriage and hauled like Phaethon from my car, after getting pretty well abused by the mob, and we thought proper to decamp, and got on board our ships about five o'clock in the morning.

About twelve o'clock on Saturday, the 2nd of June, our signals were made for sailing, but we did not get under weigh till near six. As some of the ships passed us, on board of which were part of our regiment (they being the first that got under weigh), and giving us three cheers, I must own tears rushed into my eyes, and I felt at that moment '*Je ne sais quoi*,' that I cannot express. It was very fine seeing six large ships getting under weigh at the same time, huzzaing and bands playing 'God save the King.'

23rd.—Wind still the same N W. Three weeks at sea this day. The wind changed about six o'clock in the evening to the southward, tacked and stood on a very good course about four knots an hour till six o'clock in the morning of the 24th, when it began to blow very hard at SW. with heavy rain, which continued till eight o'clock. Saw a great number of bottle-nosed porpoises. They are much larger than the common porpoise, and are generally seen in numbers together. From the heavy gale of wind this morning the sea is now running mountains high, which of course causes a great motion in the ship, and rather detrimental to writing a good hand. At best mine is not the most intelligible I ever saw; but as no person but myself or wife (if the Almighty should ever allow me to take one) is to peruse this history, detail, journal, account, work, *Je ne sais quoi,* little does it matter whether written in legible letters and in the vulgar tongue or in Arabic; if that in threescore years I am able to entertain myself and family with perusing the transactions of my juvenile days (the sole purpose of this my journal, etc.), I shall be perfectly satisfied.

July 4.—Wind south-west, blew fresh, very foggy, and unpleasant all day. In the evening the captain discovered land, but from the thickness of the weather he was afraid to run in. It was so cold there was no staying on deck.

5th.—Wind still SW. Very hazy. Spoke a small brig, informed us we were four leagues from Cape Broyle. We stood on, and about ten o'clock came in sight of land; which after being near five weeks at sea was a most grateful prospect. Soon after making the land, the smell of the pines, which we experienced at least six miles, was most charming; and on approaching nearer, the warm breezes from the shore made it very comfortable. Ten months out of twelve the coast of Newfoundland is enveloped in a prodigious thick fog; it breaks near the shore frequently, and the breeze is then so warm that it feels like the steam from a large boiler; at least in appearance so to me, after being petrified almost with cold at sea.

The agent and the captain agreed to go into harbour in New-foundland, as they found the wind so very unfair; and not being able to make anything of it at sea, they thought it as well to go into port, as to be wearing the vessel to no purpose, the wind having been contrary so long. Accordingly they took a pilot from a small fishing vessel that was come out from Cape Broyle Harbour, and desired him to pilot the ship in. The agent sent the boatswain on the fishing vessel with the three men (there being four only on board), and a letter to the *Lord Shelburne*, desiring her and the other two ships to follow us. As the fog went off and on our coming near the shore, that is into Cape Broyle Harbour, it was very beautiful. The hills which quite surround the bay are not very high, and are covered to the top with pine trees or spruce firs with parts of the rock appearing in different places. There was seen nature in its purest state; it put me in mind of the Lake of Killarney, but more rude and uncultivated.

In sailing into the harbour the country had not the least appearance of being inhabited. We anchored about two o'clock, and as soon as I could get a boat went on shore. Was rather anxious to set foot on American land for the first time. I landed in a small creek, and was more astonished than I can express at the wonderful quantity of small fish in shoals near the beach. They call them capelins, and make use of them for bait to catch cod. They were exactly what we call smelts, and just as good eating. The swell from the sea threw up vast numbers of them on the shore. But to give an idea of the numbers, I shall only remark that I took up a handkerchief full in three minutes with my hand, and brought them on board for dinner. In the evening we rowed up to the end of the bay, and went on shore to a factory, where we learnt that the English merchants sent out agents in the spring to prepare the fish, etc., who return in autumn; and that the only people who remained during the winter were Irish fishermen employed in the fishery on the Bank, and to cure the fish when brought in.

The habitations are very curious, they are built of fir-tree poles placed in the ground as close as possible and between them stuffed with moss. The roof and floor made in the same way; only on the tops of the houses they lay the branches of the spruce firs. They live entirely on salt provisions and their beverage spruce beer. We did not stay on shore very long, as it was getting late, and the fogs are so thick in the evening that it is sometimes difficult to find the ship from the shore, though not twenty yards distance.

6th.—I went on shore in the evening, and saw the whole process of the factory. A vessel is fitted out in England and sails to the Banks. The bait they make use of is in general salted mackerel; if they are at all successful they get a cargo in about three weeks; which they bring into some port in Newfoundland to be dried and to get fresh bait. The places they are dried upon are built by the side of a hill. It is a stage supported by the pine-tree poles; the stage is pine poles with the branches of the spruce laid upon it, and on which the fish is laid after being salted. The process of the fish caught in the harbour is as follows. They are landed from the vessel on to a wharf built out into the water, from whence they are thrown into a covered place (also over the water), where men are ready to receive them, who immediately open them, put the livers on one side to make oil, and the remaining part of the inside and the head are thrown through a hole betwixt the man's legs into the water.

The man then gives them over to another dresser or table, where they are received by a person who takes out the bone; the fish are then laid along the floor to be salted, which is done by a layer of fish and a layer of salt; in which state they remain five or six days; they are then washed in brine and carried out to the stages to dry. They have nothing to do with the fish caught at sea but to wash them in the brine and then dry them. The time they take to dry depends entirely upon the weather. A great deal of the fish is taken to Portugal and up the Mediterranean. I walked about a good deal in the woods, which was quite a wilderness. There is nothing like a village. A few scattered habitations (houses I can't call them) seemed all the settlement.

9th.—The captain of the ship and I went to the upper end of the harbour, which is about two miles from the entrance, surrounded by a fine hanging wood of spruce fir, variegated with mountain ash and other flowering shrubs. There are two very pretty rivers which discharge themselves into the basin. They roll over the rocks in a very beautiful manner. One of them in particular falls a considerable height over the rocks, the sides of which are very thickly covered with wood, and form a most beautiful cascade. I was much entertained with the method of catching flat-fish in the shoal waters. You see them quite plain lying at the bottom, and with a small spear we killed numbers; as also lobsters (with a hook) in abundance.

Round the upper part of the harbour there are several factories, and two or three neat-looking cabins, but no signs of cultivation, except a small piece of ground for potatoes and other vegetables. I returned about four, and dined on board the brig. On shore in the evening, and walked about the woods for an hour. The walking is very indifferent on account of the large loose stones. The paths are very narrow, and of course but little frequented.

We were agreeably awoke at six o'clock in the morning of the 22nd, and informed that we were in the Bay of Halifax, and should be at anchor by ten o'clock. We all got up happy in the idea of being released from seven weeks' confinement.

The entrance into the harbour of Halifax has nothing very pleasing. It lies nearly east and west. The west side is a rock partly covered with wood, and has at the extremity a lighthouse, there being a very dangerous reef of rocks running some distance into the sea. The east side is pretty enough. There is a large island called Cornwallis Island, which has some cultivation and a good deal of wood. Near the town, and about the centre of the harbour, there is a small island called Georges Island, where the signals are made for the shipping, and on which there are works. It is very well situated for guarding the harbour. We came to anchor close to the town about twelve o'clock. I never was more rejoiced. The colonel immediately went on shore to wait upon the governor. In the afternoon I dressed and went on shore, after being seven weeks in filth and rags. A clean coat appeared quite awkward and strange.

The town of Halifax is prettily enough situated on a hillside, at the top of which there is a citadel and block-house. The houses are all built of wood, and in general painted white or yellow, which has a very pleasing effect, particularly in summer. The streets extend from north to south along the side of the hill, and are intersected by cross streets, extending from the shore up the hill towards the blockhouse. The governor, Parr, and the commissioner of the dockyard have both very good houses. There are three barracks, which would contain from 600 to 1000 men. There are also two churches, both very neat buildings of wood, and one or two meeting-houses.

There is a square in town called the Grand Parade, where the troops in garrison parade every evening during the summer; and where all the *belles* and *beaux* of the place promenade, and the bands remain to play as long as they walk. I went to the parade; the first person I saw was Mr. Cartwright, late lieutenant in the Staffordshire Militia. He was an ensign in the 60th, acting adjutant. We disembarked the next day, the 23rd, about two o'clock, and dined with the 60th regiment. They were going to Quebec. We were not able to get into our barrack-rooms, as the 60th did not embark till Thursday. However, we got an empty room in the barracks, and four of us laid our beds on the floor, and enjoyed most heartily our repose, hard as it was.

July 27.—We began our mess. From the high price of provisions, beef being eightpence and mutton sixpence per pound, we were obliged to pay high for messing. Two dollars a week and our rations equal to three shillings and sixpence more. Port wine from fifteen to twenty pence per bottle; sherry nearly the same.

August 11.—I went on a fishing party with Captain August Devernet of the artillery. It is one of the principal summer amusements of this place, and a very pleasant one indeed. There were ten of us; we had a large boat, allowed the artillery by government, and also a smaller one for the eatables. We set out about eleven o'clock, and sailed down the harbour to a place called the haddock bank, about two miles distance. We anchored and began to fish. Such astounding quantities of haddock I never saw. I believe in about one hour and a half we caught one hundred and fifty, and I took a large skate. The people have such a profusion of fish that they will scarce eat skate. When we had tired ourselves with fishing, we sailed to an island two miles lower down, where we landed; and as the principal thing in these parts is to eat chowder, we set the cooks to work to prepare dinner.

A Mr. Roberts of the 57th regiment was to superintend the cooking the chowder. As it would necessarily take some time, Captain Devernet and I went into the woods to see if we could meet with any partridge, which are different in this country to what they are in England. They are found in woods, and perch upon the trees. The island we were upon is called Cornwallis Island, and was sold by the Bishop of Lichfield, Dr. James Cornwallis, (fourth Earl Cornwallis—1742-1824; Bishop of Lichfield and Coventry 1781-1824; succeeded as Earl Cornwallis 1823), to a shoemaker of Halifax a few years ago. It contains about six hundred acres. There is but a small proportion of it cultivated at present. Wherever it has been at all cleared, it is astonishing what fine clover springs up spontaneously. The wood is chiefly birch and spruce fir. We did not venture far into the wood, it was so astonishingly hot, and the '*moschetos*' are very troublesome. Did not meet any game at all.

On our return we found the table spread under the shade of a large birch and a fir, in a spot of about an acre, near a small cottage belonging to a poor fisherman, and close to the shore. The island formed a small bay in this place. The surrounding wood, which covered the hills on every side the bay, and a most beautiful small island entirely covered with the spruce fir to the very water's edge about a league distance from the entrance of the bay, formed altogether a most beautiful prospect. We sat down about four o'clock, and of all the dishes I ever tasted, I never met so exquisitely good a thing as the chowder. (The first Baron Vivian, writing in 1813, remarks that 'chowder' was made of salt fish and potatoes).

We attempted to make it on board ship, but nothing like this. It is a soup, and better in my opinion than turtle. The recipe I don't exactly know, but the principal ingredients are cod and haddock, pork, onions, sea-biscuit, butter, and a large quantity of cayenne pepper. In short, the *tout ensemble* was the best thing I ever ate. We had some excellent Madeira, of which we drank a bottle each, and some very good lime punch with dinner. We rowed round the island, and returned home by nine o'clock. I never spent a more pleasant day. There are frequent parties of this kind.

Aug. 20.—A duel was fought between Captain Dalrymple of the 42nd and Lieutenant Roberts of the 57th, owing to the former having two years prior to the duel said in a company that Mr. Roberts was not fit for the Grenadiers; at the same time hinting that he had sold some of his brother's books. Lieutenant Roberts at the time this discourse took place was in Europe, and not meeting with Captain Dalrymple till now, he being quartered at Cape Breton, had not an opportunity of demanding satisfaction. They fired only one pistol each, as Captain Dalrymple was wounded in the right arm, but not dangerously.

Sept. 2.—His Excellency Brigadier-General Thomas Carleton, (lieutenant-governor of New Brunswick, brother of the first Baron Dorchester). arrived from Fredericton, New Brunswick, by land. We fully expected him to have come by sea, as the *Brandy Wine* brig was for that purpose gone up the Bay of Fundy. He did not arrive till the evening, was received by a sub.'s guard from the King's Own, and next morning was honoured with a salute of thirteen guns from the artillery. At one o'clock the officers in garrison were introduced to his Excellency at the Government House, a very formal business.

On the 5th I went to see a moose deer that was brought alive to the town. It was a very curious animal, though very common in America. They are between a horse and a cow, at least they have that appearance. The head resembles the horse (except having immense ears), a small body, long legs, and cloven feet. They eat them in the winter, and reckon their flesh good venison.

Oct. 1.—A small party with the commissioner in his yacht to fish, etc., but it was rather too late; however, we managed to get sufficient for chowder. We went on shore at Cornwallis Island (down the harbour). It has been purchased within these few years by a Scotsman, who is making use of his utmost endeavours to clear it. There are not more than twenty to thirty acres free from wood. What has been improved turns out very well.

I saw a curious kind of a fence on that island, which I am informed is very common in America; it can only answer in a country abounding with wood. It is made of the poles of the fir-tree in this form **XXX;** there is no post. At the angle the fence is about six feet high, and the only advantage it has of a direct line is, they save the trouble of mortising holes in posts to put the rails in, and indeed save posts altogether. We have had lately partridge in abundance; both the spruce and the beech, the former are the best; they are as full large as a grouse, and eat very much like a pheasant. The plumage is not at all like the partridge of Britain, nor have they the least similitude. They are spotted on the breast brown and white, and perch on the trees.

Friday, Oct. 26.—I dined at the commissioner's. That same day the fleet from Quebec under the command of Commodore Herbert Sawyer, (1731?-98, commodore and commander-in-chief at Halifax; admiral 1795), arrived here; consisting of the *Leander*, 50 guns; Captain Sir James Barclay, (captain R.N., seventh baronet, died 1793), with the broad pennant; the *Pegasus*, 28, Captain His Royal Highness Prince William Henry; the *Resource*; 28, Captain Minchin, and the *Weazel* sloop, Captain Wood. On their passage from Quebec, the *Leander* struck on a rock in the Gulf of St. Lawrence, and was very near being lost. It was a most dismal situation, as all the commodore's family were with him on board. They were obliged to quit the ship, and went on board His Royal Highnesses' ship.

★★★★★★

Afterwards William IV., King of Great Britain and Ireland; born 1765, third son of George III., served as 'able seaman' at relief of Gibraltar 1780; rear-admiral 1790; married Adelaide, eldest daughter of the Duke of Saxe-Coburg Meiningen, 1818; succeeded George IV. as King, 26th June 1830; died 1837.

★★★★★★

When the *Leander* came in she was obliged to be towed up the harbour to the dockyard and hove down. Her bottom was found to be in a most shattered condition. His Royal Highness was rather expected in the evening at the commissioner's, but he did not quit his ship. On his coming to anchor the brigadier-general waited upon him; he positively declined any compliments as a prince.

Saturday,—He dined with the governor. (Sir John Wentworth— 1737-1820—surveyor of the King's forests, Halifax, Nova Scotia, 1783-92; governor of Nova Scotia 1792-1808; created baronet 1795).

Sunday—He dined with the commodore, who lives at the Navy Hospital.

As His Royal Highness had signified his intention to the brigadier that he would review our regiment on Tuesday, I was totally taken up making the necessary preparations. Had the regiment out on Sunday afternoon and Monday morning. Sunday, His Royal Highness dined at the commodore's; Monday, at the commissioner's; Tuesday, he reviewed the regiment at 11 o'clock. It was the first time I had seen him, and little expected to have received such marks of his condescension as I afterwards did.

Our review was nothing more than the common form; His Royal Highness expressed much satisfaction at the appearance of the men. After the review was over the officers were all presented to him on the parade. His Royal Highness is very much like His Majesty, but better looking. He is about 5 foot 7 or 8 inches high, good complexion and fair hair. He did the regiment the honour to dine with them; I sang several songs with which he was much entertained. He dislikes drinking very much, but that day he drank near two bottles of Madeira. When we broke up from the mess he went to my room and got my cloak to go to his barge, as it rained a good deal. I accompanied him to the boat and wished him a goodnight.

Wednesday morning.—I met him walking in the street by himself. I was with Major Vesey of the 6th regiment. His Royal Highness made us walk with him; he took hold of my arm, and we visited all the young ladies in town. During our walk he told Vesey and I he had taken the liberty of sending us a card to dine with him on Sunday (a great liberty). Vesey and I walked with him till he went on board. He dined *en famille* with the commodore. I dined with Vesey at O'Brien's.

In the evening a ball at the governor's. We went about seven; His

Royal Highness came about half after, and almost immediately began country dances with Miss Parr, the governor's daughter. We changed partners every dance; he danced with all the pretty women in the room, and was just as affable as any other man.

He did me the honour to talk a great deal to me before supper during the dance. We went to supper about twelve, a most elegant thing, near sixty people sat down. We had scarce begun supper when he called out, 'Dyott, fill your glass' (before he asked any person in the room to drink); when I told His Royal Highness my glass was full, he said, 'Dyott, your good health, and your family.' About half an hour after he called out, 'Dyott, fill a bumper,' then, 'Dyott, here's a bumper toast.'

After supper he gave five or six bumper toasts, and always called to me to see them filled at my table. We had a most jolly evening, and he retired about two o'clock. The ladies all stood up when he came into the room, and remained so till he sat down.

Thursday morning.—I met him on the Parade. He, Major Vesey, and myself walked about the town all morning. He would go into any house where he saw a pretty girl, and was perfectly acquainted with every house of a certain description in the town. He dined with the commodore and captain of the fleet at O' Brien's Tavern.

Friday, Nov. 2.—I met him in the morning; we walked. I got a live hare, and we went to the common, where we ran it with my terriers, which he enjoyed much. Always made a point of accompanying him to his barge at all hours. He dined with the commodore.

Saturday.—I met him at Parade, and attended him all the morning. He dined with the captain of the *Resource*. Vesey dined with me, and we had a good deal of company at the mess, and got very drunk.

Sunday morning.—I met him after church at Mrs. Wentworth's, Governor Wentworth's lady. He was gone up the country on business, as he is surveyor-general of the woods of this province. Mrs. Wentworth is, I believe, a lady fonder of our sex than her own, and His Royal Highness used to be there frequently. I attended him from thence to his barge; as we went along he told me he would send his cutter for me to any place I chose, to come to dinner. I told His Royal Highness I was to go on board with Captain Minchin in his barge. We went a little after three, all in boots at his particular wish (he dined everywhere in boots himself).

He received us on the quarter-deck with all possible attention, and showed us into the cabin himself. His cabin is rather small and neatly furnished. The company at dinner was: the governor; the general; two of the captains of the fleet; Major Vesey; Captain Gladstanes, 57th regiment; Captain Dalrymple, 42nd; Hodgson of ours, and myself.

A most elegant dinner; I did not think it possible to have had anything like it on board ship. Two courses, removes, and a most elegant dessert. Wines of all sorts, such Madeira I never tasted. It had been twenty-eight years in bottle; was sent a present to His Royal Highness from the East Indies by Sir Archibald Campbell, (1739-91; served in America 1757-64; governor of Madras 1786-9).

We had two servants out of livery, and four in the King's livery. His Royal Highness sat at the head of the table, and one of the captains of the navy at the foot. No officer of his ship, as it is a rule he has laid down never to dine in company with any subaltern officer in the navy. We dined at half-past three and drank pretty freely till eight, when we had coffee, and after noyau, etc. He found out I had never been on board so large a ship, and before I came away he told me to come and breakfast with him the next morning at eight o'clock, and he would show me all over the ship.

I went ashore that evening with Captain Minchin, who has a house in town. Gladstanes, Dalrymple, Hodgson, and I supped with him. Before I went there I met His Royal Highness and Sir James Barclay, captain of the *Leander*, walking about the streets. He made me walk with him till near ten o'clock, and some pretty scenes we had.

The next day, Monday the 5th November, he had fixed to land as a prince of the blood to receive the address from the governor and council, to dine with them, and to go to a ball given by the town. I went to breakfast with him at eight, found the cutter waiting for me at the dockyard and a royal midshipman attending. His Royal Highness was on the quarter-deck when I went on board. We immediately went below to breakfast, and which consisted of tea, coffee, and all sorts of cold meat, cold game, etc. etc. His Highness breakfasted almost entirely on cold turkey. His purser made breakfast, and his first lieutenant and two of the midshipmen (who take it in turn) breakfasted. They did not stay two minutes after.

And then His Royal Highness, with the greatest condescension possible, showed me first of all the different clothing of his barge's crew for the different climates. He made the coxswain put on each of the dresses and cap. Then he showed me his orderly books, and the books belonging to the lieutenants and midshipmen. Then he explained the whole business of the ship and the different stations in every possible situation for every man and officer in the ship, all under different heads, in the most exact manner; a copy of which all the officers have (in a book). He then showed me the ship' s books kept by the purser of all the men's accounts, necessaries and clothing, forms of the different returns, etc. etc.

I went home to get ready the regiment to receive His Royal Highness.

At two o'clock the garrison marched down and lined the streets from the wharf to the Government House, A captain's guard with colours was formed on the right to receive him, and a detachment of artillery with three field pieces fired a royal salute on his landing. His Royal Highness left the commodore's ship about a quarter after two in his own barge (which was steered by an officer). His barge's crew most elegantly dressed, and the handsomest caps I ever saw. Black velvet, and all except the coxswain's with a silver ornament in front and the King's arms most elegantly cast. The coxswain's was of gold, and His Royal Highness told me it cost fifty guineas.

As he was steered by an officer, what is termed the strokesman wore the coxswain's cap. The commodore's ship lay about half a mile from the wharf where he landed, and as he passed the ships, followed by the commodore and captains of the fleet in their barges, His Royal Highness and the commodore each having the standard of England hoisted in their barge, he was saluted by each of them separately, having their yards manned, etc. When he came within a hundred yards of the wharf his barge dropped astern, and the commodore's and captains' pushed on and landed to receive him immediately on his stepping out of his barge (the governor, Council, House of Assembly, etc., and all the great people being there to receive him). He was saluted by the field pieces on the wharf and proceeded through the line of troops to the Government House, the soldiers with presented arms, the officers and colours saluting him as he passed, and all the bands playing 'God save the King.'

When he entered the Government House he was saluted by the twenty-four pounders on the Citadel Hill. On his being arrived in the *levée* room, the different branches of the legislature being there assembled and all the officers allowed to be present, the governor presented the address, to which His Royal Highness read his answer, and read it with more energy and emphasis than anything I ever heard. At the same time he had the most majestic and manly appearance I ever beheld.

Immediately he had finished, the officers went out to change the position of the troops from the wharf to the tavern where he was to dine. He passed up the line and was saluted as before. The troops then marched to their barracks, and in the evening fired a *feu de joie* on the Citadel Hill.

At eight o'clock His Royal Highness went to the ball, where, I do suppose, there must have been near three hundred people. The business much better conducted than I imagined it would. The supper was quite a crowd, and some such figures I never saw. His Royal Highness danced a good deal. He began with Miss Parr, the governor's daughter. He did me the honour to converse with me frequently, and walked arm-in-arm about the room for half an hour. He retired about one o'clock and appeared much pleased with the entertainment.

Tuesday.—He came on shore about twelve, and was made a member of the Loyal and Friendly Society of the Blue and Orange, and dined with the society at our mess-room. All our officers were members and invited the governor, the commodore, the commissioner, and Major Vesey of the 6th regiment to meet the prince. We gave him a very good dinner, and he was in very good spirits. He is not fond of drinking himself, but has no objection to seeing other people. I was vice-president, and sung, etc. He got up about nine, and as he left the room he called 'Dyott,' on which I followed and had the honour of walking with him alone to his barge, as he wished the general and the rest a goodnight. On our way through the street he talked a great deal, asked me who my father was, where he lived, and why I came so late into the army. I informed him of all circumstantially. Just before he got to his barge he told me I must dine with him again before he sailed, and that he would have a small snug party and none of the great people.

Wednesday.—I met him in the street and walked about all morning. That day I had the honour to meet His Royal Highness at dinner at Governor Wentworth's, or rather Mrs. Wentworth's, the governor being away from home. Mrs. Wentworth is a most charming woman, but unhappily for her husband, rather more partial to our sex than her own. But he, poor man, cannot see her foibles, and they live very happy. I believe there was a mutual passion which subsisted between His Royal Highness and her. She is an American, but lived a good deal in England and with people of the first fashion.

As I was pretty intimate in the house, she desired me to dine there. The company was, His Royal Highness, Major Vesey, Captain Gladstanes, Hodgson of ours, a Mr. and Mrs. Brindley, the latter a sister of Mrs. Wentworth, and myself I never laughed so much in my life; he was in vast spirits and pleasanter than anything I ever saw. We had a most elegant dinner and coffee, and then went to dress, as he always dines in boots, and the commissioner gave a ball in honour of His Royal Highness. He dressed at Mrs. Wentworth's and went in her carriage, but not with her, as the ladies of Halifax are a little scrupulous of their virtue and think it in danger if they were to visit Mrs. Wentworth.

For my part I think her the best-bred woman in the province. I was obliged to go early, as the commissioner requested I would manage the dancing, etc., that is, that I would act as a master of the ceremonies. I went about eight. The commissioner's house and the dockyard was most beautifully illuminated and made a fine appearance.

His Royal Highness arrived about nine. Everybody stands up when he enters, and remains so till he desires the mistress of the house to sit down. Soon after he came we began dancing. I forgot to mention that at Mrs. Wentworth's he told me I was to dine with him on Friday. He is very fond of dancing; we changed partners every dance. He always began, and generally called to me to tell him a dance.

The last dance before supper at the governor's and at the commissioner's, His Royal Highness, Major Vesey, myself, and six very pretty women danced Country Bumpkin for near an hour. We went to supper about one. He called to me from the top of the table to drink a glass of wine, and joked me all the evening on our party at dinner; but I must say I never in my life saw him in the smallest degree lose his dignity or forget his princely situation. His character is, where he takes a liking he will be very free, but always guarded, and if ever any man takes the smallest liberty he cuts instantly. We had a very excellent supper and very pleasant. His Royal Highness retired about two; I accompanied him to his barge, which lay at the dockyard wharf. The governor, commissioner, and all the great people attended him to his barge. Just as he pushed off he called out, 'Dyott, I shall send the cutter here on Friday at three.' I cannot avoid mentioning these little circumstances; it is so very flattering to be taken such particular notice of by so great a person.

Thursday morning.—I met him in town, and walked in the dock-yard with him all morning. He dined that day with the 57th regiment. I had the honour of an invitation to meet him. We had an amazing company; all the great people, but not very pleasant. His Royal Highness retired about eight; and as he went out he called me to accompany him. We strolled about the town, went to some of the houses of a certain description, and to be sure had some pretty scenes. He did me the honour to say it was very seldom he took so much notice of a subaltern. He said it was not from any dislike he had to them, but that he was in a situation where everybody had an eye on him, and it would be expected he should form acquaintance with people high in rank. I attended him to his barge; he went aboard about ten.

Friday morning.—I met him at Mrs. Wentworth's. We stayed there more than an hour. Then walked the town till two o'clock, as he dined at three. He always desired everybody to come to him in boots. The cutter was waiting at the dockyard a little before three. The company: Colonel Brownlow of the 57th, who had arrived from England the day before. Major Vesey, Hodgson, Captain Hood of the navy, and myself. His Royal Highness received us on the quarter-deck and we went to dinner immediately. Not quite so great a dinner as before, but vastly elegant. He was in great spirits and we all got a little inebriated.

We went ashore about seven to dress for a ball at the commodore's. He dressed at Mrs. Wentworth's. When we first came on shore, he was very much out indeed, shouted and talked to every person he met. I was rather late at the commodore's. The company not quite so numerous as at the governor's; the house not being large. We had a very pleasant ball; Country Bumpkin, the same set, and a devilish good supper. We danced after supper and till four o'clock. He dances vastly well and is very fond of it I never saw people so completely tired as they all were. I saw His Royal Highness to his barge and ran home as fast as I could

Saturday morning.—We had a meeting of the Blue and Orange, as His Royal Highness gave a dinner to the Society that day at our mess-room, and was chosen Superior of the Order. He, Major Vesey, and myself walked about all morning visiting the ladies, etc. He desired to dine at half-past three. He took the chair himself and ordered me to be his vice. We had a very good dinner, and he sent wine of his own; the very best claret I ever tasted. We had the grenadiers drawn up in front of the mess-room windows to fire a volley in honour of the toasts.

As soon as dinner was over he began. He did not drink himself; he always drinks Madeira. He took very good care to see everybody fill, and he gave twenty-three bumpers without a halt. In the course of my experience I never saw such fair drinking. When he had finished his list of bumpers, I begged leave as vice to give the Superior, and recommended it to the Society to stand upon our chairs with three times three, taking their time from the vice. I think it was the most laughable sight I ever beheld, to see the governor, our general and the commodore, all so drunk they could scarce stand on the floor, hoisted up on their chairs with each a bumper in his hand; and the three times three cheers was what they were afraid to attempt for fear of falling.

I then proposed His Royal Highness and a good wind whenever he sailed (as he intended sailing on Monday), with the same ceremony. He stood at the head of the table during both these toasts, and I never saw a man laugh so in my life. When we had drunk the last, the old governor desired to know if we had any more, as he said if he once got down, he should never get up again. His Royal Highness saw we were all pretty well done and he walked off. There were just twenty dined, and we drank sixty-three bottles of wine.

When he went out he called me and told me he would go to my room and have some tea. The general, Colonel Brownlow, and myself were at tea. The general and colonel as drunk as two drummers. I was tolerably well myself and knew what I was about perfectly. He laughed at them very much. After tea we left them in my room and went on a cruise, as he calls it, till eleven, when he went on board. I don't recollect ever to have spent so pleasant a day. His Royal Highness, whenever any person did not fill a bumper, always called out, 'I see some of God Almighty's daylight in that glass. Sir; banish it.'

Monday morning.—At seven o'clock His Royal Highness sailed. I got up to take a last view of his ship as she went out, and as a tribute of respect to His Royal Highness, from whom I had received such flattering marks of condescension. I think I never spent a time so joyously in my life; and very sorry when he left us.

New Year's Day, January 1, 1788.—I dined at Mr. Brindley's; brother-in-law to Mrs. Wentworth. The same party as on Christmas Day at Governor Wentworth's. I cannot say I was in very good spirits. Was asked to dine the next day at a Mr. Townsend's and at the commissioner's, but as it was the day on which I lost my dear father, I refused them both and did not leave the barracks all day.

January 20.—I was made a Free and Accepted Mason at the Lodge in the 37th regiment. Wrote to my brother, mother, and Mrs. Wood.

On the 30th January poor Miss S. Sawyer, daughter to the admiral, died, universally regretted by all ranks, as a most amiable, good, deserving young woman. She had had a swelling in her arm for some months. The faculty agreed it should be opened, which was done accordingly. It continued in that state, not healing or mending, for near two months. That at length brought on a fever, of which she languished for twenty-one days. I was much hurt, knowing her to be so good a creature. She was only eighteen years of age, and a very handsome, fine woman. I was desired to attend her funeral as a bearer. I cannot say I ever felt more in my life, than on the occasion, when I reflected that about three months before I was dancing with her, and that now I was attending her to her grave. It really made me as melancholy as anything I ever experienced. The funeral was a handsome one as follows:—

At the head of the procession was the bishop and rector; then the body with eight bearers. That is, on the right side. Lieutenant Nicholson, 57th regiment; Captain Gladstanes, *ditto*; Lieutenant Lawford, R,N.; Captain Sir James Barclay, *ditto*; on the left side, Lieutenant Dyott, 4th; Captain Hodgson, *ditto*; Lieutenant d' Acres, R.N.; Captain Hood, *ditto*. The under bearers were the admiral's barge's crew in white trousers, white shirts, with a piece of love ribbon tied round the left arm, black velvet caps and white ribbons tied round them. The coffin covered with white cloth handsomely ornamented. On a silver plate:

Sophia Sawyer. Born 10th March '70. Died 31st Jan. '88.

After the body, Mr. d'Acres, secretary to the admiral as chief mourner; next the nurse and Miss Sawyer's maid in deep mourning and white hoods. The bearers had on full uniform; white hat-bands and scarves, black sword-knots, cockades, and crape round the left arm. After the two women followed Colonel Brownlow, 57th, and Captain Minchin, R.N., General Ogilvie and the commissioner, and the governor by himself. All with white hat-bands and scarves. There were also three or four of the family, and some officers belonging to the admiral's ship with hatbands and scarves.

After them followed almost all the officers belonging to the fleet; many of the garrison; all the people in town that were acquainted with the admiral, and to close up the whole, a long string of empty carriages. As we entered the church (which is a full mile from the Admiralty) the organ began a most solemn dirge, which continued near a quarter of an hour. The service was then performed, and I think in my life I never saw so much grief as throughout the whole congregation. I must own I have not shed so many tears since I left school. I believe sorrow was never more universal than on the occasion. It was a very cold day, and walking so slow in silk stockings and thin shoes, I was almost perished.

The following Sunday, all the people who had been invited to the funeral attended church, as the bishop was to preach an occasional sermon. His text was most admirably adapted from the Thessalonians, and his discourse the most affecting I ever heard. He frequently pointed to her grave and admonished the younger part of his hearers, and more particularly those who had attended the interment, to prepare to meet death, not knowing how soon they might be cut off. On the whole it was a most admirable sermon, and called up the passions more forcibly than anything I ever heard.

Feb. 12.—Yesterday the post arrived from Quebec, and by letters received they mention that on the 14th December there was no snow on the ground, nor was there any frost; a circumstance not known in the memory of man. We have had in this province hitherto a most favourable winter. Now and then some severe days, but the frost has never continued more than six or seven days at a time; and the sun is now getting so much power, we are not to expect any very cold weather. I had a very long letter from my dear brother by the brig, and as usual full of most generous offers. I do think there never existed in the breast of man so good a heart as he possesses. God only knows if it will ever be in my power to repay his kindness; if it should I shall be truly happy to do it tenfold.

All the month of March, cold nasty weather. Nothing but whist and eating and drinking. April brought us rather better weather.

On the 1st August Admiral Sawyer sailed for England. The command of the fleet remained with Captain Sandys in the *Dido*.

On the 17th, to the surprise of everybody, arrived His Royal Highness, Prince William Henry, in the *Andromeda*. I had dined with the governor, and was engaged to spend the evening at Mrs. Wentworth's. When we had done supper there was a loud rap at the door, and the servant brought in a letter and said it was from His Royal Highness, who was just arrived. The man had scarce delivered the message, when in came the prince, He did me the honour to shake me by the hand, and said he was glad to see me. He was very entertaining for two hours, told us all the news in England, etc. I had the honour to light him to his chamber, as he had got a bed from Mrs. Wentworth. He said he had been cruising with the Channel Fleet for three weeks, and was sent away at a day's notice when at sea, and that of course he was come to America rather ill provided.

The next day, Monday, he visited the commodore (Sandys); on going aboard his ship, the standard of England was hoisted and he was saluted by twenty-one guns. The governor, general, etc., all waited upon him, which took up the greatest part of the morning. He dined privately with Captain Buller of the *Brisk*. In the evening he came to the Parade, and after making his bow, he called me, took me by the arm, and walked the Parade for an hour. He then came up to my room, had tea, stayed till nine o'clock, and then went on board.

Wednesday.—I met him in the morning. The hottest day I almost ever felt. He told me to attend him, and he would stretch my legs. Accordingly we set forward, and walked four miles as hard as he could. I never was so hot in my life or more fagged. I never met a man more entertaining *tête-à-tête*. He dined at the general's. The company the same as the day before. Sat till near eight, then I attended him to my room, where he had tea. He told me this evening that if I wished it, he intended visiting Shelburn, etc. etc., and would be very glad of my company on the cruise. I was highly honoured, and told his Highness I should with the greatest pleasure accept the honour he offered.

Friday.—He dined at the chief justice's; a most excellent dinner. And how it was, I don't know; but His Royal Highness set to immediately after dinner, and I never saw a man get so completely drunk. He desired the general to order the whole garrison up to the Citadel Hill, to fire a *feu de joie*; but His Highness was not able to attend it, as he was obliged to go to bed at Pemberton's, where he slept for three hours, and then went to his ship.

Monday, August 25.—He dined on board, I was obliged to go out to exercise with the regiment at two o'clock preparing for our review, or should have dined with him. He came to parade in the evening; I attended him to Mrs. Wentworth's, where he drank tea and stayed till nine o'clock. His Royal Highness was pretty constant to the parade, and I think would prefer our profession to his own. It is astonishing how he remembers and knows almost all the officers of any rank in the army. If an officer has ever been presented to him, he never forgets his name or his character.

Tuesday, August 26.—He reviewed the King's Own at eleven o'clock, and I have the vanity to think the regiment never made a better review. His Highness was much pleased with their appearance. He went on board soon after the review. At three o'clock the standard of England was hoisted on board his ship; immediately on which a royal salute was fired from all the ships in the harbour. His Royal Highness intended landing this day as a Prince of the Blood, to meet the Loyal Society of the Blue and Orange at dinner, as their Royal Highnesses the Prince of Wales and the Duke of York were to honour the Society this day by being admitted members.

About half an hour after three a standard was hoisted in His Royal Highness's barge. Soon after he left his ship, on which another salute was fired from the fleet. He was attended on shore by the captains and commodore, the latter with his broad pennant, the former with theirs in the different barges. On his landing he was received by a royal salute from the garrison. The wharf and the streets were lined from the ship to the barracks where he dined, the officers and colours saluting him as he passed along, the bands playing 'God save the King.'

On his entering the mess-room he was again saluted from the citadel. We sat down twenty to a very good dinner. His Royal Highness presided as Superior, and I had the honour of being his vice. After dinner we had the three-pounders to salute. After the royal toasts, and after he had given the Prince of Wales and the Duke of York, we had three times twenty-one, and two bands playing 'Rule Britannia.' We drank twenty-eight bumper toasts, by which time, as may be well supposed, we were in pretty good order. At nine o'clock a *feu de joie* was fired by the garrison from the citadel. Those that could walk attended. I was one of the number that got up the hill. Went afterwards to the Governor's, and then attended His Royal Highness to his boat.

Saturday.—He dined with Captain Duvernet commanding the artillery, who gave us a most excellent dinner and a good deal of wine. In the evening His Royal Highness was amused with a set of fireworks designed by Duvernet which was very pretty. Also he ordered a number of live shells to be thrown which had a very good effect.

Monday, Sept, 1.—He gave a dinner at our mess-room to the Blue and Orange Society; it was as handsome a thing as I ever saw. The room was emptied for the occasion. He had all his own servants on shore, cooks, confectioners, etc. etc. His plate, glass, in short, the same as on board his ship. We had ninety dishes, fifty-five the first course and relieves, and thirty-five the second course; a most elegant dessert, champagnes, etc. I was his vice, and a most joyous day we had. The whole was the most elegant thing I ever saw.

Friday.—The *Thisbe*, Captain Hood, and the *Weazel*, Captain Sawyer, came in. His Royal Highness dined on board. We had the same party as the last day with the addition of Hood and Sawyer. In the evening His Royal Highness gave a ball on board his ship. The company assembled at seven o'clock. The quarter-deck was divided at the mizzen-mast; between it and the main-mast was for dancing, and abaft it for supper, the whole covered in with a frame and canvas, and lined with white colours and blue festoons. There were near fourteen ladies and thirty gentlemen. All the officers of his own ship, and they are the most genteel set of young men I ever saw.

We danced till one o'clock. His Highness did not dance, but paid the greatest attention possible to everybody. The ladies went below, and the colours that divided the quarterdeck were drawn up in festoons and displayed the most completely elegant supper I ever saw. At the end of the deck were two transparent paintings, the one representing the Scottish motto and thistle, the other St. George's Cross and the Garter. Upwards of sixty people sat down to supper at a table almost in the form of a horse-shoe. The supper was chiefly cold, except soups and removes, with partridges, etc., champagne, hock, etc. In short, the whole was by far the most elegant thing I ever saw. We remained more than an hour at supper, and it was wonderful to see the attention His Royal Highness paid to every one present, not neglecting a single midshipman. We danced till three o'clock, when the champagne began to operate with some of the gentlemen, and the ladies thought it near time to go on shore. I never spent a more joyous night.

Monday.—His Royal Highness gave a grand dinner in honour of their Majesties' Coronation. The garrison fired at twelve, and the fleet at one, a royal salute. We dined twenty; a superb dinner, and after the first eight toasts the ship was manned, and they fired twenty-one rounds each time. We got pretty tipsy. At nine o'clock a salute was fired by the great guns on the Citadel Hill, and answered by a *feu de joie* from the regiment drawn out on the works of the hill. We were all on board the *Andromeda* during the *feu de joie*, which had a most beautiful effect. When that was over His Royal Highness went on shore to see a most extensive display of fireworks on the exercise ground.

They were by far the finest things of the kind I had ever seen, and His Royal Highness appeared much delighted.

Friday.—Dined on board the *Andromeda*. Mrs. Minchin and Mrs. Dalrymple were there, the only ladies. A famous feed, and champagne *à l'abondance.* Came on shore about seven; tea at Minchin's. His Royal Highness told me when he came on shore that he would sup at my room. I took it as a very great honour, he having never stayed on shore after nine since his arrival. The party at supper was Le Prince, the Commodore, Brownlow, Minchin, Hood, Buller, Dalrymple, and myself. After supper we set to Burton ale. The Prince in the greatest spirits I ever saw him in my life, sang two or three songs, and as all the company did their possible to make it pleasant, in my life I never spent so joyous an evening, and for three hours laughed most incessantly. I believe our risible faculties were considerably assisted and supported by the Burton, as seven of us (the prince included) drank fourteen bottles; that mixed with champagne and claret must have made a pretty fermentation in our stomachs. We all (with stumbling and tumbling) attended His Highness to the barge, and parted, I believe, well satisfied with the evening's entertainment.

Wednesday morning,—At seven o'clock the prince made the signal for sailing; accordingly we got under weigh—*Andromeda, Thisbe,* and *Brisk*: the *Resource* waited for the commodore's despatches to carry to England.

The next day about nine we made the lighthouse off Shelburn. The entrance is something like Halifax, but much more desolate. On the west side, after you enter the harbour, there is a point called Point Carleton. After you pass that point you get a view of the town, which to be sure has as poor an appearance as anything I ever saw. The barracks are on the opposite side the harbour from the town. We came to an anchor about four, and immediately the prince did us the honour to send for us to dinner. We met my friend Vesey there, and also Major Edwards of the 6th. We spent a very pleasant day. Drank as usual rather freely of the *vin de Bordeaux;* went on shore in the evening to the barracks and came off about ten o'clock.

Friday morning.—I went on shore to breakfast with Vesey. The barracks are extremely good, but the situation the most wretched I ever beheld. Nothing on the surface of the ground but immense large stones and stumps of trees. The commanding officer's quarters are remarkably good. After breakfast I walked to town. They in general cross the harbour, as the distance is little more than half a mile, and by land it is two miles. The walk has nothing very inviting, as it is a small path made through the woods, which are in part cut down for firewood.

The town has only been settled four years, at which time there was not a single tree cut down. Indeed, from the present appearance of the place, you may easily conceive what it must have been; for in the town streets the stumps of the trees are not taken up. There are computed to be near 3000 inhabitants, blacks and whites. Some tolerably good houses, but from an account taken by the commanding engineer last winter, there are 360 uninhabited houses, which clearly proves the rapid decline of the settlement. We dined with the 6th regiment, and had a very jolly day.

Sunday.—His Royal Highness reviewed the 6th regiment. The morning was so boisterous, it was with difficulty we could get on shore, and blew so hard that half the grenadiers lost their caps, so that it was impossible to judge of the discipline of the regiment. They made a handsome appearance, but their ground was so limited (having nothing but a parade of about 120 yards by 50) that they laboured under every disadvantage of time and place. After the review, Hood, Buller, and myself walked through the woods about two miles from the barracks to a negro town called Birch Town. At the evacuation of New York there were a great number of these poor devils given lands and settled here. The place is beyond description wretched, situated on the coast in the middle of barren rocks, and partly surrounded by a thick impenetrable wood.

Their huts miserable to guard against the inclemency of a Nova Scotia winter, and their existence almost depending on what they could lay up in summer. I think I never saw wretchedness and poverty so strongly perceptible In the garb and the countenance of the human species as in these miserable outcasts. I cannot say I was sorry to quit so melancholy a dwelling. We returned by the barracks and dined again with His Royal Highness. There was a Mr. Bruce and a Mr. Skinner, American Royalists, dined; they are the only people tolerably decent in Shelburn.

Wednesday.—About three o'clock we came to an anchor in Spanish River (Cape Breton), having had a remarkably fine run from Shelburn. Immediately on our coming to anchor, the Prince sent for us to dinner. The entrance into the harbour has nothing very striking. In the afternoon we went on shore to the coal-mines, which were just opposite to where the ships lay. We all went down by the bucket into the pit, and to be sure a most infernal hole it was. The chief of the governors of Cape Breton's (*sic*) salary arises from a duty upon the coal got here. The next morning we weighed and went about nine miles up the harbour, and anchored off the new settlement called Sydney. The harbour from the mines is about three miles broad, and the shores entirely covered with wood to the water's edge.

The French, I believe, had a small settlement here at the time Louisburg was taken in '57, since when it has been quite deserted till the year '83, at which period a governor, etc., was sent out from England, a man of the name of Des Barres, a captain in the 60th regiment; a great surveyor, having published a survey of the coast of North America from Florida, but a most eccentric genius.

★★★★★★

Dyott makes a mistake here. Mr. Bradley in his life of Wolfe writes: 'A town of four thousand people, a big place for the period and locality, had grown up under the protection of the massy ramparts and frowning cannon.' Louisburg was not taken in '57, but on July 27, 1758.

Joseph Frederick Walsh or Wallet Des Barres (1722-1824}; military engineer; made successful expedition against the North American Indians 1757; surveyed the coast of Nova Scotia 1763-73; lieutenant-governor of Cape Breton 1 7841 805; colonel 1798; governor of Prince Edward Island 1805-13$ published charts of the Atlantic and North American coasts. Cf. Prowse, *History of Newfoundland.*

★★★★★★

He fixed the seat of government at Sydney, and I am sorry to say that their improvements have not a very propitious appearance at present. He dined with His Royal Highness; Lieut.-Colonel Graham, who commands a part of the 42nd regiment quartered at Sydney, dined on board. We got pretty hearty, and went on shore in the evening and supped at Colonel Graham's. The town of Sydney consists of about fifty houses situated on the banks of Spanish River, and surrounded to the very sides of the buildings by an almost impenetrable wood. There is a narrow path from the barracks just to keep up a communication, and that's all the clear country I saw. The barracks are shamefully bad; the troops have cleared a good parade and made themselves as comfortable as their situation would allow. The officers had no rooms in

57

the barracks, and were obliged to build huts and log-houses.

Monday.—We dined at a Mr. Cayler's, who has a small house and about an acre of cleared land on the opposite side of the harbour. He is an American loyalist, and possesses a considerable property in the province of New York. He is secretary to the Government of Cape Breton. We had a good dinner, and got outrageously drunk, prince and subject.

Thursday.—We left Sydney after having spent a very pleasant week; rather more wine than was good for our constitutions. The prince intended to have gone to the island of St. John's, (now Prince Edward Island), in the gulf of St. Lawrence; but the weather coming tempestuous, and contrary winds, he thought it most advisable to return to Halifax. We were unfortunate in the winds, as we did not get back till Monday following, the 20th.

Saturday.—We dined at the commissioner's; a large party, and all got wondrous drunk. On our way into town in the evening we met the chief justice's chariot. I immediately stopped it and mounted the box; His Royal Highness, the chief justice, the general, and the commissioner got inside; Brownlow, Vesey, and three others got up behind; away I set, but as it was necessary to turn round, I, in attempting that part of the charioteering, was within an inch of oversetting all the party into the harbour from one of the quays. By great good luck we escaped and away I drove like fury to town.

Wednesday.—Dined at the general's, and supped at the commodore's to take our leave of the prince, as he was to sail the next morning. We drank his health on our knees, and then attended him to his barge. He shook hands with us all, and expressed his sorrow at leaving us. When I shook him by the hand and bade him farewell, I really felt an unpleasant sensation; parting with him as a man, and more especially as a Prince of the Blood from whom I had received such repeated marks of attention. Take him altogether, I think I never saw or heard of a finer character. He is, I will venture to say, from experience, as honourable a man as ever held a commission in the British service. He has a generous and noble spirit, and will, I am convinced, when an opportunity may offer, render an essential service to his king and country. I had the honour, I may say, of living with him for three months, and in that time one may be able to judge of a man's character. I believe I never shall spend three months in that way again, for such a time of dissipation, etc. etc., I cannot suppose possible to happen. I must own I thought it time as agreeably employed as I ever experienced, and to be sure the company of a prince added not a little to the joyous hours.

Thursday morning.—At six o'clock His Royal Highness sailed for Jamaica. He was saluted from the citadel as he went out.

On the 16th, December, was performed, by the officers of the garrison and fleet, the comedy of the *School for Scandal.* The female parts were done by two young boys of the town. On the whole I declare I never saw a play better performed out of London. I was appointed treasurer and master of the ceremonies, as I did not feel equal to taking a part; my talents not at all suiting the theatrical line.

January 1, 1789.—I dined at Governor Wentworth's. Spent a very jolly day. Had rain and thaw for a week.

8th.—I was seized with a bad sore throat, which confined me a week.

22nd.—A ball and supper given by the navy and army to the town. A very jolly evening; danced after supper. Just as the company was departing, they were alarmed by a cry of fire, which proceeded from the stores and warehouses of the greatest tradesmen in town, being in flames. The garrison were immediately ordered to attend; the seamen from the fleet also assisted, and by very great exertion the threatened dreadful conflagration was in some degree prevented. As it was expected, a great part of the town had been destroyed. A large lot, containing four houses, were entirely consumed. They were detached, and it was with great difficulty the flames were prevented catching the houses opposite, amongst which stood the Government House. The buildings are all of wood, and a most dreadful appearance the fire had, as it burnt like paper. I thought at one time a great part of the town must have been consumed. The damage is supposed to amount to near £20,000. Happily no lives were lost.

February.—The officers in garrison fitted up a new theatre. On the 26th opened it with the *Merchant of Venice.* It was as complete a thing for the size as I ever saw. Boxes and a first and second pit. The plays were very entertaining, as some of the characters were vastly well supported. This month we had a good deal of snow and dirty tempestuous weather. But what with whist and good eating and drinking (as our markets were well supplied), we endeavoured to drive away all gloomy thoughts, and to enjoy life in the best manner the dreary regions of Nova Scotia would allow. We had much more snow this winter than the preceding one.

March.—We had a packet arrived, which brought us the first European news we had had for some months, and also the melancholy account of the king's indisposition.

★★★★★★

On November 5, 1788, the king, who for some time had been in poor health, became mad. February 1789, Pitt brought in the Regency Bill. On March 10 it was announced to Parliament that the king had recovered.

★★★★★★

Our harbour was frozen up for some days, and on the 10th and 12th we had very good skating in many parts of it. This month was fatal to the moose and caribou; great quantities were brought to market; but in my opinion it is very little better than carrion.

April 16.—We had a jolly meeting of the Blue and Orange. We continued our plays at the New Theatre to crowded audiences through the winter. They went off remarkably well. We collected £400, almost the whole of which was expended on the house. Closed in June.

June.—Our fishing amusement commenced. No occurrence worthy of note.

July 21.—We received an order to march four companies of the regiment to Fort Edward, near Windsor, to be headquarters.

We left Halifax on the 24th; marched through the woods to Falkner's, fifteen miles; from thence to Woodworth's, fifteen more; and sixteen from that to Windsor. The middle stage the very worst road I ever saw, and the places we stopped at all single houses with an adjoining barn, where the men and their ladies all pigged together, where gods met gods and jostled in the dark.

The country round Windsor for about a mile or two is cleared, and is very pretty, particularly after coming through such a wilderness. The tide from the Bay of Fundy rises at Windsor upwards of fifty feet, and at low water it leaves as disagreeable a sight as I ever saw. You have nothing to look upon but a filthy sand and most dirty mud-banks, as the water almost entirely quits the river. Windsor was settled by the French a considerable time back; but on this province becoming a part of the British dominions, they were literally driven out of the country.

There are some tolerably good farms in the neighbourhood, and some very pleasant rides. The town of Windsor consists of, I believe, about forty houses. The fort is an old mud-work with a block-house and barracks for about one hundred men at most. We found our people much crowded, as we had near double that number. I was very unpleasantly situated, being obliged to double up with a jolly ensign, or to take lodgings in town.

On the 24th of August I was ordered to Halifax to August prepare the three companies for their review, which took place the 15th September, and I may say positively that no part of the regiment ever made a better appearance or gained greater credit.

March 1790.—They were very gay at Halifax—plays, balls, and assemblies; not near so much whist as usual, but an abundance of good eating and drinking. We were much longer this winter without hearing from Europe than we had ever been since our arrival.

I returned to Fort Edward the 27th February, when no accounts had arrived. The first week in March was as severe weather as I ever felt, almost a perpetual storm of snow and hail. The Windsor river at this season is quite a curiosity. Vast quantities of ice of an amazing size floating up with the flood tide, and at low water leaving perfect mountains all over the river; the very look is sufficient to petrify one.

I dined with Governor Wentworth during my stay at Halifax on some caribou (the reindeer of this country). It is nearly the size of a yearling calf, with stronger legs, the head and body resembling the fallow deer. I thought it but very poor eating; indeed, any animal that lives in the woods during this season of the year cannot be very fat, and of course, in my opinion, not very palatable. We had also some venison of the fallow deer from New England, but very inferior to a good haunch of English doe.

To my astonishment, on the 18th of this month I was informed by letter that Dick Beresford, who had got a second-lieutenancy in the 21st regiment, was arrived in Halifax on his way to join. I set forward the next morning to see him, and stayed four days in town, when he returned with me to the fort and remained near a week. It is a most pleasing satisfaction that of meeting with a particular acquaintance in a distant country, and who has recently quitted your connections. It cannot be described; it is the next enjoyment to 'a return to your native country after an age of absence.'

My hope of experiencing that felicity appears to me in a very glimmering light; nor can I determine what limits to fix for my duration in this most inhospitable clime. All I can conclude definitely is to remain with my regiment till I acquire the first step an officer can consider as real promotion in the profession I am embarked in. Towards the end of this month the season began to get rather milder, and for the four first days of April the snow and frost began to disappear very perceptibly, and we had every reason to expect an early spring.

The 6th was as fine a day as you commonly find in England about the beginning of May, when lo and behold, on the 7th we had as violent a snowstorm, and of much longer duration, than any we had the whole winter. It must have fallen on a level near five inches, but as it blew a gale of wind, it drifted in many places as many feet.

On the 8th we had a northwester, with some showers of snow and hard frost; and on the 9th spring again returned, and the weather as temperate as on the 5th and 6th. It is impossible to depend on the weather for four-and-twenty hours in this country, and the sudden change is most wonderful.

On the 12th we had another severe snowstorm; it continued the whole day and fell near a foot deep. The roads near this place are beyond anything I ever saw; scarcely passable either on foot or horseback. A farmer brought a very great natural curiosity to the fort. It was the produce of a ewe. It had one head, two necks, one windpipe, one stomach, one heart, and in all other particulars two distinct animals. It was alive when it came into the world, but expired soon after. The ewe had another fine lamb soon after that lived and did very well.

On the 4th September Forbes and a party of friends from the 6th regiment paid us a visit. On their return I rode with them as far as Horton, sixteen miles through the woods, and a most villainous road over a prodigious mountain. The township of Horton is situated in a valley, on one side of which is the Basin of Mines, and what they call the Grand Pre or great meadow. It is the most extensive flat I ever saw, consisting of upwards of 2300 acres of dyked and salt marsh. The settlers are chiefly New Englanders and veritable Yankees.

The country is pretty, though no great extent cleared, except the Grand Pre. There is a tide river like the one at Windsor, and on the opposite side is the settlement of Cornwallis, which is considerably larger than Horton, and much more land cultivated. I did not cross the water, but on the whole I think the valley of Horton and Cornwallis much more picturesque than Windsor; but the farms are not so extensive, nor are the inhabitants so industrious—the former possessing either too much of the levelling and indolent indisposition of the New Englanders, and the latter what they called country folks, or, by way of explanation, from Great Britain or Ireland.

August, 1791.—We had fine weather this month. About the middle of it I made a party to take a view of the Basin of Mines at the head of the Bay of Fundy, and so called from the supposition of their being mines of silver in the neighbourhood, and also mines of copper. The Duke of York has the exclusive right to them all by a grant from the Crown, and has some people now in Nova Scotia employed to investigate them. The Basin of Mines is eighteen miles in length one way and fourteen the other, surrounded entirely by woods. On one side is a remarkably bluff hill called Cape Blomidon, a great curiosity from its stupendous appearance, being perpendicular from the sea, which washes its base, and is near a thousand yards high.

We endeavoured to scramble to the top, but in vain, as we were prevented by what exactly resembled a stone fortification when we had got within about thirty yards of the top. We had a most extensive view of sea and woods.

On the beach we picked up a number of pieces of copper ore and some very curious stones. We were entirely guided by the tides, which rise in the Basin and the adjacent rivers near forty feet, so that we were obliged to go with one tide and return with the next. We did not get back to Windsor till near an hour after high water, so that we had three miles to row against the tide, and very hard work we found it.

On the 25th of August I went to Halifax to meet my friend Dickson, who was returned from the States, but by no means reinstated in his health. He wished to get to the fort to settle his accounts in order to his going to Europe in the fall, which made my stay in town but short. I returned to the fort on the 30th instant. The day after I left Halifax, to the great surprise of the bigwigs and natives. Lord Dorchester arrived. His lordship had sailed from Quebec on board a frigate (the *Alligator*), had met with a gale of wind off the coast, and on account of having received some damage, she was obliged to put into Halifax to repair. His stay was very short, as the frigate was repaired without loss of time and proceeded to sea on the 3rd September.

On the 22nd October I set forward for Annapolis Royal to pay a visit to the three companies of the regiment. The distance from Windsor is eighty-six miles. Some part of the country for a distance of two miles on each side of the road is tolerably well cultivated. The town of

Annapolis is a very old settlement, and originally the seat of government of this province. It is situated on a river which empties itself into the Bay of Fundy twenty-one miles below the town. There is a fort with some outworks to defend the river, but the works are all suffered to go to ruin. There have been most excellent barracks built of brick, but they are in the same state as the fortifications, and the troops at present but ill accommodated.

Since the American revolution a number of loyalists have come to settle in the neighbourhood from the States. The trade very trifling, the exports chiefly to the West Indies of horses, fish, and timber. I returned to Fort Edward on the 27th. December Saturday.—I dined with Major Boyd of the 20th regiment; a party at his quarters, and to be sure I finished the week as I began, and never was more inebriated in my life.

January 1, 1792.—A fine day, a little snow on the ground and a slight frost. We had some severe weather about the 20th.

The 23rd, the coldest day we had felt. I was obliged to go to Halifax on business. The 24th, I dined with Major Rawdon; the 25th, at Mr. Morden's, and returned to the fort on the 26th.

On the 28th Major Rawdon, Parkhill of the 16th, Neale of the 21st, and John Hodgson, (1757-1846; served in North America; wounded in Holland 1799; governor of Bermuda and Curaçoa; general 1830), of ours, arrived. Our commanding officer had ordered two cases of claret, and for three days that the party remained I never saw such hard drinking. Rawdon is without exception the most determined fellow at a bottle of claret I ever knew. They left us on the 31st, Hodgson for Annapolis, the others for Halifax. I had fully determined to pay a visit to Annapolis in the course of this month, but was prevented by reason of my waiting to accompany Major Rawdon.

I never saw finer weather than we had till the 21st, when there fell in the course of eight-and-forty hours the greatest quantity of snow I ever remember. The very day it began Rawdon, Parkhill, and Neale arrived in order to proceed to Annapolis, but found it impracticable on account of the great depth of snow. They remained with us till Friday the 25th, and returned to town. We had four most violent hard-going days of course.

On the 15th I went to Halifax, and on the 17th was admitted a member of the Society of friendly brothers in a knot belonging to the 16th regiment. We kept the day in honour of St. Patrick by dining together at the coffee-house, and a pretty scene of drunkenness it was. I stayed in town till the 25th, leading a life of debauchery. The March packet from New York arrived on the 19th, which gave me some business to answer my letters.

The *Circe* frigate, commanded by Captain Gardiner, was lying at Halifax. I got very intimate with the captain, a most gentlemanlike fellow, and I suppose the youngest man for a post-captain in the navy. We had a most sumptuous entertainment at the Government House in honour of the Prince of Wales's birthday. Kept it up till four o'clock next morning.

On the evening of the 17th a fire broke out in town, which raged with great violence, and consumed six dwelling-houses and an ordnance store. Luckily it was a calm evening, or the town must have been consumed.

On the 25th September, I received the account of the death of my ever-lamented sister, Mrs. Lee. I don't think on any occasion I ever suffered so much or felt more real grief than when I read the account.

On the 12th November I dined at Commissioner Duncan's. I had a toothache in the morning; after dinner the pain increased to a violent degree, and in the evening I was so ill as to be obliged to go to bed and send for the surgeon, who found me in a high fever. I was obliged to remain at the commissioner's four days till the fever abated, when I was moved to quarters in his carriage. Recovered in about ten days.

December.—On Monday at twelve o'clock on the 3rd we sailed from the wharf in Halifax with a fine north wind. I must own I felt rather sorry to leave a place where I had spent many very pleasant days, and also grief to part with some friends of the regiment for whom I had a most sincere regard. We had a fine wind all day; I did not suffer much from sea-sickness, though a little squeamish from taking too much of Gregory Townsend's wine the day before sailing.

Monday.—A fine day and fair wind. I could not help remarking the singular superstition of the captain of the ship, though I know that character is attributed to sailors in general. Two years ago they lost a man overboard from the ship in the latitude we were in this day. The captain remarked to me that every time he had passed that latitude since, which I believe was four or five times, he had always observed a small bird swimming about on the water, as near as he could possibly conjecture to the spot where he lost his man. I never was more astonished than at his remark.

On Wednesday at twelve o'clock we sounded again, and found bottom, sixty fathoms water. Sounded again at eight o'clock, and imagined ourselves off Scilly. We stood on all night, and sounded on Thursday morning at eight o'clock. Imagined ourselves in the Channel. At ten o'clock we made the land to our great joy, and which was conjectured to be the Start Point, about thirty leagues up Channel; but on getting in with it it proved to be the Land's End at the entrance of the Channel.

Friday.—A most charming morning, close in with the land, and running ten and eleven knots we made the Isle of Wight about ten o'clock, and at twelve spoke a pilot boat, who agreed to take the passengers on shore to Portsmouth, to which we most cheerfully consented, though we did not suppose the ship was so far distant from Portsmouth as we found her to be, which was upward of forty miles. However, we landed by ten o'clock. The transport I felt on setting my foot on British ground after an absence of six years cannot easily be described.

I was astonished to find they were arming, supposing from the accounts when I left Nova Scotia that the French business would be all settled.

★★★★★★

The danger of Holland and the activity of the revolutionists stirred the English Government to take measures of defence. On December 1, 1792, a part of the militia was embodied, and naval preparations were made.

★★★★★★

I left Portsmouth Saturday evening in the mail coach, and got to London on Sunday morning the 30th December, where I remained till Tuesday, 8th January, and got into the mail coach, and arrived at Freeford on Wednesday the 9th to my great joy and satisfaction. On account of an augmentation of the army, General George Morrison, (1704?-1799; lieutenant-general 1782; general 1796), directed me to employ myself on the recruiting service, and at request made Lichfield my quarters, and that I should have a party as soon as possible.

I remained at Freeford till the 26th March; went to Ashburn for two days, and to Misterton and Leicester the 30th. Stayed there till the 4th April, and on the 6th went to Newcastle to receive the out-pensioners in the counties of Stafford and Chester fit for garrison duty.

Stayed there till the 8th, and at Keel till the 12th; halted at Freeford one day, and proceeded to London the 14th. During the month of February, and till the regiment marched, I was employed at the request of Lord Uxbridge to drill the Stafford militia, then embodied on account of the war.

When in town I was employed in effecting a purchase of a company in the regiment from Rose, in which I succeeded. I had great difficulty in being able to get leave to stay at home. General Morrison being very pressing that I should repair to Newfoundland. He at last consented that I should remain on the recruiting service. My principal reason for going to London was at the request of Lord Uxbridge, (created Earl of Uxbridge 1784; died 1812), who solicited me in strong terms to give my aid to the drilling of his regiment at Plymouth. I was very much averse to that duty, but as I considered myself under particular obligations to his lordship, I consented.

On the 4th June, in honour of His Majesty's birthday, all the people employed in the dockyard walk in procession through the town with bands of musick and emblems or models of their different business. The custom is annual, and the concourse of people assembled is immense. There were upwards of two thousand marched in order. Some of the models and devices were extremely beautiful. The different companies had flags emblematical of their employ. Lord Uxbridge gave a dinner to the whole regiment, and a quart of ale to each man. There were tables laid out in the barrack square, and the whole dined together. Unfortunately the weather was not very good; however it went off vastly well, and the men were very happy.

Lord Uxbridge applied to Major-General Hotham, to appoint me his Major of Brigade for the brigade he was to command on Maker-heights near Plymouth, which the general complied with, and I became a major accordingly. (Probably George Hotham—born 1741— son of Sir Beaumont Hotham; a general officer in the army; colonel of the 14th regiment of Foot; died 1806).

Our brigade was a very small one; it only consisted of the Glamorgan Militia and a park of artillery. However I considered it as a feather in my cap, and was much pleased with the appointment.

September.—On the 6th I went with Lord Granville Leveson-Gower, (1773-1846; youngest son of the first Marquis of Stafford; created Viscount Granville 1815; advanced to an earldom 1833), into Staffordshire to attend Lichfield races, a thing I had not seen for nine years. We got to Freeford on the Sunday to dinner. Lord G. stayed till Tuesday, then went to Lichfield. The balls were thinly attended, but a wonderful crowd on the race-ground. I was quite delighted, as it put me so much in mind of old times.

Our camp broke up on the 12th October, and I went to October London on the 14th, stayed at Uxbridge House ten days with Lord Paget, and went with him to Leicester to hunt.

★★★★★★

Lord Henry William Paget, first Marquis of Anglesey (1768–1854); raised a regiment of infantry in 1793, chiefly from the Earl of Uxbridge's Staffordshire tenants, which on the outbreak of the war became the 80th Foot; commanded the cavalry in Spain under Sir John Moore, and the cavalry and horse artillery at Waterloo, where he lost a leg.

★★★★★★

I remained there a week. He mounted me two days. From Leicester I went to Beaudesert, and on my arrival there found an order to go to Plymouth to attend as a member of a general court-martial.

Arrived there on the 17th November, it continued till the 26th for the trial of Lieutenant Ford of the Invalios.

On the 7th December I again quitted Plymouth for Staffordshire (General Hotham having leave of absence), came through Bath, saw several of my old friends, and amongst the rest Lord Enniskillen, Mrs. Colville (late Miss Ford), and my old captain, Gouldney. Got to Freeford the 15th December. Soon after my return I spent some days at Beaudesert, and also at Ravenhill with Colonel Sneyd. We had some very pleasant parties at Fisherwick, and in December a masquerade and ball at Drakelow, a most excellent night.

Christmas Day I spent at Freeford, and went to pass New Year's Day at Beaudesert. For the first time saw a baron of beef roasted; it was as much as two servants could carry, and reminded one of the old English hospitality. The house was full and very pleasant; a grand ball there on the 16th, good supper and plenty of dancing.

In February 1794 I paid a visit into Leicestershire for a week. In the beginning of March I went to Keel, and from thence with the Sneyds to Caperthorn, Mr. Davenport's, a very pretty place in Cheshire. Was out a fortnight.

On the 28th I received a letter from Lord Charles Henry Somerset, (1767–1831; son of the fifth Duke of Beaufort; colonel of the 1st West India Regiment; governor of the Cape of Good Hope), offering me the majority of a regiment he was going to raise, if I chose to purchase it. I accordingly went to London on the business, where I arrived the 1st April, but from his lordship's terms I found it would not do; indeed it did not appear very certain government would allow him to raise a regiment, and in case I had purchased the majority I was to be allowed only £1100 for my company.

I was in Westminster Hall when Lord Cornwallis gave his evidence respecting Hastings; there surely never was a more persecuted man.

★★★★★★

The impeachment of Warren Hastings began in 1788. Lord Cornwallis, in 1794, gave timely evidence in Hastings' favour, and he was acquitted on the 23rd of April 1795.

★★★★★★

On the 11th April I had the honour of being presented to His Majesty at the *levée* by my noble friend Lord Uxbridge, Some people have certainly profited by attending on Courts, but I fear my visit will not be of that nature. My friend Hodgson returned with me into the country on the 15th April, and stayed at Freeford till the 20th.

On the 7th May I left Freeford to commence the campaign at Plymouth, where I arrived on the 9th. Found all things as usual.

The garrison consisting of the 25th, 40th, Stafford, West May York, and Glamorgan. Our camps did not take place till the 20th May at Roborough, and 23rd at Maker, the former consisting of the Monmouth, Worcester, West York, and Northampton regiments; the other camp, the Cornwall, Glamorgan, and 96th regiments.

The latter end of May I received a letter from Lord Charles Somerset to say that the business of his regiment went on, and again offering me the majority. I hesitated for some time. However, I went again to London on the business, and as Lord Uxbridge and Lord G. Leveson were going to town by way of Portsmouth in Lord U.'s yacht, I accompanied them. We were at Portsmouth just in time to see the grand ceremony of the king's visit; it was a most magnificent sight.

I got to town on the 26th June, and had the business of the majority arranged to my satisfaction. I left London on the 2nd July, and joined the Loyal British at Devizes the next day; found Lord Charles there with about two hundred—not men—say recruits. However, numbers is the object, and in that we were very successful for the time.

On the 9th July my friend Lord Granville Leveson called on me in his way back to Plymouth, and on the 10th I accompanied him in his chaise to my old quarters, where I stayed three weeks, and never passed so pleasant a time; being in love, and having the object of your adoration present, makes any place cheerful; this was my case; I certainly never knew what it was to love till I saw the best creature existing (Lovely Fanny).

I was obliged to quit Plymouth in order to join the Loyal British again at Devizes, and to my great grief left it on Wednesday the 30th July, as miserable as mortal could be possible, and got to my regiment the next day. I marched two hundred of the regiment on the 4th August to Trowbridge, ten miles, where I remained alone till the 15th, as dull and as heavy as possible.

Trowbridge is a place of great manufactory for broadcloths and kersymeres; and the country about is very beautiful. On my return to Devizes on the 15th I found Sir Robert Sloper, (genera] 1796; died 1802), was arrived to inspect the regiment, which he did that and the next day. His report was not very favourable for us, indeed he had reason for it.

On the 21st I left Devizes for Plymouth, where I arrived on the 22nd to dinner; found all my friends glad to see me.

September 17th.—Lord Huntley's and General Ley's regiments were lying in Cawsand Bay to go to Gibraltar, and a part of Lord Richard Howe's fleet, (Earl Howe, (1726-99), admiral of the fleet), was in the Sound, so that Plymouth was quite gay.

★★★★★★

George Gordon, fifth Duke of Gordon, Marquis of Huntly (1770-1836); as Marquis of Huntly served with the Guards in Flanders, 1793-45 raised a regiment, now known as the Gordon Highlanders, and commanded it 1795-9, in Spain, Corsica, Ireland, and Holland; commanded a division in the Walcheren expedition, 1809.

★★★★★★

The day I got there I dined with a large party at Lord Uxbridge's. The Marquisses Worcester, (Henry Charles Somerset, Marquis of Worcester, sixth Duke of Beaufort, 1766-1835), and Huntley; Colonels Hope, Campbell, Hervey, Aston, Sneyd, and Captains Legge, Pakenham, and Tilson of the navy.

I went from Plymouth by way of Bristol to Freeford, just to bid farewell before I went to Ireland; got there on Tuesday the 30th September, and only stayed till Friday. Arrived at Bristol on Saturday morning, time enough to October attend the regiment's embarkation, which took place at Pill, five miles from Bristol. The men, on account of being the Bristol regiment, did not altogether approve of marching through the town without halting; however we got them on with fair words and some foul blows. We lay windbound at Pill from the 4th to the 13th, and of all the tedious things I ever experienced, it was the most unpleasant. We had a fine passage. We sailed about eleven o'clock on Monday, and got up to the quay in Dublin by daybreak on Wednesday. I went on shore after breakfast and waited on the commander-in-chief, (General Robert Cunninghame, afterwards Lord Rossmore). Was much surprised to find the regiment was not to remain in Dublin, but to march to Clonmell, eighty-two miles south. We were to march in two divisions, the first to disembark on Friday and the second on Saturday. I chose to go with the second division, as I wished to see all off before me.

We had a continuation of rain for near six weeks after our arrival, such persevering rain I never saw; so constant that it was with difficulty we could ever get a parade. Our men were extremely sickly, and we lost twelve by death in two months. After Christmas the weather cleared up and we had a spell of frost and dry season. I made the best use possible of my time, and worked the regiment as hard as I could to get them into some order. I can't say much for Clonmell as a quarter; there are only one or two pleasant families in the neighbourhood; but their being three or four miles from the town makes the visiting not only expensive, but uncomfortable. The desertion from the regiment at Clonmell was infamous, and the way we were taken in by rascals enlisting and immediately deserting was the most iniquitous business I ever saw.

The winter was rather severe for this part of the world, but very much preferable to the incessant rain we had in November and December.

On the 27th March, 1795, Lord Charles Somerset arrived at Clonmell to take the command of the regiment. On the 31st he reviewed his regiment, and I believe no man was ever more pleased or surprised than he was at the discipline, dress, appearance, etc., of the corps.

The day after the review I left the regiment to go to England in order to forward our recruits for an augmentation, on the completion of which I expected the rank of Lieutenant-Colonel. I left Clonmell on the 1st April and travelled to Waterford; saw Lord Waterford's place at Curraghmore. (George-de-la-Poer, second Earl of Tyrone—1735-1800; created Marquis of Waterford in the peerage of Ireland 1789).

The situation is very fine, the house but indifferent and not at all in the style of neatness of an English nobleman's place. Waterford is a large populous town, and the new bridge across the River Suir, a very fine piece of architecture; it is 1300 feet long and built by Cox the American. The quay at Waterford is very extensive and handsome, some very good houses, and a most elegant and magnificent assembly-room.

I sailed from Waterford on the 4th, and landed next morning at Hubberston in Milford Haven; stepped into the mail coach at six o'clock on Monday morning and arrived at Bristol by twelve next day. Travelled through Monmouthshire, which is the most picturesque beautiful county I ever saw, and crossed the Severn at the New Passage. I left Bristol at seven o'clock on Monday, and got to Freeford at one the next day. Our recruiting parties completed our numbers, and on the 25th May I set out from Freeford for London in order to get my step established.

During my stay in London I made an application to Lord George Henry Lennox, (1737-1805; son of the second Duke of Richmond; ensign 1754; general 1793), to get appointed his Brigade Major-General, to which his lordship in most kind manner consented. I stayed in London till the 6th June without having accomplished my wish respecting the step of Lieutenant-Colonel, and returned to Freeford with Will Inge, where I remained till the 13th, and then took my departure for Plymouth to enter on my new office of Brigade Major-General.

Got there on the 15th June, waited on Lord George and was received most kindly. I found my situation very different from what it had been when I was on the staff at Plymouth before. I lived entirely at Lord George's, and a more pleasant family does not exist on the earth. I had plenty of employ, as most of the business of the district went through my hands. In the beginning of August I got my rank of Lieutenant-Colonel. I renewed my visits to Maristow with a pleasure that I cannot express. I found a stray garrison at Plymouth, the 17th, 25th, 31st, 32nd, 48th; they all embarked in July to prepare for the West Indies; the 25th, 31st, and 48th to Portsmouth; the 17th, 32nd, and 67th for Cork.

Plymouth was this summer to me more pleasant than ever, as I lived in the most comfortable and happy manner possible with the Governor's family, and three such people in one house are not to be found in the whole world as Lord George, Lady Louisa, and Miss

Lennox.

September and October.—In September the 103rd regiment was drafted, and I was attached to the 28th regiment, and in consequence of an order for all officers to join their regiments going or on foreign service I was under the necessity of giving up the most enviable situation in the world. His R.H. the Duke of York arrived at Plymouth on the 3rd October and reviewed the camps, etc. He stayed only two days and lived at the Government House, which was rather a curious circumstance considering the business of Lennox and his Highness; however nothing disagreeable appeared. (This refers to a duel fought in 1789 between Frederick Augustus, Duke of York, and Charles Lennox, eldest son of George Henry Lennox. Cf. Wilkins, *Mrs, Fitzherbert and George IV*).

From the time it was determined I was to leave Plymouth I was wretched, principally on account of parting from the woman of all others I ever did or ever shall love, and also the Lennoxes and Sneyds gave me some pangs, as I have extreme affection for them all. The melancholy day at length arrived when the woeful parting was to take place. Wednesday the 21st October was the wretched day. The Stafford militia set out on their march for Winchester, and I and Markham (?), the finest fellow in the world, after a sorry parting at the governor's house, got into a chaise and proceeded to Maristow, where we dined and supped, and afterwards I passed the most dreadful trial I ever experienced. I cannot—words cannot—express what I felt on taking leave of Sweet Fanny.

Lord March (?) and I bent our way towards Portsmouth in as melancholy a mood as ever two fellows journied, for although he was not in love, still he had that worth about him, that he had a fellow-feeling for a friend in misery, and indeed suffered on his own account at parting with a number of people for whom he had a great regard. March and I parted at Southampton, and I got to Portsmouth on Friday evening in order to join the 28th regiment, which had been embarked some time for the West Indies.

An opportunity offering I made an exchange into the 25th regiment, which was a circumstance I much wished, as it kept up closely the connexion with Lord George. The first battalion of the regiment was already in the West Indies, and the detachment embarked with the rest of the (*illegible*) was going out as an augmentation.

I effected my exchange into the 25th and embarked at Portsmouth on Monday the 9th November for the West Indies. During my stay at Portsmouth I never was so tired of a place in my life. I went to Captain Berkley for two days, which was the first moment of comfort I felt after leaving dear Devonshire.

Tuesday the 10th.—All the fleet dropped down to St. Helen's and expected to sail positively on Wednesday, but notwithstanding the most delightful wind we did not proceed to sea, and on Thursday the wind changed, and we returned to Spithead, where we remained till the 13th, when we put to sea; light winds all day.

The 16th from the eastward and till the 17th in the afternoon, when it changed to the south-west. The admiral (Sir Hugh Cloberry Christian—1747-98; rear-admiral; served in the West Indies 1779-82; knighted 1796; commander-in-chief at the Cape of Good Hope 1798), in consequence made the signal to rendezvous in Torbay, but only eleven sail could fetch in; our ship was fortunately one of the number, as a most violent gale of wind came on that evening which did material damage to a number of ships and obliged the fleet to return to Portsmouth. Several of the ships were lost and crews perished; one of them, with a number of officers and 200 men of the 63rd regiment, perished on the rocks of Portland.

★★★★★★

Richard Hussey Vivian writes in November 30, 1795: 'The 63rd lost a transport and 180 men. . . . Captain Godley tells me that there were 14 officers and 235 bodies of soldiers lying on the beach of Portland at the same time.' Cf *Lord Vivian, a Memoir*)..

★★★★★★

Finding there was a possibility of our ship lying a few days in Torbay, on the 21st I went to Maristow, where I remained till 23rd, and four happier days no man ever passed. Our transport had sailed from Torbay, but I got a passage to Portsmouth with the 10th regiment, and arrived at Spithead the 26th November. Found the fleet was again preparing for sea, but from the damage that had been sustained and want of fair wind, we did not again put to sea till the 9th December. Whilst the fleet was lying at Spithead I went over to Stoke, Lord George Lennox's, and passed several most pleasant days. I cannot too often repeat what a charming family they are.

From the 14th to the 24th constant gales of wind from the south-west. On the 20th a tolerably clear day, and we saw the greatest part of the fleet, and also on the 21st in the afternoon, but parted from them in the night.

On the 24th we could see only four sail, the weather still continuing very foggy. A ship hoisted a signal of distress in the morning: we bore down to speak her, but she fired a gun and bore away, as we supposed, for a port. As we considered ourselves completely separated from the fleet, I proposed to the master of the ship to open the private instructions, which he did, and found the directions to be that in case of separation the rendezvous was Carlisle Bay, Barbadoes. The cabin-boy alarmed us with a report that the ship had sprung a leak forward and was making a good deal of water; but on our examining, it was found to be nothing more than a bolt that had started in the upper part of the bows and was of no consequence. In the evening the wind veered to WNW.

25th.—Christmas Day brought us the wind to NNE. with hazy weather. We saw in the morning eight sail, but could not distinguish any men-of-war. We spoke a ship, the captain of which told us that in the gale of the 22nd he saw two ships totally dismasted. It being a day of great hilarity on shore, I ordered the men an allowance of porter in addition to their grog, as also the best dinner the situation would afford. I was glad to find we had no man sick or an appearance of illness from our first sailing; this I attributed to the great precaution I caused to be observed as to cleanliness in every particular.

The first January 1796 proved tolerable fine with the wind west and by north. Spoke a ship, the *Europa*, belonging to the fleet, a transport, but had no troops.

On the 6th we had been out one month, and melancholy to say we were not more than four days' sail from England, notwithstanding we had been out as many weeks. I don't suppose any people ever had such a continuation of contrary wind for so long a time. We had only one sail in sight for the last three days. Indeed, we had almost constant rain and thick weather.

10th.—I read prayers to all the people, which indeed I never failed doing on a Sunday morning when the weather would permit. The morning remarkably fine, but the wind had got to the south of west. I could feel a most perceptible change of climate for the last two or three days that we had been running to the south, and this day was quite warm on the deck. I got a large tub by way of bathing machine, which I had filled in my cabin with salt water and managed to give myself a most complete lavage, in which I stood great need, as the dirt

(I may say filth) accumulates most wonderfully on board all ships, and ours was by no means a very cleanly one. Indeed, much could not be said in that particular in favour of my companions embarked. I mean to continue my bathing both for comfort, as the climate gets warm, and for the preservation of health. I had tubs prepared and fixed on the forecastle of the ship in order that the men, when the weather is sufficiently warm, may wash themselves all over.

From the 10th to the 17th we had a continuation of contrary wind from west and by south to SSW. with squally and two or three heavy gales. Our latitude on the 17th was nearly the same as on the 10th, so that we had passed as unpleasant a week as it was possible without getting at all nearer the place of our destination. In the course of the week we saw several of the hawk's-bill turtle floating on the surface of the water. We only observed one ship all this week. I think in my existence I never passed so melancholy a week. Day after day foul wind with the sea so much agitated as to make it a service both of difficulty and danger to walk the deck.

However, as I am a great believer in Mr. Pope's idea, 'Whatever is, is right,' I comforted and consoled myself with that thought, together with the first of all blessings, the hope of returning and enjoying my friends in old England. No situation can possibly be more unpleasant than being embarked in a transport with eight or ten men you never saw till the day you got on board, and these men, though well meaning in every particular, still some of them being very young, and of course inexperienced, their not having lived at all in the society to which you have been accustomed, and not finding one, who from particular circumstances you could form a friendship, makes the time appear extremely dull and extremely tedious. Captain Bushey I always found a most worthy good man, and had it not been for his society on board, I don't know what would have become of me.

19th.—A most charming day and very sultry in the morning. I set the people to dance in the evening, all the officers assisted at the ball, and it put everybody in good spirits. It was the first day since our departure that was at all calculated for this kind of amusement. A small flying fish chopped on board the ship, which was a very great curiosity to those who had never seen anything of the kind. I preserved it in spirits in a phial.

26th.—The wind continued to the eastward and had every appearance of continuing, so that we concluded we had reached what we had long been looking for, the trade winds, as by observation our latitude was 28. The cause of the trade winds (as they are called from continuing the same way) has not been assigned. They generally extend to 28 or 29 degrees of latitude from the line and universally blow from the eastward. The sailing in these latitudes before the wind (as far as sailing can be called pleasant) is certainly a very great improvement in this mode of travelling when compared with the perpetual adverse retrograde jumbling infernal motions and movements we had experienced.

The weather and wind still continuing, and the master of the ship having pronounced us fairly in the trades, I had the between-decks where the men sleep most thoroughly scoured and cleansed, and as our climate began to warm and must be expected to increase in heat daily, I gave out some instructions and regulations relative to what arrangements I judged necessary in order to preserve health. From a scrupulous exactness and attention to cleanliness, and by giving encouragement to all sorts of amusements, I alone attribute the very healthy state of the men, not having more than one or two in the surgeon's report, and even these of little consequence.

27th.—Charming fine weather, and not near so hot as we had felt it before we got into the trades, owing to a brisk breeze at ENE.; notwithstanding the sun had very great power, still the breeze was much more refreshing and cool than when we were in more northerly latitudes and had southerly winds. The ship we spoke on the 25th kept company with us. In the afternoon of this day we passed the tropic. In the course of the morning saw several tropical birds, and in the afternoon a ceremony, with which the sailors always treat their brethren that have not passed the line, was performed. It is a very old custom, and practised by, I believe, all nations. One of the sailors is made to personate Neptune, who is supposed to rise from the sea, accompanied by his wife Amphitrite. They are clad in a most ridiculous manner, in order to represent the high and mighty god and goddess of the ocean. These deities have two attendants, one of which is supposed to be a very humble inhabitant of the deep, on earth yclept a barber.

Mister Neptune greets you with a welcome to the tropic and an offer of a *bottle of milk* and a newspaper that he is supposed to have got a few days before from ashore, adding he shall order a prosperous gale to carry you to your intended port. This is what passes in the cabin and with the passengers, who order according to custom some rum, etc., by way of treat to Neptune and his party for his visit. But the ceremony observed to the poor devils of sailors who have never passed the line is not quite so courteous. One of the Neptune's attendants seizes the unfortunate man, and after blindfolding him, they place him on a pole put across a large tub of water. The attendant then puts the small end of a speaking trumpet in his mouth, which obliges the poor wretch to stretch it open pretty wide.

Some questions are then asked, such as, 'What countryman are you?' 'Where are you bound to?' etc. etc. On his making the reply a quantity of salt water is poured down the trumpet, a part of which of course finds its way towards the stomach. An oath is then administered purporting that he is never to suffer any person to pass the line without undergoing the like ceremony. As the person initiated into these Deistical mysteries of the tropical latitudes is obliged to repeat this oath, he is the whole time saluted with libations of the god's element, which very much against his inclination he is doomed to partake.

Then comes on the barber's work, who after daubing the face and head of the fast-bound stranger with the vilest of all possible compositions, of tar, grease, etc. etc., proceeds to shave him with a piece of old iron, which not only takes away the sweet-scented fine oily lather, but scrapes the face (carrying some particles of skin with it) to that degree to cause howlings most hideous. The barber and attendant, by way of *conge*, and considering it absolutely necessary that the face, etc., should undergo a washing, on a sudden pull away the pole on which the victim was seated, and souse he goes into the tub of water; thus ends the ceremony.

The god and goddess take no share except being spectators of the mischief they have made. The master of the transport told me that in some ships, instead of letting the man fall into the tub, he has seen a rope made fast round a sailor, and the poor mortal thrown over the side and towed for some yards. This part of the ceremony the watery god did not execute from our ship, as she was travelling rather too fast—going at least seven knots an hour. This same business was repeated on five of the sailors, to the no small amusement of the redcoats. Barbarous as the ceremony was, I own I laughed most immoderately.

30th.—In the morning we passed a piece of a wreck supposed to be the main-mast of a man-of-war, which must have been in the water a long time from the great quantities of barnacles that were adhering to it. These are a species of shell-fish that fix themselves to ships, etc. etc., that are long at sea. From the size of the mast it was conjectured by the captain of our ship to have belonged to a first-rate, and probably had been floating since the action of the 1st June 1794, as no three-deckers had been damaged since that time. We saw a number of flying fish and the dolphins in pursuit of them. A line and bait was put out in hopes to tempt the latter, but as yet without success. The Saturday evening's amusement of dancing was prevented by the indisposition of the musician (a fifer); however, an allowance, or rather donation, of grog brought forward some diversions and some songs, etc., to make up for the disappointment.

From the 1st to the 6th February, most delightful weather and a most prosperous breeze, seldom going less than seven knots an hour. Nothing particular occurred during the week. The people entertained themselves on Saturday evening as usual, and on the 7th I read prayers. By the observation we made the latitude of Barbadoes this day. This week I finished my stock of vegetables, consisting of carrots and tur-nips, which had been preserved as good as when they came on board. I kept them in a cask on the deck open at the top except a covering of canvas. The carrots were excellent and of infinite service to the pres-ervation of health. I also brought on board a hamper of apples, which kept tolerably well till this week notwithstanding the hot weather.

I ordered my servant to examine them every day and to pick out any that were the least decayed, to which precaution I attribute their holding out so long. I found them a great luxury. Since we have been in the trades, where the wind is always cast, I have observed every night the sea to appear with a great deal of the fiery particles, and which I imagined seldom was seen but with a southerly wind, at least I have heard old sailors make the remark, and indeed have been at sea many days together without seeing a spark. And before we came into the trades we always considered this appearance overnight as an indication of southerly wind the next day. Philosophers are undeter-mined how to account for this; some say it is animalcule, others that it is phosphoric fire.

During the heavy gale of wind the night we left the Channel the sea, and indeed the ship's sails, appeared all on fire; the former was most completely illuminated from the prodigious quantity of the fire. This day a ship was seen ahead of us. On the 11th, as soon as it was light, we discovered the long-wished-for island of Barbadoes. We made sail at four o'clock, and in about an hour after we saw the land. The morning early was cloudy with a heavy shower of rain, but cleared away about nine o'clock. The appearance of the island as you come from sea is in general low land, but on getting nearer on the north side there are some hills. It is quite a new scene for a European. The island is picturesque almost to a degree of enchantment, and really makes you fancy it a fairy island.

We got into the bay about twelve o'clock, and I immediately went on shore. Very few of the transports had arrived, not more than ten, and no man-of-war. The quartermaster-general, Brigadier Knox, commanded on shore, on whom I waited to report my arrival. I found Colonel Hope, the adjutant-general, also on shore.

★★★★★★

John Hope, fourth Earl of Hopetoun (1765-1823); adjutant-general under Abercromby in the West Indies 1796; wounded at Alexandria 1801; second in command under Sir John Moore at Corunna; headed division in the Walcheren expedition 1809; succeeded his half-brother James, third Earl of Hopetoun, 1816; general 1819.

★★★★★★

Bridge Town is a large straggling town, with narrow sandy streets; many of the houses large and constructed for the climate with an open gallery in front, and a shed over it to keep off the rays of the sun. The white people all appear sickly, and look extremely pallid, but almost *tout le monde* is of the sable race. The county round the town appears like an unenclosed common in England, excepting the cocoa and cabbage trees, which are very beautiful, and grown in abundance immediately adjoining the place. I expected to have had fruit in great abundance, but was disappointed, as I found nothing but oranges and shaddocks, and they not very good. It was not exactly the fruit season, and I am told Barbadoes is not famous. I felt the weather very warm, and for some days had some fever and headache. I took calomel pills and rhubarb, which I found of great use.

I met with great civility from General Knox and from Hope. I also met an old acquaintance, Sir Francis Ford, (of Ember Court, county Surrey, born 1758; member of council in Barbadoes; created a baronet 1793; died at Barbadoes 1801), who has a large property in the island, and was come out to look after it. He was very kind in getting me poultry, etc., which, as we were ordered to Grenada, where provisions of all kinds are very scarce, and as the price and the plenty was daily altering for the worse as the fleet increased, I derived great benefit from his attention. I paid him a visit at his house in the country, about two miles from Bridge Town, to dinner. I met there Major-General Leigh (the commander-in-chief in the West Indies till Sir Ralph's arrival; he arrived from Martinique on Sunday the 14th).

★★★★★★

Sir Ralph Abercromby (1734-1801); commanded expedition against the French in the West Indies 1795-6, reduced St. Lucia and Trinidad; commanded troops in the Mediterranean 1800; defeated the French, but was killed at the Battle of Alexandria, 1801.

★★★★★★

The dinner was quite West Indian, consisting principally of poultry; there was one joint of mutton, which some people said was as good as they ever ate. I pitied their taste. The country round Sir Francis's house, and indeed every part of the island, is one open field, as there are no fences, and the division of property is distinguished by a road or path with a stone set up at one angle and a particular mark upon it. The principal things I saw growing were cotton, Indian and Guinea corn, and sugar. The former is a pretty shrub, and not unlike a white rose-tree in bloom.

The sugar is cultivated by plants, which are put in the ground in November, and cut the January twelvemonth following, about the size of a fruiting pine. They put out a stalk which runs up as high as a tall raspberry-tree, but as thick as a carrot. From this cane a juice is extracted by the power of mills, and by a process is made sugar. Cocoa-trees are plenty. They are very handsome, and the fresh cocoanut much better than what you eat in England. Cucumbers are plenty, and at Sir Francis Ford's I saw peas and beans of the island, moderate eating. We had English green peas, very good. Also salad, lettuces, etc. Fish is tolerably plenty, but no sauce, as butter is a thing not to be had in the West Indies. There is little or none made in the islands, and what is imported becomes rancid immediately of course. Pickles are had in abundance, and very good. The beef and mutton are both very indifferent, but pork and poultry are tolerably plenty and as good as I ever ate.

After I had been at Barbadoes a few days, I found the great utility that must attend wearing flannel; for, as in the tropical climates the heat must be very great, the perspiration must also be copious; and as every house is calculated as much as possible to draw every breath of air, when a person after ever so short a walk goes into a house, his shirt acts exactly in the manner they use linen bags to cool their wine, which is by keeping them constantly wet and hung up in a draught of wind; that is, the bottles in linen bags. Flannel prevents this, as it naturally absorbs the perspiration, and at the same time encourages it.

I went on board two slave-ships in Carlisle Bay from the coast of Guinea. The name on the stern of one of them was curious, considering the trade in which she was employed, *The Liberty of Providence*. She was an American. The other was a Liverpool ship, and in my life I never saw a vessel more clean in every particular. The females were all in the after part of the ship, and the males forward. They all appeared very happy, and in a state of perfect nature nearly as to clothing. I observed the females had all a number of different-coloured glass beads hung round their necks. The master of the ship told me the chief employment, and indeed amusement, they had was in new-stringing their beads, and that he very frequently broke the string on purpose to set them to work.

Some of the girls I really thought very good-looking (as far as the sable race could be so), and the finest made creatures I ever beheld. Not all the powers of the first dancing-master could give such attitude as some of them had. Indeed, all the negroes I have seen in the West Indies are uncommonly straight, upright, and well made. Those we see in Europe are in general the reverse. These poor wretches were taken on shore and sold just as a flock of sheep are sold in a fair in England. However, I have seen nothing like the barbarity that has been talked of as to the treatment of the slaves on shore. Their huts are comfortable, and their food good and wholesome.

Their labour in the eye of an Englishman must appear excessive hard; working in the fields under a meridian sun. But I firmly believe they don't experience more than an English labourer during harvest, as they live to as great age, and have the appearance of as good health. Long experience has fully proved that no European constitution can stand fatigue in this country. I am therefore for employing negroes for every purpose, both civil and military, and I wish the British Government would garrison all the West India Islands with black soldiers only.

I was much delighted with the dress of the negro girls in Bridge Town, which is exactly that of the fine ladies when I left England; short-waisted and turbans, the latter made of white or coloured handkerchiefs, but displayed and put on with better taste than anything I ever saw. Really and truly I never beheld that part of the female dress (and which I much admire) so well disposed as in some of the black women in Bridge Town. The negro dances are most curious, and their music still more so.

The dance is a kind of reel performed by two or three of each sex; and the music consists of the head of a cask or tub on which they beat with something like a drumstick. The other instrument is made of two cocoanut shells, which they strike together in time with the tambourine. These dolorous sounds are accompanied by the voices of half the surrounding circle, making on the whole but a most dismal concert. It is astonishing with what very exact movements they keep time, and though they display wonderful agility in their motions, still there is so great an appearance of lasciviousness in the whole dance, that it gives one the idea of the Timeradee dance performed by the natives of Otaheite as described by John Hawkesworth, (1715?-1773; published an account of voyages in the South Seas).

The mornings and evenings are pleasant at Barbadoes, the former in particular, though it is of short continuance, as there is very little twilight, and as soon as the sun makes his appearance, he of course brings with him all his fires, and when he sinks into the lap of Thetis, darkness almost immediately follows. There is a fine sandy beach for bathing, and the sea is so clear that in most parts of Carlisle Bay you, can see the bottom in ten fathom water.

On the 1st of March the regiment was ordered to proceed without delay to the island of Grenada, in consequence of an application for an immediate reinforcement. We were disembarked from the *Boddington*, and put on board three small schooners, in which we proceeded on the 3rd, and made the land of St. Vincent's on the 4th. Shortly after we could see the islands of St. Lucia, St. Vincent's, and Grenada at the same time. These islands all appear very high from the sea. We were at a great distance from St. Lucia, which looked exactly like three sugar loaves.

In the morning of the 4th we passed between St Vincent's and the island of Bequia, one of the Grenadines. The reinforcement that sailed from Barbadoes with us consisted of a detachment from the 10th and 88th regiments, making in all about 500 men, and was intended to assist Major Wright of the 25th, who commanded a post in the island called La Baye, and which had been violently assaulted by the enemy.

Brigadier-General M'Kenzie commanded the reinforcement, and his orders were to wait off the island of Grenada till he received instructions from Brigadier-General Nicholls commanding at St. George's.

After passing the island of Bequia, we sailed by two or three other of the Grenadines. One in particular, Isle Ronde, singularly pretty, and which almost joins Grenada. We fell in with the *Alarm* frigate off Isle Ronde with despatches from General Nicholls, to say that Major Wright had been obliged to evacuate La Baye, and that he had got away without any loss. We therefore proceeded to St. George's, the capital of the island. The sailing down by the island is the most beautiful thing I ever saw; infinitely superior to anything at Barbadoes. The island consists of a great number of hills rising one above another and covered with wood to the very pinnacle. They are all extremely steep and varied in figure so curiously as to make it the most picturesque scene imaginable. We got into the bay of St. George's just as it was dark, and landed the next morning, and marched up to the barracks on Richmond Hill about two miles above the town; a very strong place, with barracks for 600 or 800 men. We found the 9th and 29th regiments; the former was sent to take the duty in town and we occupied their barracks.

The town of St. George's is not so large as Bridge Town, but more compact and neater; situated close to the waterside, with a hill that projects and divides it. On the hill is a fortification and barracks; one side of the hill is called 'The Carénage,' (a fine harbour in which ships of war could moor in safety during the hurricane months), the other 'The Bay.' The road from town to Richmond Hill is but indifferent, and as the hill is very steep, it's a great fag to get up it. The view of the town, the sea, and the appearance of the island from the Hill is one of the most picturesque beautiful things I ever saw.

The Brigands, (emancipated slaves and whites of extreme democratic principles), as they are called, we found in possession of every post of the island, excepting the very neighbourhood of the town of St. George's.

On the 7th the enemy collected in some numbers on a hill commanding the town, and about the same height of Richmond Hill. It was judged necessary by General Nicholls to dislodge them from there; as otherwise, if they had effected a post, they would have annoyed us a good deal; and accordingly a party was sent out, on the first appearance of which they scampered off. This party, consisting of a captain and 50 men, with 100 men belonging to a black corps in town, was relieved daily; but as the enemy had harassed the relief going up two or three times, and the general having received information of their intending to attack the post in force on the night of the 12th, a field officer with a captain and 50 men was ordered to reinforce the post.

I being senior field officer was ordered for the duty (my first essay in real service). The party marched at four o'clock, and had to scramble up a hill more than a mile high, and in many places so steep as to make it necessary to use the bushes and trees to climb the precipice. This under a burning sun was a complete duty of fatigue. The party got up to the post without any attack, although they appeared in numbers on the adjacent hills. The enemy consist chiefly of the rebel negroes of the island, aided by a few French, and mulattoes from Guadaloupe, and encouraged and assisted by a great number of mulattoes of the island who are united with the negroes.

An alarm was made in the night by some of their scouts having fired on our advanced sentry; but on the piquets returning the fire they went off.

On the 13th a reinforcement arrived from Barbadoes on the windward side of the island, consisting of 700 men, part of the 3rd, 8th, and 63rd regiments. They were ordered to remain off the windward side of the island till a plan was concerted for their operations. General Nicholls despatched a vessel to Barbadoes on the 14th with his plans, to be submitted to the commander-in-chief, General Leigh.

The return of the vessel was most anxiously looked for till the 21st, when she arrived, and in consequence a part of the army from St. George's and Richmond Hill marched on the 22nd at seven o'clock p.m., consisting as follows: 500 of the black island corps; two troops 17th dragoons; 200 of the 9th regiment; 200 of the 10th; 100, 25th; 200 of the 29th, and proceeded with an intention of joining the reinforcement that had arrived from Barbadoes on the windward side of the island. Brigadier-General Nicholls took the command, and Brigadier-General Campbell, Lieutenant-Colonel of the 29th, was second in command.

We marched all night and till four o'clock next morning, when we halted for two hours at a sugar work called Madam Sagesses, which had been burnt and almost totally destroyed by the brigands, about eight miles from St. George's. This march determined me in an opinion I had always entertained of the improbability of any military operations being performed by night marches; for although one half of the distance was a tolerably good road, we were near ten hours getting eight miles, and that not without much confusion. We moved on at six o'clock about three miles, and halted four hours.

A few shots fired by the black corps in front, at some wretched poor devils in the cane fields, killed two of them. We came in sight of a party of the enemy about two o'clock, and attacked their advanced post, which was carried with the loss of a few men. The black corps had the principal share in dislodging them. I was ordered on to their support with the 9th and 25th regiments. After we had got possession of the post they at first occupied (called Madam Hooks), where they had some huts and a piquet, that gave us a full view of their grand post at Post Royal, General Nicholls determined to move forward and attack Post Royal that night with the 9th and 29th regiments. I had got his permission to accompany them.

We had proceeded about half a mile, when Brigadier-General Campbell, who was in front, finding the night coming on very fast, and knowing how much the troops had suffered from being under arms almost twenty-four hours, the 9th regiment in particular, as that corps and the 25th under my command had marched, I should write run, three miles as fast as it was possible for them, and had only halted an hour, and that on account of a most tremendous shower of rain, when it was ordered forward (the 9th on the storming party, the 25th being left to guard the hill where the huts, etc., were), Brigadier Campbell, as I mentioned before, proposed to defer the attack on Post Royal till next morning.

The column therefore returned to Madam Hooks, where the 10th had been left, about seven o'clock, and I do suppose no troops ever were more completely fatigued; for myself, I am very certain after I had once lain down, if we had been attacked I should have been cut to pieces, as it was impossible I could move. I was very far past eating. I had in the course of the day taken a copious share of drink, as I am very certain that in my whole life altogether I had never drank so much grog as during the last four-and-twenty hours. Sleep made me a new man.

The next day, the 24th, threw up a work for our guns and mortars to bear on Post Royal. I should have mentioned that at the attack of yesterday, it was the first time I had heard the sound of great guns on service; the music of the six and nine pound shot was at times rather too close to be pleasant. During the night of the 24th our battery was completed and in the morning of the 25th opened a fire on Post Royal. The regiments stationed at the battery were the 3rd, 8th, and 63rd, which had landed under command of Lieut.-Colonel Dawson of the 8th, early in the morning at Hook's Bay, and moved forward immediately. The 9th regiment had been at the battery since the 23rd, and the 25th regiment remained on the hill we drove the enemy from the first day. The reserve, consisting of the 17th dragoons, the 10th and 29th and 88th regiments and black corps under my command, remained at Madam Hooks. Our stores that had been landed, etc., also were there.

On the morning of the 25th General Nicholls, who had remained at Madam Hooks since the 23rd, left it about nine o'clock to go to the battery where my guns were. I went up with him to see what was going on. We had a most perfect view of the enemy at Post Royal, the distance not being more than a thousand yards. They did not fire so much at our battery as was expected, though their shot had done some execution, and our people exposed themselves more than was necessary.

General Nicholls called the commanding officers of the regiments together to consult on the best method of attacking and storming the hill. We were assembled in a most conspicuous place for the enemy to have taken a shot at us. It was under our own battery and in a wide red road in full view from their work. I shall never forget Dawson, in the most profound part of the council of war, bursting out laughing with, 'By God, now's their time! one round of grape carries off the general and all his council, and defeats the mighty battle.' The plan of attack was determined notwithstanding, but I believe Dawson's remark hastened our consultation.

On our return to the battery we perceived a considerable detachment of the enemy endeavouring to get possession of some high ground on the left of our work, as if with an intention of attacking that flank. The 88th regiment and black corps under the command of Major Houstone, which had been brought up from Hooks, were ordered to attack them. Just as they began to engage, which was at about half a mile distance from the battery, an alarm was given of a fire having broken out at my post at Madam Hooks. This post consisted of the remains of a large sugar-house and a number of negro huts, the latter of which, by the soldiers having made fires to cook, by some accident had taken fire, and as they were built of dry wood and thatched with sugar-cane, they blazed away most furiously. This alarm made me ride off as fast as I could to Madam Hooks. After securing the stores, provisions, etc. etc., I was intending to return to see what was going forward at the battery, but in consequence of the two men-of-war (the *Mermaid* and *Favourite*) who had convoyed the three regiments from

Barbadoes and also an Indiaman, in which a part of them had been embarked, beginning a heavy fire, I was obliged to turn my attention towards them.

The flames from the huts and the heavy fire from the ships alarmed the general much. He told me he really concluded the enemy had attacked us in force and had set fire to the works. The firing from the shipping turned out to be in consequence of two French schooners with troops trying to get into the next bay to land their men as a reinforcement to Post Royal. General Nicholls, on seeing the flames from Hooks, hearing the fire from the ships and observing the reinforcement in the schooners, determined to lose no time in storming the post. The storming party consisted of the light infantry of the 3rd regiment, 100 strong; 100 of the 29th regiment and the 63rd regiment; Colonel Dawson, as senior field officer, had the command.

I forgot to remark that the party on the left under the command of Major Houstone had met with much greater resistance than was expected, and the 8th regiment was therefore sent to their support, which had the desired effect; though I believe the enemy retreated towards Post Royal more on account of their seeing our people moving to the attack than in consequence of any defeat they dreaded from us on the left.

Colonel Dawson had not advanced more than two hundred yards down the hill from our battery when he received a wound from a musket ball through the neck, and was obliged to fall back. The column suffered severely going down the hill, as it was exposed to the enemy's fire from their work, and also the enemy themselves, who were drawn out under cover of their guns on the hillside of Post Royal and firing small arms at our people as they advanced. After the column had got to the bottom of the hill (that is, between the two—one on which our battery was and Post Royal), they halted a short time as they got under a part of Post Royal Hill that was so steep they were secured from the enemy's fire; unfortunately the guide they had did not when they advanced conduct them the proper path; the consequence was the light infantry of the 3rd regiment suffered most severely; all the officers were killed or wounded, and between twenty and thirty men knocked down; and as the enemy appeared determined to dispute every inch, it was some time dubious how the affair would end; but British valour, perseverance, and resolution, as it does on all occasions, triumphed at last.

As the column ascended the hill the 17th dragoons were ordered forward to get round to the opposite side, which had the effect desired, as they made dreadful slaughter with their swords on the enemy that were endeavouring to make their escape down the opposite side of the hill from where they were attacked. The post was carried about two o'clock.

Our loss consisted of Major Edwards and two subalterns of the 3rd regiment killed and about fifteen or twenty men, and three officers and forty men wounded. No troops could behave better than ours did in general; and I was told the enemy never were known to make so good a stand. The day was intensely hot, and as the army was under arms for eight hours and some of them for twelve, everybody was rejoiced when the affair was over.

The unfortunate officers and men that were wounded in the action were brought on negroes' shoulders on litters to my post at Hooks Bay, and all put together in a long building. The sight of them (many having been most dreadfully wounded) was shocking. The first officer brought was my friend Dawson, having been shot through the neck by a musket ball as he went down the hill from our battery.

March 26th.—Employed in burying the dead, and sending away the wounded by sea to St. George's. I never beheld such a sight as Post Royal Hill, etc. The number of dead bodies and the smell was dreadful. The side of the hill on which the enemy endeavoured to make their retreat was extremely steep and thickly covered with wood, and the only method of discovering the killed was from the smell. It was near a fortnight after the action that many bodies were found. Nine days after the post was taken a *mulatto* man was discovered in the woods that had been wounded in three places—two shots through his thigh. The only thing he had tasted was water, but to the astonishment of everybody he recovered. The negroes and people of colour can certainly suffer and endure far greater torture than white people.

I have seen two or three instances of this kind that astonished me. One in particular at Hooks Bay. Two negroes were taken prisoners the day we got possession of the post, and in order to secure them they were forced into a sort of arched place something like what I have seen under steps made use of to tie up a dog. There was just room for the poor devils to creep in on their hands and knees and to lie down. After they had got in, two soldiers of the 29th regiment put the muzzles of their firelocks to the door-place and fired at them. I ran to see what the firing was, but before I got to the place they had fired a second round.

On reaching the spot I made a negro draw out these miserable victims of enraged brutality. One of them was mangled in a horrid manner. The other was shot through the hip, the body, and one thigh, and notwithstanding all, he was able to sit up and to answer a number of questions that were asked him respecting the enemy. The poor wretch held his hand on the wound in his thigh, as if that only was the place he suffered from. The thigh bone must have been shattered to pieces, as his leg and foot were turned under him. The miserable being was not suffered to continue long in his wretchedness, as one of his own colour came up and blew his brains out *sans ceremonie*.

This account does no credit to the discipline of the army. I own I was most completely ashamed of the whole proceeding, and said all I could to the general of the necessity of making an example to put a stop to these acts of wanton cruelty, being certain that nothing leads to anarchy and confusion in an army so soon as suffering a soldier in any instance to trespass the bounds of strict regularity, or to permit him to be guilty of an act of cruelty or injustice.

During the night of the 26th the enemy set fire to their works on Pilot Hill and evacuated the post. This post was situated about two miles from Post Royal on the coast. There was a most unfortunate accident happened in Hooks Bay on the 26th. The *Ponsburne* East Indiaman, that had brought part of the reinforcement from Barbadoes, drove from her anchors and went to pieces in a very short time. All the hands were saved, but every article of stores, ammunition, etc., was lost. It was an awful sight seeing the power of the element dashing to atoms in the space of two hours so stately a production of man's art. This with the loss of a schooner drove on shore made it necessary to retain the post at Madam Hooks longer than was intended to my very great annoy, as a great quantity of provisions, etc. etc., were drifted on shore, which it was thought proper to destroy to prevent it falling into the enemy's hands.

11th.—Evacuated Madam Hooks and was ordered to take post in front of Post Royal; to encamp and hut on a ridge called Morne Soubige, covered with cotton trees, and overrun with brushwood and all kinds of rubbish. My camp consisted of the park of artillery, the 3rd, 10th, 25th, and 88th detachments. The 29th and 30th employed in clearing the hill, etc. It was a most dreadful spot. The tents were pitched on the ridge of a hill with a fine hanging wood down to the sea on each side. To experience misery in extreme is to live in a tent in the West Indies.

We were perfectly quiet here, and in a state of inactivity. Some regimental business requiring me at St. George's I went there in one of the quartermaster-general's vessels (the run only six hours) on the 5th April, where I remained till the 11th and returned in the same vessel, but the time to return was different than to go, as we were upwards of twenty-four hours on the passage, having to beat to windward. Getting into the bay at Post Royal, our pilot got us on shore on the breakers, a reef of rocks, and we were in some danger of being lost; but boats came off and took us out of the vessel.

Nothing new had occurred during my absence. The part of the island we were on is called the windward side, and the post we occupied reckoned very unhealthy. We had as yet perceived nothing of that nature. The 8th regiment took the post at Pilot Hill, one mile from Morne Soubige, which the enemy evacuated on the night of the 26th March. This was the place the 25th regiment had been quartered at and from whence Major Wright made his escape when besieged by the enemy. The regiment, in the course of a few months, lost three or four officers and upwards of three hundred men. There was a town near the post called La Baye, which the negroes burnt in the beginning of the insurrection, and this place is so notorious for being unhealthy even to the inhabitants of the island, that the La Baye fever is one of the diseases of the country.

Having nothing to dread from any attack from the enemy after it was light, I always had the line out half an hour before day and remained under arms till daylight. Bathed three times a week, and rode on the beach between Soubige and La Baye till seven o'clock, when I got breakfast. Sat in my tent till one, and then rode to headquarters on Post Royal Hill. Dined at three (salt pork and peas), and generally took a ride in an evening after the piquets were mounted. In this way with little alteration the same daily dull scene passed for ten weeks. For some time after we had taken post at Soubige, there was seldom a night passed but what some of our sentries fired and alarmed the line. We were in general young soldiers, and imagination raised variety of appearances on a dark night.

We had a curious and laughable alarm one night. A soldier on piquet had lain down in the tent allowed for the men and officer, and in consequence either of a dream or a fit, he suddenly jumped up and roared out, 'We shall all be cut to pieces; here they are, we are surrounded, fire away.' The noise and violence of his cries caused such a tremor that the sentry at the tent and also one that was advanced fired. This set others firing at they knew not what. The line all turned out, the battery with lighted matches, and from the noise and firing at the piquet I concluded a serious attack was made. It was some time before the officer commanding the piquet could make his men convinced what had made the alarm.

The sea crawfish we got sometimes is curiously spotted, and marked like tortoiseshell when highly polished. They resemble in shape the sea crawfish in Europe, but their claws much longer. We got river crawfish now and then; very large, the great claws long and all the same thickness.

May 13.—A field officer's party marched at night with an expectation of surprising an advanced camp of the enemy's, but did not succeed. The party lost men, and an officer of the 3rd regiment wounded. Three villains (Dutchmen) deserted from the 25th regiment to the enemy. One of them was afterwards taken at Goyave, and we had him hung up on the highest tree we could find without any ceremony. About the same time that the men deserted nine soldiers that were straying rather too far from the camp were taken by the enemy.

14th.—A vessel with Spanish colours came close in with the land, as if she intended going into Hooks Bay. On the supposition of her having a reinforcement for the brigands on board from the island of Trinidad, a party was sent to oppose their landing, but the vessel did not run into the bay. My tent was, I believe, infested with every species of reptile the island produces: a scorpion, lizard, tarantula, land-crab, and centipede had been caught by my black boy, and the mice were innumerable.

I was prevented bathing in consequence of what is called in the West Indies the prickly heat. It is an eruption that breaks out all over the body, and from the violent itching and prickly sensation it has got the above appellation. All new-comers to the West Indies are subject to it, and when it is out it is considered as a sign of health. Bathing, I was told, was liable to drive it in. Nothing can equal the extreme unpleasant sensation, and people sometimes scratch themselves to that degree as to occasion sores. About this time our part of the army was suffering in a most shameful manner for the want of numerable articles in which it stood much in need. Neither wine or medicine for the sick, and not a comfort of any one kind for the good duty soldier; salt pork, without either peas or rice, for a considerable time, and for three days nothing but hard, dry, bad biscuit for the whole army, officers and men. Two days without (the soldiers' grand comfort) grog.

On the 23rd day we had so much rain as to make us imagine the rainy season had commenced, as there was also thunder and lightning, which the natives say is a certain forerunner.

On the 30th we heard of the surrender of St. Lucia, and in consequence of the joyful news in the evening fired a *feu de joie*.

June 1.—Brigadier Nicholls returned to the army from St. George's, where he had been since a short time after the action of Post Royal, leaving the command with Brigadier-General Campbell. General Nicholls came for the purpose of making arrangements for the further prosecuting the campaign, the adjutant-general having been sent from St. Lucia to Grenada to assist and forward such plans as might be judged necessary.

3rd.—An express arrived at Post Royal from Sir Ralph Abercrombie to General Nicholls from the island of Carriacou, about six leagues to windward of Grenada, Sir Ralph having come there from St. Lucia in order to consult with the general, who set out to meet him immediately. We understood a reinforcement was to arrive in four or five days, which God knows we had long expected. We were much alarmed for the weather, as it had been very showery since the 23rd May. All very anxious to get away from the post we had so long occupied, not only from a wish to draw the campaign nearer to a conclusion, but from the desire every soldier, I believe, has for active service when on a campaign, in preference to remaining inactive and unemployed.

The long-looked-for reinforcement having arrived under the command of Brigadier-General Campbell, the army quitted the post of Post Royal, Morne Soubige, and La Baye (Pilot Hill) at seven o'clock in the evening of the 9th, leaving two hundred men at Post Royal, and after marching twenty-one hours without scarce a halt through thick woods, deep rivers, etc., took post on some rising ground about three o'clock in the afternoon of the next day with an intention of attacking a hill in our front called Madam Chadeaus, where the enemy appeared in some force, next morning.

Our march for the last three miles was literally up and down precipices, halfway up the leg in clay, and through a wood where I believe no human foot had ever before stepped. A party from the enemy had attacked our advanced guard, and disputed the ground we halted upon, but they made no stand; however, they annoyed us all the evening with their bush fighting from the woods with which we were surrounded, and killed and wounded several men. We lay on our arms all night in a plantain walk.

The plantain-tree is an annual bearing a vegetable of the same name, on which the negroes feed. It grows to the height of from ten to fifteen or twenty feet. The stem is about eight inches in circumference, but the leaf is the largest and most beautiful I ever saw. I had the curiosity to measure one of the common size. It was six feet long exclusive of the stem, and two feet three inches broad. The stem of the leaf is fluted, and the colour a most charming dark green. The vegetable grows in hunches or large clusters, very moderate eating. The negroes very soon compose a temporary shed with the leaves, which not only answers as a shade from the sun, but also keeps off the rain.

At daybreak on the morning of the 11th three columns under my command were ordered to take possession of the heights occupied by the enemy at Chadeaus. They did not wait for our arrival, but trusted to their legs for their escape. We found the top of the hill a large space just cleared in the wood, with plantains and Indian corn growing. On this spot we were ordered to pitch our tents for the ensuing night— such as had them. I had lost mine, the mule on which it was packed having fallen lame soon after quitting Soubige, and was obliged to be left. The consequence was I lost my tent, etc., and all the liquor I had except what I carried in my canteen, which I believe amounted to about a pint of rum.

The reinforcement that had arrived from St. Lucia, consisting of the 27th and 57th regiments, the *corps étrangers*, and Lowenstein Yougers,(Lowenstein *Jagers,* mentioned frequently in the *Diary of Sir John Moore*), under the command of General Nicholls, were to land on the opposite side of the island from whence we had marched, the day after our part of the army moved, with an intention of attacking a post the enemy had on the coast called Goyave, which they had fortified strongly, and where all their supplies were received.

The officer who commanded the Republican French troops appointed by Victor Hugues, (partisan of Robespierre, came out to the West Indies in 1794, and gave a great impulse to the cause of the French Republic), which did not consist of more than two hundred men, was stationed at Goyave.

Soon after our arrival at Madam Chadeaus a negro came from

General Nicholls with a note to say Citoyen Jossée, the French commander, had surrendered Goyave on their first appearance, but that Fidon, the brigand general, had gone off to Mount Quoca with a thousand of his people. Mount Quoca, (2500 feet high, now called Mount St. Catherine), is the highest mountain in the island of Grenada, extremely strong by nature, as it is a ridge, one end of which is almost perpendicular. The enemy had added greatly to its natural strength, having by dint of negro labour got some heavy cannon to the top. This place from the beginning of the insurrection had been their grand camp and principal place of assembling, and it is a most remarkable situation. It consists of three heights, one rising above another, on each of which they had cannon. The lower one at the end of the ridge was, I suppose, more than 500 yards high, and, as I mentioned, nearly perpendicular.

These three heights they had separate names for. The first Camp La Liberté, the next Camp L'Egalité, and the upper one Camp La Mort. This last the villains called the Camp of Death, as it was the spot where they massacred all the prisoners they took, and where in the very commencement of their brutality they put to death in the most horrid manner the Governor of the island and ten of the inhabitants they had made prisoners.

Outpost at Madam Chadeaus (the different estates having retained the name of the proprietors only, as there was scarce on any of them a vestige of a building, the black rascals having burned and destroyed the estates of all they conceived inimical to their proceeding) was situated on the next and almost adjoining hill to Mount Quoca, and within shot of their cannon from the guns at the lower works, but they did not fire at us; the reason, we concluded, was their being in want of ammunition. It rained almost incessantly the night of the 11th in the true West India style. Our encampment was in a ploughed field, what tents we had, and they were of very little service. I got into a soldier's tent with our officers; we were all just as wet as if we had lain in a river, and both under the tents and all round them was half-way up the leg in mud.

On the 12th two negroes came in from the enemy, and told us they were in great confusion in their camp, and that many of the negroes were leaving it. General Nicholls came from Goyave, six miles from us, after having settled the business of the capitulation with Monsieur Jossée, and had ordered a column to move forward from Goyave to join us. The general only remained at Chadeaus an hour, and returned to Goyave.

June 13.—The brigand general Fidon sent in a flag of truce with proposals to surrender his post at Mount Quoca. His conditions were that he and his associates were to be sent unmolested to Guadaloupe; but no terms would be listened to, (because Fidon had brutally murdered twenty Europeans). Brigadier-General Hope, the adjutant-general who came with the reinforcement that landed at Goyave, was ordered to move with a brigade consisting as follows: the 8th, 9th, and 25th British to be under my command; the *corps étrangers*, 500 of Lowenstein Yougers, and 200 of the island black corps. The intention of this column was in order to get possession of two posts the enemy had in the rear of Mount Quoca, by the taking of which we should surround their camp. We found a very great change in the weather from our high situation in the centre of the island to what it had been on the coast, the nights particularly so cold.

We made large fires, and rolled our blankets close round us, our lodging not much calculated to keep out either wet or cold. A large fire at night and smoking a cigar a great preventative. Almost constant rain or thick fog, which caused sickness to appear amongst our people; not a thing to eat but royal salt pork and biscuit. Generally half the day in the clouds.

On the 14th and 15th constant rain; the latter day not a morsel of provisions in the line. Oh shame, shame, good soldiers dropping down from hard duty and from the inclemency of the worst climate in the universe, and for twenty-four hours nothing to eat or to drink. We had certainly no manner of business to have halted more than one day at Chadeaus. As to the weather, it could be no excuse. A man collects full as much rain when he is sitting down unsheltered as when moving forward. I am very certain neither officer or private soldier had ever lain down dry from the day the column came to Chadeaus; so constant was the rain that the ammunition in the men's pouches was totally useless.

The principal reason why General Hope had not moved on with his brigade was in consequence of his being taken with the fever and ague, which obliged him to go to St. George's. However, on the 16th, the commander-in-chief, Sir Ralph, arrived at Chadeaus, and ordered the movement that Hope was to have made to take place under the command of Brigadier-General Campbell, and instead of the foreign troops the 27th regiment under the command of Lieut.-Colonel Gilman formed the right brigade. (Sir John Moore wrote praising Lieut.-Colonel Gilman, and remarked on the 'good conduct and regularity of the 27th regiment.') We were ordered to be under arms at three o'clock in the morning of the 17th, but as usual no provisions had arrived, and it was absolutely necessary each man should carry one day's entire; indeed it ought to have been two, for the distance we had to march and the business to accomplish; not having one day complete, we could not stir.

On the 18th in the morning General Campbell did not think of moving unless he got the two days' provisions; however, I took the liberty of representing to him that as we had one day complete, and the men breakfasted and got a glass of rum, I thought it would be advisable to move on, as the enemy were gaining a victory by our delay and from the sickness that would prevail from inactivity; the enemy were also gaining time either to strengthen their positions or to make their escape, both of which was equally bad. And worst of all, the army was getting dissatisfied from not being suffered to proceed. I don't know whether it was in consequence of what I said, but we moved in two brigades from the left (I had the left, and Gilman the right) at seven o'clock on the morning of the 18th. About the same time Lowenstein Yougers commenced an attack on Mount Quoca by scrambling through the woods, getting behind trees, and taking a shot when they could get an opportunity.

The first three miles I had to take my brigade was through a thick wood with a negro for my guide, as there was neither path or anything by which I could have made out the way, had it not been for my sable conductor. After fording a tolerably deep river, we joined the right brigade on what had formerly been the great road across the island, but was rendered almost impassable by being cut up and having trees felled across it in all directions. The line continued its march through a country of wood, without any material obstruction (except two or three rivers, deep, rapid, and full of rocks), till about five o'clock, when the enemy appeared in front of their post called Mitchell's Camp, with an appearance as if they intended to make a stand. We had a company of *Yougers* in front with the 25th and 27th light infantry companies.

These commenced the attack, supported by the left brigade; we carried the hill without much trouble, although the enemy were very well posted, and might have annoyed us much, particularly in our approach, as we marched up a road exposed to their fire the whole way, and the hill in some parts very steep. General Campbell was with me at the head of the left brigade. As we were going up the hill a villain levelled and fired at us; the ball struck the ground close to the general. Brigade-Major Johnston called to us to say a man on the hill was levelling his musket at us. A soldier of the 9th regiment, just behind us, was wounded about the same time. Immediately that we got to the top of the hill the villains ran off to the woods. We took possession of their camp (which consisted of about fifty wretched huts) between seven and eight o'clock, and the two brigades halted for the night.

There was a curious circumstance happened on the march, which shows what determined soldiers by trade the Germans are. As the head of a column came near a plantation of plantain-trees, we saw a negro hut about one hundred yards below us, and a poor black devil run out of it. We called to him to come to us, but Massa rather chose to trust to his heels. The captain of the *Yougers*, who had a double-barrelled fuzil, immediately levelled at him, dodging him through the trees (just as you do a woodcock after it has taken wing), and killed the wretch as dead as Julius Caesar, I am sorry to say to the great entertainment not only of the Germans, but of all our people that saw it.

On searching the house we found the poor fellow's wife as cool and as unconcerned as if nothing had happened. Blackey, it was found out, was a great brigand, and had been with Fidon the day before. After we had got into our huts at Mitchell's, several shots were fired from the woods, one of which struck an officer of the 9th regiment, and as a piquet of the 27th regiment were sitting round their fire, one of the privates was wounded in the thigh by a shot from one of these rascals in the woods, and bled to death in five minutes.

My old regiment, the 103rd, had been drafted into the 27th. I therefore had an opportunity of seeing many of my old friends and acquaintances amongst the privates of that regiment. We had a very fatiguing march from Chadeaus to Mitchell's. The day was very hot, and from the excessive rains up to our ankles in mud. A great number of the men lost their shoes.

June 19.—Marched from Mitchell's at daybreak, the right brigade in front. A good road for four miles, but through a wild uncultivated country. We passed what is called the Grand Etang (*Anglice* Great Pond). This is a circular lake of about twenty acres, situated in the very centre of the island, surrounded by high mountains covered with woods from the very edge of the lake to their summit.

★★★★★★

Mr. C. P. Lucas in his volume on the West Indies (*Historical Geography of the British Colonies*, vol. ii.) describes this Great Pond 'as one of the natural curiosities of Grenada . . . it is said to be thirteen acres in extent, and is 1740 feet above the sea . . . and is apparently the site of an old crater.'

★★★★★★

The *Yougers* and light infantry companies attacked the enemy's second post called Asche's Camp about nine o'clock, which they carried with difficulty and some loss of men. The enemy was strongly posted at this place; indeed, as a position of natural defence, nothing could be stronger. After we quitted the road we entered a thick wood without a track or path; halfway up the leg in clay, and to pass up and down two or three mountains almost perpendicular in order to gain possession of a very high ridge literally in the form of a pig's back, the enemy firing from behind trees and retreating all the way.

After getting on the ridge, it was not possible for more than one man, and that with some difficulty, to advance in front; and as the brigands were posted behind the trees, they picked off several of the *Yougers*, and killed and wounded some men of the 8th Light Infantry company that were in front. Had not our light companies pressed the *Yougers* to move on much faster than what they are used to, they would have played the very game the brigands were practising, and have bush-fought them all along the ridge.

After the enemy were driven from the ridge, they had still possession of a high pinnacle at the extremity of it, with some light ordnance (swivels and a three-pounder), but between the ridge and the pinnacle there was a deep ravine. The light companies passed the *Yougers*, and with great perseverance scrambled up and took the hill. I was with General Campbell at the end of the ridge, having come up from the rear to see what was going on, and I believe, as far as I can judge, that no men ever showed more zeal or intrepidity than the light companies in the attack this day, which was made under many great difficulties, and had the enemy shown half their courage must have been attended with great loss of men.

It is astonishing with what incredible alacrity the negroes got through the woods, and how nimbly they scrambled up and down the hills. The business was all over by twelve o'clock, and we got into some tolerable good huts. But, oh shame to tell, never did anything equal the neglect of this army in the article of provisions. After two days' severe, harassing marches, at the end of each a sharp action, and notwithstanding this post at Asche's that we had just taken was only four miles from St. George's, and that many people came out during the engagement, there was not a drop of rum to give the men as a reward of their exertions.

A soldier never murmurs at the want of provisions, but if his grog is stopped, he is completely defeated. We had received a small supply after taking Mitchell's on the 18th, but on the 20th there was not a morsel of provisions of any kind for either officer or private man. Neglect and infamous misconduct has prevailed in this particular during the whole campaign. Blame is due somewhere, and exemplary punishment ought to attach to the person in fault.

Heavy rain during the night of the 19th and all the following day. The 27th regiment returned to the post at Mitchell's under the command of Colonel Gilman, to remain till further orders. General Campbell and I lived together, that is, I got into the same quarters with him at Mitchell's and again at Asche's. Our living was salt pork, which my black man (Allan M'Cray) cooked for us.

We got into a hut where the 25th regiment was posted on the top of a hill, and though it was not very high, it was absolutely so steep that both hands and knees were obliged to go to work to get up it. The side was clay, and as slippy as that substance when well wet usually is.

On the 20th, the day after we took Asche's, the general got a letter from the Governor at St. George's to say that the enemy's camp at Mount Quoca had been taken on the 19th, but that Fidon and most of his people had got away. The *Yougers* commanded by Count D' Heilgmer, consisting of near five hundred men, had practised their usual mode of attack with success, having crept up the sides of the mountains in very small parties, hiding themselves behind the trees, till they got beyond the enemy's upper work. This so alarmed Fidon and his black companions that they made no stand, and the loss the *Yougers* sustained was very inconsiderable.

I believe what contributed to make Fidon move off so rapidly was the 57th regiment having possession of a strong post and commanding ground within half a mile of him, added to the appearance of the *Yougers* still nearer him; he dreaded the idea of being taken, well knowing that the most ignominious death must attend his exit. Brigadier-General Nicholls remained all this time at Goyave with the 29th regiment, and Brigadier-General M'Kenzie the small garrison at Richmond Hill; indeed, he had remained there from the time of his arrival with us from Barbadoes. I conclude his warlike abilities were well known from his being kept constantly in garrison. Lord help the British army, if it is to be commanded by such a general as M'Kenzie. He is the poorest man of war I ever met with.

The morning after we took Asche's, the line, *viz.* the 8th, 9th, and 25th regiments and a company of *Yougers*, were under arms; and as a proof what state the roads, or rather the country, was in through which we had marched, scarce a soldier had a pair of shoes to his feet, having been dragged off by the stiff mess and depth of the clay. Latterly the men who had shoes did not attempt to put them on, knowing they were of little use, as the spot we were on at Asche's, from the constant rain, was in such a state that if you attempted to stir from your hut, you were nearly halfway up the leg in mud and wet. Some bodies were found of black men that had no appearance of shot, but must have been killed in endeavouring to make their escape down the hills, which were so steep that they must have fallen and broke their necks.

On the 21st orders arrived respecting the regiments that were to be drafted to go to Europe. I concluded, of course, the 25th was one of the number, especially as Lady Louisa, (wife of Lord George Henry Lennox, and daughter of the fourth Marquess of Lothian), had wrote to say the regiment was certainly to go home at the end of the campaign. But to my no small mortification, I found by the orders that instead of being 'draughted,' the regiment was to be completed with 'draughts' from other corps. I cannot say I ever felt much greater disappointment than on receiving this intelligence, having made up my mind as certain of embarking for old England at the end of the campaign.

As there was not the smallest prospect of the enemy making any attack on us at Asche's and nothing offensive to be carried on, I got General Campbell's leave to go to St. George's on the 22nd, in order to write to the adjutant-general for him to lay before the commander-in-chief the state the regiment was in, and how very unfit to receive drafts. I returned early next morning, as General Campbell was ordered to St. George's and I was left in command. Incessant rain from the time we took post at Asche's.

In the afternoon of the 24th I received an order from General Nicholls to move the corps from Asche's to St George's, excepting a captain and two hundred men for the defence of the post.

Accordingly on the 25th I arrived at Richmond Hill with the bri-

101

gade, and closed a long, severe, and fatiguing campaign.

From the almost constant rain the troops in the field were becoming very unhealthy. I had been obliged to send forty men to the general hospital of the 25th regiment from Asche's. After the rains have begun in that country it is impossible to carry on any warlike operations. The day I came in I got a letter from Brigadier Hope, the adjutant-general, to say the regiment was to be drafted, and to go home in the fleet, in consequence of an arrangement that had taken place. Whether this change was owing to my representation, or to instructions from England, I can't say. It might be the latter, a packet having arrived between the first order for drafting and the time of the new arrangement taking place. I did not care from what cause it proceeded, being so overjoyed with the idea of quitting the horrid climate.

The regiment was to be drafted into the 53rd, and the officers and sergeants to embark for Europe on the 12th July. I was fully employed in getting all the necessary arrangements made for turning over the men, which took place on the 9th July, without a murmur from any soldier, and not a man had a claim to make on the regiment, as I had taken particular care to have every man's accounts made up in the clearest manner possible, and his balance paid him.

On Tuesday the 12th July the sad remains of the 25th July regiment marched from Richmond Hill, and embarked on board the *Atlantic* transport, having lost by the disease of the country only, in the space of fifteen months, 11 officers, 30 sergeants, 15 drummers, and upwards of 500 rank and file. We embarked at a most fortunate time, as the sickness was becoming extremely alarming.

In consequence of all the posts the enemy had possession of in the island being taken, a great number of prisoners were made, and among the rest many persons of property to a very considerable amount, most of the French families in the island having joined the insurgents. It is not possible to account for the infatuation of these people suffering themselves to be led not only to countenance crimes of the greatest cruelty, but to be aiding and abetting a mulatto fellow in the most horrid murders and massacres it is possible to describe. This comes of equality and fraternization. In all their transactions the modern French vocabulary is made use of. We found a number of letters, papers, etc., of Fidon's and other officers of the sable army. They all had the same preface: '*Liberté, Egalité, La Loi*,' copied from the disciples of Robespierre and true followers of all his hellish doctrines.

We got under weigh from the island of Grenada at eight o'clock in the morning of the 20th, about twenty-five sail, convoyed by the *Mermaid* frigate and *Favourite* sloop-of-war, with an intention of join-ing the West India convoy at St. Kitts, which was to sail from thence on the 16th August. The regiments embarked were the 8th, 9th, 10th, 25th, 29th, 63rd, and 88th.

On the 24th I went on board the *Mermaid* at sea (Captain Otway), and drank part of a bottle of claret with him. He told us, from the way the wind was, he did not think we should make St. Kitts, and must therefore stand away for Tortola, which island we made on the 27th, and got to anchor in Tortola Road the same evening. As the ships lay seven miles from the town, I did not go ashore on the island. It is but small, the produce but sugar only. The hills so high that the sugar-canes are put into wooden troughs at the top, and slide down without the labour of carriage. I went on shore on a small island op-posite Tortola called St. James', near which our ship lay. But as there was nothing worth looking at and as the weather was excessively hot, and my curiosity for seeing the West Indies pretty well satisfied, I did not remain long on shore.

Many of the transports were very unhealthy at Tortola, and on their passive from Grenada the 8th regiment in two days after their arrival lost four officers. I felt myself unwell from the day after we got to Tortola with a headache and constant fever on me; but our people continued tolerably well. Tortola is one of the Virgin Islands; there are more than twenty of them all in a cluster.

On the 19th we made Scilly Island and fell in with Sir September Edward Pellew's squadron of frigates.

★★★★★★

Sir Edward Pellew, first Viscount Exmouth (1757-1833); took the first frigate in the French war 1793; famous for repeated acts of gallantry; bombarded Algiers 1816; commander-in-chief at Plymouth 1817-21; vice-admiral of the United Kingdom 1832.

★★★★★★

20th.—Fine wind up Channel though thick weather, and got into Plymouth Sound; went ashore immediately and found all the Len-noxes all well at Government House. The transport was put into quar-antine on account of our having had the fever on board. The men did not land till the 30th September, and the regiment was ordered to be quartered in the barracks at Plymouth.

The 24th January, 1797, I left Plymouth and arrived at Freeford on the 26th. The 10th February went to Keel, and was taken ill the day after my arrival. I remained there a fortnight, and was only three times out of the house. Returned to Freeford the 22nd, and had remains of my old cursed West India complaint hanging about me.

On the 28th March 1797 I left Freeford and arrived at Plymouth on the 31st. Found the regiment in dock barracks, which were much more comfortable than the town of Plymouth.

The 22nd June a court-martial assembled, consisting of officers of the line and marines for the trial of four private marines on a charge of mutiny. They were all found guilty and three sentenced to death, which was executed on the 5th July. I was a member of the court. It seldom happens for the officers of the line and marines to sit together in general courts-martial. I had received an invitation from Lord Hugh Fortescue, (1753-1841; third baron; created Viscount Ebrington and Earl Fortescue 1789), who was quartered with his regiment at Plymouth, to pay him a visit at Castle Hill in the north of Devon, which I accepted, and set out for his lordship's seat on the 14th August. It is sixty miles from Plymouth and near Barnstaple.

The house is comfortable, but nothing grand, the park and the grounds are very fine. He lives in a good style, and I never passed a more pleasant week. The country in the north of Devon is infinitely better than in the south, and it is famous for a breed of cattle, of the large red kind. The last ten days in August rain incessantly. This summer in the month of May a mutiny of a most serious and alarming nature broke out in the navy at Plymouth. It was carried to extreme excess; most of the captains were turned on shore from their ships, and the command given to a sailor who was called a delegate. A sailor of this description was chosen from each ship, and these when assembled formed a congress to form regulations and project plans of operation. Ropes were reeved at the yards of the ships to intimidate, as they threatened to hang any person that was refractory, and also any officer who attempted to resist them. This horrid business was only settled by means of great concessions on the part of the government.

★★★★★★

This was suppressed by Lord Keith, but the mutinies at Spithead and the Nore were more serious: the former was suppressed by Lord Howe, the latter came to an end after the execution of the ringleader William Parker.

★★★★★★

In August, September, and October I passed a good deal of time at Saltram, Lord Boringdon's, (John, 1772-1840; second baron; Earl of Morley 1815), and generally a house full of people. A very pleasant and one of the prettiest women in England there most of the summer, Lady Elizabeth Monck.

The beginning of January set in with sharp frost. On the 11th I left the regiment on leave of absence to pay a visit to my friends in Staffordshire, etc. Slept at Exeter and at Bath, and reached Freeford on the 14th.

On the 28th March I accompanied my brother, who was High Sheriff, to Stafford to attend the assizes in the capacity of grand juror; quite a new employment for me. A full assize, and the High Sheriff much flattered by the extreme respectable attendance that accompanied him into Stafford. We returned to Freeford on the 31st.

In the month of June an order came for the Lancashire June Militia to embark for Ireland on account of the dreadful state of that country from the rebellion that raged with fury at that time. (The Irish rebellion of 1798. The rebels were routed on Vinegar Hill by General Lake with 13,000 men on June 21).

The regiment embarked on board two men-of-war, but were detained for some days by contrary winds; and on account of the troubles having taken a favourable turn, the Lancashire regiment was disembarked. However, about this time two regiments of militia went from Liverpool to Ireland, *viz.* the Warwick and Buckingham, and remained some time.

On the 28th July I received an order to hold the regiment in readiness to embark for the island of Jersey, and on the 8th August we embarked on board the *Dictator*, a 64, and *Charm*, a, 44, and sailed in the afternoon. Arrived off Jersey the next day, and disembarked on the 10th and 11th, and went into barracks at Belle Vue, near the small town of St. Aubin. I was extremely sorry to part with my much esteemed friends at Government House, but otherwise, considering the length of time the regiment had been at Plymouth and the vice it had naturally imbibed, I can't say I was sorry for a change of quarters.

The island of Jersey is extremely pretty, the houses neat and the inhabitants hospitable. A bad situation for soldiers on account of the abundance of gin, which is so cheap that a man gets drunk for twopence. I found an old friend of mine commanding the island—Major-General Andrew Gordon; the second in command, Major-General Monson. The regiments on the island, the 49th, 88th, Loyal Irish Fencibles, and garrison battalion. We relieved the 58th regiment, who embarked in the ships that we left. We had most delightful weather after our arrival, and no alarms or disturbance from our neighbours, although the French coast is within fifteen miles of us.

The 88th regiment was relieved in November by the 69th, the former ordered for the East Indies. Our regiment was reviewed by Major General Gordon on the 7th December. Every man (officers, etc.) had on new clothing. The former short coats, the latter long. I never saw any regiment look better; it was as fine a day as ever was seen. The general was highly pleased; returned his thanks in the handsomest and most flattering manner; and assured me he never saw so good a review in his life. After the review, etc., was over, I made application for a short leave of absence; and on Thursday morning the 20th December I embarked in the packet from Jersey, called at Guernsey and went on shore for two hours.

Saw the parade of the 8th, 23rd, 27th, and 79th; none of them in very high order. I waited on the commander-in-chief, Sir Hew Dalrymple. (Bart; 1750-1830; lieutenant-governor of Guernsey 1796-1801). The island is not so large as Jersey, but vastly more trade, and the town considerably larger than St. Heliers at Jersey. Left Guernsey about two o'clock Thursday, and next morning was off the coast of England near Portland, when we were chased by a French privateer, but she did not come up with us.

I landed at Weymouth about two o'clock, found Colonel Elliott and the Staffordshire supplementary militia quartered there. Proceeded that night to Shaftesbury; the next morning to Warminster, Bath, Bristol, and in the mail to Birmingham; arrived at Freeford on Sunday the 23rd, where I found everybody in very good health. Went to Leicester on Monday the 31st, and passed the next week. Returned into Staffordshire with Mr. Lee and Mr. Walker on Monday the 7th.

We had a subscription ball and supper at the George on the 23rd, in honour of Her Majesty's birthday. Sir Robert Williams and I officiated as managers or stewards on the occasion. It was extremely splendid. There never was a more severe winter than this; remarkable deep snow and severe frost. We had a very good party used to meet daily at the George at Lichfield at eleven o'clock and play whist the whole day. Had several very pleasant balls and assemblies.

Captain Callander, 25th regiment, came to Freeford and stayed a month with us; he arrived the 15th January.

In consequence of Lord Granville Leveson, having vacated a seat for Lichfield and offering himself for the county of Stafford (Lord

Gower being made a peer), we had a contested election for the city, which commenced on March the 2nd March. Sir John Wrottesley was proposed by Lord Stafford's friends, and Sir Nigel Gresley by my brother on the independent interest. The contest was a warm one, but Sir John carried the day.

★★★★★★

Lord Gower, second Marquis of Stafford (1758-1833); summoned to Parliament as Baron Gower in the lifetime of his father.

Sir John Wrottesley, first baron (1771-1867); whig M.P. for Lichfield 1799-1802; M.P. for Staffordshire 1822; for South Staffordshire 1825-37; created Baron Wrottesley 1838.

Sir Nigel Bowyer .Gresley, son of Sir Nigel Gresley; succeeded his father 1787; died 1808.

★★★★★★

On the 3rd March I received a letter from the department adjutant-general to say the Duke of York had recommended me to the king to be assistant adjutant-general to the troops in the South-West district, under the orders of Sir William Pitt, (1728-1809; entered the army 1744; K.B. 1792; general 1793; governor of Portsmouth 1794-1809). This was highly gratifying to me, and the appointment of all others I wished for. I continued at Freeford till the election was over at Lichfield, and set out for London on the 20th March, where I arrived the next day.

I called on the adjutant-general, who told me I was to meet a board of field officers on Saturday at the Horse Guards to consider and report our opinion on the subject of clothing for the army in the West Indies. We continued sitting three days, which was tiresome enough for a man who went to London for only seven. On Tuesday the 26th I had the honour of an audience of the Duke of York, to thank him for my new appointment. Found H.R.H. very gracious. I had intended to have gone to the King's *levée*, but it being Passion Week there was not any.

I left London on the 30th, and went to Windsor to see my old friends of the Stafford Militia. As Prince Edward was in Sir William Pitt's district on the staff, I waited on him at Windsor. Found him affable and good-humoured. (Edward Augustus, Duke of Kent and Strathearn—1767-1820; fourth son of George III., father of Queen Victoria).

On the 31st I went to Highfield, Sir William Pitt's. A very comfortable house and pretty place four miles from Hertford Bridge in Hampshire. I found Sir William and Lady Pitt extremely friendly and very pleasant. Sir William made Highfield the headquarters of the district till he moved to Portsmouth. Sir William's family consisted of three *aides-de-camp*, Addenbrooke, Coleman, and Vigoreux. Lord Rivers, Sir William's brother, has a very pretty place about two miles from Highfield, a large old house. A remarkable good riding house attached to the stables. His lordship is a very fine gentleman-like old peer as I ever saw. (Lord Rivers—1722 ?-1803; George Pitt, first Baron Rivers; whig M.P. for Shaftesbury 1742; Dorset 1747-74; created baron 1776; filled several diplomatic posts).

On the 18th April I left Highfield and proceeded through Odiham and Alton, Wickham, Fareham to Portsmouth, where I arrived in the evening, fifty miles. Major-General Murray, the Lieutenant-Governor, was commanding in the absence of Sir William Pitt. I did not enter on my new duty till Sir William's arrival.

June, on the rumour of an armament being about to be collected, I made an offer to the Duke of York to be employed on service; and received a very flattering answer, with a promise if opportunity offered my application should be attended to.

The 25th was ordered to form part of the expedition under Sir Ralph Abercrombie; I was in hopes to have attended them, but Sir Ralph advised me by no means to think of it. I therefore remained contented with Sir August William. On the 4th August we left Portsmouth to prepare for the Weymouth campaign. I went to London, and on the 7th went to the *levée* to kiss the king's hand on my appointment as Assistant Adjutant-General. Was presented by my old colonel, Lord Charles Somerset.

Left town on the 8th, and stayed at Highfield till the 19th, when I proceeded to Winchester to pass a day with Colonel and Mrs. Maden. Joined Sir William at Stockbridge on the 20th, and arrived at Weymouth on the 22nd. His Majesty had been there since the 17th, but in consequence of Lord Howe's death, (5th of August 1799), Sir William did not make Weymouth headquarters till the 22nd. We found the Royal Family all arrived, that is the King, Queen, Princesses Augusta, Elizabeth, Sophia, Amelia, and Mary. Their attendants consisted of Generals Garth and Goldsworthy, Lady Elizabeth Bellasys, Lady Matilda Wynyard, and Miss Townsend.

★★★★★★

Princess Augusta Sophia (1768-1840), daughter of George III.

Princess Elizabeth (1770-1840), daughter of George III.; married 1818 Frederick Joseph of Hesse-Homburg; artist.

Princess Sophia (1777-1848), fifth daughter of George III.

Princess Amelia (1783-1810), youngest child of George III.

Princess Mary (1776-1857), fourth daughter of George III.; married William Frederick, second Duke of Gloucester, 1816.

General Garth, cf. *The Creevey Papers*, vol. ii.

Lady Matilda Wynyard, daughter of the second Earl Delawarr; married 1793 General Henry Wynyard; and died 1843.

★★★★★★

His Majesty is out walking on the Esplanade every morning by half-past seven o'clock, where he continues till near nine. He then gets his breakfast, and if the weather admits, the whole family go on board a frigate, the *St. Fiorenzo*, and sail till evening, when the king regularly attends the parade of the piquets in front of the lodge. Four times a week the family go to the play, and twice a week a party of the nobility are invited to the lodge. On the whole it's but a tiresome kind of life we lead. The king converses with almost everybody he knows, and talks to all the children he meets.

Left Weymouth the 14th October and went to Plymouth October for a few days to see my friend Lady Louisa. Never was I so thoroughly tired of a place in my life as Weymouth. The same sameness is more tiresome than anything ever was. I slept at Ashburton and got to Plymouth about three o'clock on the 15th. Found Lady Louisa alone and rather low spirited on account of the action in Holland, in which the 25th regiment had been engaged.

We got the details of the action whilst I was at Plymouth, in which the loss to the 25th was very considerable.

★★★★★★

This refers to the expedition to the Helder. Sir Ralph Abercromby had landed a British force of 10,000 men on August 27. On September 12 the Russian allies arrived, and reinforcements from England brought up the number of the combined army to 30,000 men. The general advance on the 18th and 19th of September was a failure. The British lost over 1000 killed and wounded.

★★★★★★

Headquarters were established at Salisbury instead of Portsmouth,

The Duke of York

the latter place was Sir William Pitt's government, which was the reason he made it headquarters. I was taken unwell a few days after my arrival at Salisbury and confined to the house for some time. Lord Radnor has a house within three miles of Salisbury; an excessive pretty place. (Lord Radnor—1750-1829; second earl; married the Hon. Anne Duncombe, daughter and co-heir of Anthony, Lord Feversham).

His lordship called on me immediately on my arrival at quarters. I was acquainted with Lady Radnor at Weymouth, one of the pleasantest women I ever knew. I also got very intimately acquainted with Lady Charlotte Durham, (Bruce she was) at Weymouth, one of the most delightful women in the world. She was on a visit to Lady Radnor, and therefore a cruel disappointment to me being confined at the time and unable to visit at Lord Radnor's whilst Lady Charlotte was there, though frequently asked. (Lady Charlotte Durham, daughter of the ninth Earl of Kincardine; married in 1799 Admiral Sir Philip Durham, G.C.B.; and died in 1816).

I recovered in about a fortnight and went several times to Lord Radnor's very old house, but comfortable.

On the 29th November I went to Highfield for three days; found Lord Howe there; Sir William and Lady Pitt both uncommon well. Wynyard and his wife were staying at Addenbrooke's. Took a ride in December to Fonthill, fifteen miles from Salisbury, the seat of Mr. Beckford, of notorious memory. The house is the most 1799 splendidly furnished of any house in England, but it did not quite strike me as a comfortable living house. The grounds were pretty, but nothing very fine. Mr. Beckford jnr. is building a curious tower about two miles from his house. It is erected on very high ground and intended to be the highest building in England, but for what purpose I did not discover. I went to see Wilton House (Lord Pembroke's), three miles from Salisbury.

★★★★★★

William Beckford (1709-70); Lord Mayor of London 1762 and 1768; ardent supporter of John Wilkes 1763 and 1770; laid first stone of Newgate 1770.

William Beckford (1759-1844), son of the above; author of *Vathek*; M.P. for Wells and Hindon; lived in almost complete seclusion at his mansion, Fonthill Giffard, where he spent large sums in fantastic decoration.

George Augustus Herbert, eleventh Earl of Pembroke (1759-1827); said to have trebled the value of his estates.

★★★★★★

The house is extremely old, part of it having been built in Harry VIII.'s time. No part of the furniture, etc., has been altered these one hundred years; therefore the house is cheerless, cold, and uncomfortable. Indeed, it is so filled with statues and ancient curiosities that it is more like a museum than the residence of a nobleman. It is said there are the finest collection of Roman antiques at Wilton in Europe. There are some fine pictures, and one in particular by Vandyke of the Pembroke family. The grounds adjoining the house are beautiful, and the prospect of Salisbury Cathedral very fine. General Goldsworthy has a house in the neighbourhood belonging to Lord Pembroke; lives most comfortably and is a most worthy good man. I dined several times with Mr. But, who has a good house near Lord Radnor's, planned by Wyatt, and who lives *comme il faut*. (James Wyatt—1746-1813; architect; studied at Rome and Venice; executed restorations at Salisbury, Lincoln, Hereford, and Lichfield cathedrals; built Royal Military College, Woolwich, 1796).

On the 22nd January I left Salisbury and went by way 1800 of Bath to Freeford, where I arrived the 23rd to dinner. I was very sorry to leave Salisbury, both on account of quitting my situation, and also because I found it a charming county, and some pleasant people in the neighbourhood.

I remained at Freeford till the 2nd February, when I went to town for the purpose of going to court on my promotion. I attended the *levée* on the 5th and the drawing-room on the 6th. His Majesty and the Queen both did me the honour to notice me, I thought particularly. I left London on the 8th and returned to Freeford the 9th, where I continued till the 14th March, when I again went to town in my way to the regiment. I stayed in town till the 31st March and rode to Ipswich to dinner the next day; the finest road in all England. Slept at Witham, thirty-nine miles, and rode on next morning thirty miles to Ipswich.

I passed through Chelmsford, Romford, Ingatestone, Witham, and Colchester. Found the 1st battalion of the King's Own or 4th regiment. Ipswich is a large, old, straggling town; a tide river, navigable for small vessels from Harwich, comes up to it. The country about it very charming, though almost wholly in tillage. Lieut. General Garth commanded in the district and was stationed at Ipswich. I went to visit Mr. Vancouver, who I had met at Sir William Pitt's in Hampshire; a sensible, pleasant man. He had just made a purchase of a vast tract of heath, and was enclosing and breaking it up; but from the wretched appearance I should think it would never answer. (This may possibly be Charles Vancouver, an American agriculturalist, who published a work on the drainage of the fens in 1801).

The regiment marched from Ipswich the 29th April to Colchester; found in the barracks, which arc sufficient for 1800 the accommodation of 5000 men, the 49th and 85th regiments. Colchester, a large unconnected place, something like Ipswich.

I received orders to prepare the regiment for the camp June at Windsor, and marched accordingly on Friday the 6th June. I was not at all sorry to leave my quarters as, in the first place, the regiment was sickly, and in the next I had not got acquainted with a single creature in town or neighbourhood. Friday we marched twenty-three miles to Chelmsford and went into the barracks for the night. Saturday thirteen miles and encamped on Warley Common near Brentwood, where we halted Sunday, on the most beautiful spot I ever saw and the greatest extent of prospect probably in England.

Marched on Monday morning thirteen miles to Epping Forest, near the six-mile stone on the Romford Road. Tuesday to a common near the Uxbridge Road. We turned off at Whitechapel turnpike and up the new road to Paddington, and along the Harrow Road to our ground. Wednesday to Hounslow Heath near Belfont. We were just got to our ground when His Majesty made his appearance. I had exactly time to get the regiment under arms and paid His Majesty the usual compliment. Thursday we reached the Grand Camp on Bagshot Heath near the twenty-three milestone. We were very fortunate in our weather, though most excessively cold in the mornings.

His Majesty first saw the several brigades on their parade and marched past on the line of encampment; afterwards he saw each brigade in review on Wingfield Plain. The king paid me many compliments respecting the regiment. It was always a great favourite with His Majesty. Lieut.-General Dundas, who superintended the exercise of the troops, had the brigades out, and then a line and latterly the whole army, horse and foot, His Majesty always attending. The general officers were Lieut.-General Dundas, Stevens, and Gwyn. The generals Lord Chatham, Lord C. Somerset, Marshal, Burrard, Garth, Lord Cathcart, Wilford, and Manners.

★★★★★★

Sir David Dundas (1735-1820); lieutenant fireworker 1754; lieutenant-general 1797; general 1802; commander-in-chief 1809-11.

Lord Chatham (1756-183 5), second Earl of Chatham; entered the army 1778; master of the ordnance 1801-6; commanded the Walcheren expedition 1809.

Sir Harry Burrard (1755-1813); entered the army 1772; created baronet 1807; took command in Portugal 1808.

Lord Cathcart (1755-1843), tenth Baron Cathcart.

Robert Manners (1758-1823).

★★★★★★

On the 14th July we had a sham fight, and afterwards His Majesty gave a most magnificent *fête* at Frogmore; a dinner and ball, besides rural sports in the gardens, such as gipsies juying (?), lofty tumbling and tight-rope dancing. Upwards of two hundred people at dinner, and on the whole the handsomest thing I ever saw. On the 17th the whole army was assembled on Wingfield Plain to be seen by His Majesty in their new clothing, etc. etc. There were near 17,000 men assembled. The day most uncommonly fine and the greatest concourse of people that ever were assembled in England. His Majesty was received with a royal salute and presented arms. Then the King and Royal Family passed along the two lines, after which a *feu de joie* was fired three times from right to left of the first line and from left to right of the second. The whole then marched past by troops and companies.

The reviewing being over, the field officers and all the generals invited to the queen's *fête* were invited to a *fête* given by 1800 his Majesty at the Lodge in the great park. We assembled and dined by half-past one o'clock in six tents that were presented to His Majesty by Lord Cornwallis taken at Seringapatam from Tippoo. They were made of cotton of curious workmanship. (Lord Cornwallis—1738-1805; first Marquis and second Earl of Cornwallis, governor-general of India; created marquis 1792; defeated Tippoo Sultan near Seringapatam 1791).

As the camp was to break up on the 2nd September and as the 31st August was the last field day, as soon as it was August over I set out for London, having got leave for a month. The regiment marched on the 6th for Lewes, where it arrived on the 9th. I got to London on the 31st, dined with Wynyard, and went next morning to Tunbridge Wells on purpose to see Lady Donegal and her sisters. (George Augustus, second Marquis of Donegal—1769-1833; married Anna, daughter of Sir Edward May, Bart).

I continued at Tunbridge till Thursday the 4th; cannot say September I admired the gaieties of Tunbridge at all. Returned to London, and set out on the 6th for Freeford for a little shooting and to attend the races. Got to Freeford on the 7th to dinner. Took down a new chaise for my brother. The races were uncommonly well attended, and I had some famous sport shooting. I stayed in Stafford until the 29th, went to town, stayed all night, and proceeded to the regiment for the 1st October at Lewes barracks. I travelled per coach through Croydon, East Grinstead. The barracks for the officers most infamous, the accommodation for the men very good.

Brighton is thirty-seven miles from Tunbridge, a place now of great eminence in consequence of H.R.H. the Prince of Wales having a house there.

★★★★★★

The Pavilion. Cf. *Letters to Ivy from the first Earl of Dudley*, by S. H. Romilly. Writing in 1811 Lord Dudley says: 'By-the-bye, it is a curious circumstance enough that in Brighthelmstone, which, when it is full, contains twelve or fourteen thousand people, there is literally no police at all. There is neither mayor, bailiff, headborough, nor, in short, any vestige of municipal government. The nearest justice of the peace lives at Lewes, nine miles off. Yet there is no place so quiet or so completely free from crimes. The doors are all left unbarred, and yet I never heard of anything being stolen.'

★★★★★★

The Steine, which is the Mall, is a gay scene when the company are assembled about two o'clock. The Dowager Lady Donegal was there. I dined with her several times, and she did me the honour to breakfast two or three times at the barracks to hear our band. No great attention paid to us by the inhabitants or neighbourhood of Lewes. Lord Gage, (Major-General Henry Gage—1761-1808; third viscount), and a Mr. Shiffner the only gentlemen who thought proper to call at the barracks.

On the 19th November I left Lewes for the winter leave. Went to Stoke, found Lord and Lady ——— (*illegible* ?Markken?) there. Had some very good shooting, and remained there until the 28th. Went to Portsmouth, dined with General John Whitelock, (1757-1833; lieutenant-governor of Portsmouth 1799; commanded force to recover

Buenos Ayres 1807), and next day I went to Winchester to pay a visit to General Stevens.

On the 2nd December I went to Highfield and stayed with Sir William and Lady Pitt until the 5th; went to town, and remained in London until the 9th, and reached Freeford the 10th. The apparent scarcity of corn in the kingdom (whether real or imaginary is hard to determine) must bear very hard on the lower class of people. Wheat on an average is at upwards of a guinea a bushel, and barley upwards of 13 shillings.

The poor mechanics in the large manufacturing towns are in a wretched state, 1800 and I fear before the winter is over serious and alarming disturbances must take place. On Monday the 12th January 1801 I went with my brother Richard and Mrs. 1801 Dyott to Thorpe to pay a visit to Mr. Inge and Lady Eliza. (Lady Elizabeth Euphemia married William Phillips Inge, Esq. of Thorpe Constantine, co. Stafford. She was the daughter of Lord Galloway).

Remained there until Wednesday; went to Seal and passed two days with Will Gresley and his wife, and on Friday the 16th I went to Leicester, where I remained with my friends until Saturday the 24th. Returned to Freeford, hard frost and snow, but it did not continue.

I was frequently at Drakelow. I believe my visits lately March to be not so much for the company of my old friend Sir Nigel as for the sake of his dear daughter Maria, for whom I had a sincere regard and attachment, but it had grown to attachment most sound and dear. I ought to have joined my regiment on the 14th, but on dear Maria's account I asked for a prolongation of my leave to the 1st April. (Wilmot Maria Gresley married Rev. T. Levett of Packington, co. Stafford, and died December 17, 1845).

In the beginning of this month the king had an alarming attack of fever, and it was generally imagined to be a return of his former situation.

******

Lady Hamilton wrote to Nelson on February 24, 1801: 'The King, God bless him, is ill, and their (sic) are many speculations. Some say it is his old disorder.'

******

To the great joy of all his subjects His Majesty recovered his health, and the reports from the physicians were discontinued on the 12th March. Some people imagined the disagreements amongst His Majesty's Ministers, which about this time took place, had occasioned his indisposition, Mr. Pitt, Mr. Dundas, and Lord Spencer having resigned their offices.

★★★★★★

William Pitt (1759-1806), second son of the first Earl of Chatham; prime minister 1784-1801 and 1804-6.

Henry Dundas (1742-1811), first Viscount Melville; impeached 1806 for malversation; guilty of negligence but acquitted.

George John (1758-18 30), second Earl Spencer; home secretary 1806-7.

Pitt broke up a strong ministry because in honour he could not carry it on. George III. would not allow him to bring in a measure for Roman Catholic emancipation.

★★★★★★

The very high price of grain and of butcher's meat still continued. The prices as follows at Lichfield the 13th March:—

Wheat	25 shillings per bushel.
Barley	15 shillings per bushel.
Oats	8/6 to 9 shillings per bushel.
Beef	8 pence and mutton 8½ pence per lb.

On the 22nd March I left Lichfield per mail for London, where I arrived the next morning. I was as usual much *en désespoir* on bidding *adieu* to old Freeford and my much beloved brother. I remained in town until the 1st April, when I departed for headquarters at Lewes, which I reached per heavy coach to dinner. (The Gresleys were in town, which I considered a most fortunate circumstance, being an opportunity of seeing my dear Maria, for whom I felt a most ardent passion, and to whom I trust and hope some day to be united in holy bonds.) I was at the drawing-room at St. James's on the 26th March. There was no *levée*, as the king was not sufficiently recovered from his late attack. The drawing-room was as dismal a business as I ever saw.

It was a court mourning, add to which the melancholy appearance of the queen and princesses on account of His Majesty's illness made the scene a most gloomy one. London was full and thronged with Irish in consequence of the meeting of the first Imperial Parliament. I don't think the Pats appeared to associate very much with Johnny Bull. On my arrival at the regiment I found the thing going on much as when I left it. An augmentation had been ordered of two companies of 100 men each, which occasioned a considerable proportion of our people to be employed on the recruit service. During the month of April drying north-east wind and hot sun; very uncomfortable weather. I employed myself all the month in field days and getting the regiment in order after the idling of the winter. I fired three volleys and a royal salute in honour of the victory obtained over the Danes by Lord Nelson in Copenhagen Harbour. (A fleet under Sir Hyde Parker, with Nelson as second in command, defeated the Danes on April 1, 1801).

On the 3rd May I received a letter from Colonel Brownrigg to acquaint me that His Majesty had been most graciously pleased to appoint me one of his *aides-de-camp*. This I consider an honour the most flattering I could possibly hope for or expect. (Sir Robert Brownrigg—1759-1833; ensign 1775; served in the Netherlands 17931 created baronet 1816; general 1819).

I went to London on the 8th May. My visit to town was purposely to see my dear Maria G.,' and for whom I felt the most ardent love and regard.

I got to town in the evening and went to tea at Sir Nigel Gresley's, from whom I received the most friendly attention during my stay.

On the 15th May I met Colonel Brownrigg at General Whitelock's, who told me the 25th regiment was to go to Weymouth to attend His Majesty. On the 16th I had the honour of an audience of the Duke of York, and to my surprise, instead of the regiment going to Weymouth, the duke told me we were going to embark to reinforce the army in Egypt. (Accounts had just at the time arrived of a severe action having taken place near Alexandria, in which the French had been beaten, but with considerable loss on the side of the British.)

★★★★★★

The Battle of Alexandria had taken place on March 21, 1801.
The English had to deplore the loss of Sir Ralph Abercromby, but they thoroughly defeated the French.

★★★★★★

The regiment was ordered to march from Lewes on Tuesday the 19th, and I joined them at Portsmouth on Thursday the 21st. The regiment did not, however, embark until Thursday the 22nd, owing to the ships not being ready.

The 25th and 26th embarked at Southsea Beach on Thursday morning at six o'clock the 28th May. The former on board H.M. ship *Agincourt*, the latter on board the *Madras*. I must own I felt rather happy at embarking, and chiefly as it gave me hopes that it was the last regimental duty I should probably have (and that if it pleased God to let me return to my native land, I might flatter myself the first wish of my life might be accomplished, that of being united to the woman I love).

The terrible crowded state of the ship and the confusion it occasioned was the cause of some inquietude and not much comfort.

Wind still adverse, though not so much as it had hitherto been. One of our Pats, standing near the quarterdeck and looking up at the rigging soliloquised, 'Navigation—to the devil I pitch you, navigation.' Saturday, a fine summer day but nearly calm, what wind there was against us.

Little wind, Cape St. Vincent in sight. Sent a boat on board a Portuguese fishing boat, but did not get any fish. The Portuguese told us that two English seventy-four gun ships had chased two French vessels the day before into Cadiz, and that a Spanish frigate four days before had taken a Portuguese fishing boat. We saw four sail of armed vessels inshore; we supposed them to be Spaniards. We also saw a ship at a considerable distance at sea, but did not make her out. She stood towards us in the afternoon and proved to be an English line-of-battle ship, the *Superb*, of seventy-four guns. Captain Keates. He sent a boat aboard us by which we learnt that there were five Spanish sail of the line, and three French, lying in the outward road of Cadiz, and that there were 2000 French troops ready to embark on board them, supposed to be for Egypt.

The lieutenant also told us that the *Venerable*, a seventy-four (Captain S. Hood), was cruising with the *Superb*, but was at that time close in with the shore, having sent a boat into Faro to get intelligence relative to the fleet in Cadiz. This intelligence respecting the situation of the fleet in Cadiz alarmed us a little, fearing they might attempt to intercept us in the straits. Shortly after the *Superb* left us, we saw the *Venerable* and also a large fleet at a considerable distance at sea (which we learnt was a convoy from the Mediterranean, under charge of the *Sea Horse*). In the evening we spoke the *Venerable*; Captain Ryves went on board. The information respecting the fleet in Cadiz was confirmed, and, in consequence. Captain Hood, who was the senior officer, said he should accompany our two ships with the *Superb* into the straits.

June 18.—We stood in for the land, and saw the town of Tangier on the coast of Barbary. Entered the straits in the evening, and anchored about twelve o'clock in Gibraltar Bay.

19th, Friday morning.—I went on shore with Colonel Graham and Captain Ryves at six o'clock to the garrison parade, where we found the Governor-General Charles O'Hara, who invited us to breakfast. (1740?-1802; governor of Gibraltar, where he died, 1795-1802).

I was much delighted with Gibraltar, although I had but a very slight view of it, as we were only on shore two hours. They had no accounts from Egypt subsequent to what we had heard. They had a report of Monsieur Ganteaume, (Count G. H. Ganteaume—1755-1818; French admiral), being at sea with eight sail of men-of-war, but no certain intelligence. They were much in want of water; the soldiers were on an allowance of a gallon a day, owing to their having had no rain for a long time. I walked to the end of the town, but could not wait to see or examine anything, as we went on board again as soon as we had breakfast, and got under weigh. About twelve o'clock we made sail, and stood out of the bay. When you get round Europa Point, which is the southern extremity of the rock, the eastern side has a most tremendous appearance, being a perpendicular ragged surface 1400 feet high.

24th.—General O' Hara at Gibraltar remarked in a conversation respecting Sir Hyde Parker, that there were three things against him—'He was getting old, getting rich, and had married a young wife.'

29th.—The wind continued fair; in the morning made the island of Pantellaria; and at a great distance saw the island of Sardinia. About twelve o'clock observed a strange sail; did not know whether she was friend or enemy until she made the private signal; she was the *Peteril* sloop-of-war; we spoke her about two o'clock, and the captain came on board. She was two days from Malta, and about six weeks from Alexandria. When the captain left Egypt General Hutchinson was gone from Alexandria to attack Grand Cairo.

★★★★★★

John Hely-Hutchinson (1757-1832); first Baron Hutchinson and second Earl of Donoughmore; commanded first division under Abercromby in Egypt; succeeded to chief command 1801; captured Cairo and Alexandria 1801.

★★★★★★

The troops were healthy, and had plenty of provisions of all sorts brought by the Arabs. The captain of the *Peteril* also told us that Monsieur Ganteaume had been seen about a fortnight before off the island of Candia with four sail of the line and five frigates, having a considerable number of troops on board to reinforce Alexandria. Sir John Warren, (1753-1822; English admiral), with six sail of the line, had sailed from Malta a few days before the *Peteril* left it, but his destination was not known. This report respecting Monsieur Ganteaume rather alarmed us, as our captain intended to make the island of Candia rather than the coast of Egypt; at all events we had reason to fear the French would endeavour to intercept us between Malta and Alexandria.

I wrote to my brother and Lady Louisa Lennox by the *Peteril*: she was going to Minorca, and I thought she might have a chance of sending letters from thence to England. The breeze freshened in the afternoon; we were going nine knots an hour, and expected to be at Malta next morning, but were disappointed, as the wind became foul about ten at night.

July 1, Wednesday.—Made the island of Gozo early in the morning, and stood on under an easy sail. Gozo is divided from the island of Malta by only a very narrow channel; we ran down the side of Malta almost close in with the shore. The appearance of the island is quite like a barren rock, owing to the innumerable quantity of low walls intersecting the side of the island, which rises in a gradual ascent from the beach. We came to anchor off the harbour's mouth about twelve o'clock, and immediately went on shore. The fortifications of La Valette, (Valetta), the capital of the island, are reckoned the most complete in Europe; and the buildings in the town for the residence of the knights and Grand Master most magnificent. Major-General Pigot, who commanded, lived in the palace of the Grand Master.

★★★★★★

Sir Henry Pigot (1750-1840); entered the army 1769; commanded at the blockade of Malta 1800; general 1812; G.C.M.G. 1837.

★★★★★★

I waited on the general, and after eating ice cream, etc. (a most dainty delicacy in the month of July in the latitude of 25), I went to look over the different apartments of the palace. The great Consul Buonaparte, when he was there, and afterwards General Vaubois, who commanded during the time it was blockaded and taken last year, (September 15, 1800), carried off all the furniture.

★★★★★★

General Vaubois had been summoned to surrender by Admiral Saumarez, but the French general sent word that 'they are Frenchmen who are at Malta.'

****

But there is a magnificent suite of rooms and an armoury in which there are 10,000 stands of arms remaining, although the French carried away 30,000 stands. In one of the rooms there are remaining several good portraits of the different Grand Masters, as also what was said to be a striking likeness of the late Empress of Russia. The streets of the town are very narrow, but perfectly regularly built, and with good houses. There are one or two places or 1801 squares very handsome. The inside of the Church of St. John's is reckoned the finest thing in the world; built and furnished by the Knights of St. John of Jerusalem; it is hung with the finest and most beautiful tapestry, the subjects taken from Scripture; the floor paved with grand marble in the mosaic style and inscriptions on the stones to the memory of knights who have been buried.

The grand altar is the most magnificent thing I ever saw, with a white marble statue of St. John the Evangelist performing the baptismal ceremony; the figures as large as life. The silver candlesticks in front of the altar are at least eight feet and proportionally large. There are six other altars at the end of aisles that intersect the grand aisle at right angles. In a recess off one of the side aisles is a sort of urn of gold, which we were told contained the Virgin Mary, and in front of this urn is a lofty sort of palisade of solid silver, each bar of which must be at least six or eight inches in circumference, and a pair of gates of the same structure as an entrance to the recess.

The altar-piece at the end of one of the cross aisles was Our Saviour on the Cross in white marble, with two statues of white marble representing Mary Magdalene and Mary the Mother of James looking up to the Cross. The expression of grief depicted in Mary Magdalene's countenance the most agonising that it is possible to behold. Behind our Saviour is a very fine painting of the beheading of St. John. There are also in this aisle, on each side, some uncommon fine paintings from some of the most eminent masters of the old school. In another of the aisles under the altar is a sepulchre containing the skull and bones of St. Clement, one of the Grand Masters of the order, which are shown to you (with a light), ornamented with a wonderful variety of jewels and precious stones.

There are a prodigious number of magnificent monuments in statuary marble to the memory of the several Grand Masters. In the great aisle there were three chandeliers, two smaller of silver, and one very large one in the centre of gold; but Monsieur Buonaparte, imagining they might be brought into circulation, carried them off. I had not time to examine minutely this very splendid relique of antique grandeur, which very very far surpassed anything I had ever seen, and my great astonishment was that the great nation had not despoiled it more. I never was in a place of divine worship that struck me with so sublime and reverential an awe as this church did. In a place adjoining the Place where the Grand Master's palace is built, is another palace, which is called the Grand Master's winter residence; when I was there it was a sort of hotel, and the library (which was for the use of the knights) was become a kind of public coffee-room.

The books were taken down on the place surrendering to the British last year, and packed up in cases. I was surprised the French had not sent them away with their other spoils, as they carried off a very great quantity of valuable articles of furniture, paintings, etc. etc. I was only on shore two hours, and therefore had not time to see half I should wish to have seen, but I was better entertained with the sight of Malta than anything I had ever seen in my life. It is one of the disgraces of the present generation that the French politics should have influenced this order, and been the means of destroying the institution, and with it in a great degree these grand remains of religious antiquity.

The institution of the order of St. John's of Jerusalem existed before the Crusades to the Holy Land. During those memorable old battles the Knights of St. John settled at Malta, received and attended all the wounded and sick that were sent from the Holy Wars, and in the latter years of the Crusades the knights formed themselves into a military corps, and went to the Holy Land, leaving a sufficient number of their aged brethren to contribute their assistance and attendance to the sick at Malta.

After the Crusades were terminated the different powers in Europe (and almost all were concerned) contributed a large annual donation as a revenue for the support of these knights, who had essentially served them in their wars against the infidels. This revenue, to a very large amount, together with individual donations, to a great extent enabled the knights to build and decorate the town, etc., of Valetta as it appears at present. The fortifications have been improved and enlarged in more modern days, having withstood several memorable sieges from the Turks. It remained in possession of the Grand Master and knights until the year '98, when the cursed French politics divided the knights, and like the house divided the order fell, and Mr. Buonaparte got possession.

The French Army irritated the Maltese to acts of rebellion against them, and by means of assistance from Great Britain, after a blockade of two years the French surrendered La Valette to Major-General Pigot, the present commander. I should think if England knows her own interest, she will use every endeavour to gain the good-will, and reconcile the Maltese to the British Government. At present I understood they had expressed the strongest attachment to our interest, and utter detestation for the French. There is a splendid fine harbour and a fortification that may defy the power of France as long as we have command at sea, which I trust will ever be the case.

The produce of the island is almost entirely cotton, and they get all their provisions, at least a great part of them, from Sicily. There are granaries, etc., in the garrison of La Valette for seven years' consumption, all of which Buonaparte found well filled, but took care to carry off all, except sufficient for the garrison for two years. There is abundance of fruit and vegetables of all descriptions; oranges, melons, pears, apples, grapes, apricots, etc., in profusion; the fruit a dainty luxury to sea-faring people, and of which our ship's company eat voraciously.

We were informed by a cutter just arrived from Egypt, that General Hutchinson had taken Rahmanieh; that the French Army, consisting of two thousand men, had evacuated the place, and had retired to Cairo, and that the general was within two days' march of Cairo when the despatches came away. General Coote commanded the army before Alexandria. The French squadron had made an attempt to throw a reinforcement into Alexandria by endeavouring to land troops to the westward of the place, but on seeing some of our men-of-war they cut their cables and put to sea, leaving some transports with stores, which fell into our hands.

The French squadron had been pursued by some of our ships under Sir Richard Biskerton, and it was reported their sailors were very sickly. I got on board by three o'clock, and we weighed anchor immediately, but we did not sail until eight o'clock, as we had to wait for the *Madras* in consequence of the delay occasioned by sending poor Captain Hare on shore, who was extremely ill after he landed.

4th,—The breeze freshened in the morning, with a fair wind at the rate of four knots an hour. The thermometer in the shade in the after-cabin at 80°. Hailed the *Madras*, and Captain Ryves desired Mr.

Ireland, late 1st lieutenant of our ship, but who was sent into the *Madras* on Captain Hare's going on shore at Malta, to chase a brig that was seen a long way ahead of us.

I forgot to insert at the time the circumstance of one of the women of the regiment being brought to bed on board. Poor soul, nothing could equal the wretchedness of her situation from the excessive heat, noise, and constant crowd of the between-decks where she lay in. And as the young soldier was literally brought into the world under a 24-pound cannon and on board the *Agincourt*, I thought him deserving the name of that memorable battle, and therefore I requested he might be called 'Agincourt'.

9th.—In the morning saw several sail ahead; spoke the *Leda* frigate about twelve o'clock. The captain told us that Cairo was taken. Lord Keith, the admiral commanding the fleet, was at anchor in Aboukir Bay. We passed through the fleet, which was cruising off Alexandria to blockade the port. Saw the fortifications of Alexandria about one o'clock, as also Pompey's Pillar and Cleopatra's Needle.

We also saw on the African shore, to the westward of Alexandria, a very lofty building called the Tower of the Arabs. The taking of Cairo, (June 28, 1801), put us in good spirits, flattering ourselves it was an omen of good fortune. We passed Alexandria and proceeded on to Aboukir Bay, famed for the Battle of the Nile, and came to anchor close to the admiral. I waited on Lord Keith immediately to find out our destination, (George Keith Elphinstone—1746-1823; Viscount Keith; admiral 1801).

His lordship sent off to General Coote to report our arrival. Aboukir Bay was crowded with shipping, an immense number of transports and troopships; as also a fleet of Turkish men-of-war, and the Captain Pasha of Turkey or Lord High Admiral on board. As little communication as possible was held with the shore in consequence of the plague at Aboukir. It was very near communicating with our camp; a soldier's wife had taken the infection by some means; on its being discovered, she was sent away and died. Her husband found means to get her clothes sent to him in a box, which he had conveyed to his tent. This spread the infection, and all the men of the tent were taken ill. However, speedy means were taken to carry the men away, and the dreadful contagion was stopped.

The French Army at Cairo surrendered by convention and were to be sent to France. They were expected with our army under the commander-in-chief to arrive in about ten days, accompanied by 30,00 Turks. As soon as the whole were assembled, the attack on Alexandria is expected to commence. Lord Keith said it was supposed the French had not more than four thousand men in Alexandria.

It was unfortunate we did not arrive one day sooner; a sloop-of-war sailed for England as we sailed into Aboukir Bay. The thermometer was at 81°. I suppose there never was a finer passage made in the world than we had; we arrived in six weeks from the day of our embarkation and five weeks and four days from our sailing, and not-withstanding the heat and the crowded state of the ship, there was but one sick man when we disembarked.

10th.—I dined on board the *Foudroyant* with the admiral. Lord Keith keeps a very good table. I could discover by his lordship's conversation that he was not on very good terms with General Hutchinson. It is a most unfortunate circumstance whenever the two services disagree. Lord Keith told me we were to disembark next morning at two o'clock. I therefore hurried on board to give the necessary orders.

11th.—The regiment disembarked in a number of small boats at two o'clock in the morning of Saturday; rowed up to the head of Aboukir Bay and passed through the narrow that communicates to the Lake Madieh. After rowing across the lake near ten miles, we land-ed in the rear of the army encamped four miles cast of Alexandria. The distance we had to row was near twenty miles. The regiment got on shore by nine o'clock, reached camp and had our tents up by one. What surprised me most on landing was seeing the camels and the wonderful docility with which the Arabs make them lie down to be loaded.

I found the army grumbling and a little dissatisfied with the com-mander-in-chief for the apparent delay in not carrying on offensive operations against Alexandria, instead of keeping them encamped and exposed to a dreadful hot sun on a burning sand. However, nothing can be done until the return of Sir John Hutchinson with the force from Cairo. I found the army encamped on the spot where the action of the 21st March had been fought; the right of the line extending to the sea and the left to the Lake of Madieh, with a strong entrenchment in its front.

The piquets and vedettes advanced a mile or more in front of the works. Our vedettes and the vedettes of the enemy are approached within twenty yards of each other. The French vedettes will converse very civilly with our field officers whenever they ask them questions. The works in front of Alexandria appeared extremely strong, and if it is intended that we are to force them we shall find it a tough job. A market has been established in our camp, which is very tolerably supplied by the Arabs with fresh provisions, poultry, fish, as also a sort of calico linen, thread, coffee, sugar of the country, etc. etc.

The Arabs and Turks of the country are the most filthy-looking wretches I ever saw. They are of a tawny colour with long beards and turbans. The camp is on a sandy desert, and if there is much wind the sand makes sad work with the eyes. Major-General Coote commands, and has under him Major-Generals Ludlow, Lord Cavan, Finch, and Brigadier-General Stewart.

★★★★★★

Sir Eyre Coote (1762-1824); served in Egypt 1801; K.B. 1802; general 1814.

Major-General Ludlow (1758-1842) commanded the first Brigade of the Line, consisting of the 25th, 44th, and the 1st and 2nd battalions of the 27th, regiments. He succeeded his brother in the peerage 1811, and was the last Earl Ludlow.

Richard Ford William Lambart (1763-1834), seventh Earl of Cavan; present at the attack on Alexandria 1801; general 1814.

Major-General Finch commanded the 24th, 1st and 2nd battalions of the 54th, and the 26th regiments.

General Stewart commanded Stewart's, De Roll's, Dillon's, and Watteville regiments.

★★★★★★

The regiments we found in camp were a battalion of the Coldstreams and a battalion of the 3rd regiment Guards, the 23rd, 27th, two battalions 44th, 54th two battalions, and three foreign battalions, as also the 26th Light Dragoons. The day I arrived in camp I dined with my old acquaintance General Coote, not many luxuries but very comfortable. In the evening I rode with the general round our vedettes; met three French officers who were visiting their vedettes, the officers took off their hats and we returned the compliment. After the sun is down the evening gets cool, and very pleasant riding for an hour. I had the same tent with me that I had at Windsor, and found it most uncommonly useful.

13th.—Turned out at three o'clock in the morning for the first time; the army get under arms an hour before day and remain until the reveille beats. I rode to look at the market. The Arabs are a nasty-looking set as I ever saw. There appeared a great supply of poultry, sheep, etc. etc. The sheep have long ears, hanging down like spaniels'; wretchedly thin and poorish eating. I dined with Major Moore of the 26th dragoons.

15th.—Began camp-dinners at my tent. Lieut.-Colonel Busby and I lived together, and made it out very well.

We had a great want of vegetables, little being brought to market, except the Turkish cucumber and pumpkin, which are both nasty eating. The oranges and grapes are good, and nuts, like the dry Barcelona nut, to be had in abundance. The fish is palatable and good, a sort of grey mullet and also a kind of sea barbel, etc. The coffee the Arabs brought to market was very indifferent, though it is the country for coffee; I tasted most excellent several times, but it was difficult to buy. The sugar of the country very scarce and very dear; it is a sort of maple sugar, and, I believe, is grown in the Delta.

17th, Friday.—Menou, made a signal to send a flag of truce. He had for some time rejected receiving or sending a flag of truce by the land communication, and whenever it was found necessary, if he wished to send to us, he fired a gun and hoisted a white flag, and some of the men-of-war cruising off sent in a boat, if we wished to send to him.

★★★★★★

The French general, Menou had succeeded Kleber, who had been assassinated in June 1800. Menou was a general of but second-rate capacity.

★★★★★★

One of the cutters stood in towards Alexandria with a white flag flying, and he sent off a boat. When General Hutchinson entered into a convention with the army at Cairo, it was stipulated as one article by the French that, if Menou chose to accept the same terms, he should be at liberty to receive them. This article had been communicated to Menou the day we arrived, and he had ten days to send his answer. The flag of truce brought his reply, which was sent to Lord Keith. His letter was civil, and he said he was sure the English would have a bad opinion of his brave garrison, if they agreed to capitulate in the manner the *Rascal* at Cairo had done. 'We must lick him a bit.'

19th.—A packet closed for England; I wrote to my dear brother, as also to Lady Louisa Lennox, Lady Donegal, Lady Charlotte Durham,

Colonel Sneyd, Sir Nigel Gresley, Callander, General Ogilvie, and Major Gore; a serious list of letters, but as they were all on the same subject there was not much difficulty in the composition after the first was finished, and as they went to various parts of England, not much probability of the repetition being discovered.

24th, Friday.—A report of the plague having broke out in the Guards' camp; there was certainly a man died with every symptom of the plague upon him; and as the disease had been for some time in the hospital at Aboukir (only fifteen miles in our rear), it might be expected to visit the camp. I considered it a happiness for us that the plague, they say, disappears in July on the overflowing of the Nile, as it was past a suspicion, if the disease raged in any part of the country, that the Arabs, Turks, and devils that came to the market in camp with supplies must bring it with them. God knows, we had plagues enough without the real plague.

28th.—Dined with Major Power, 28th regiment. I made a rule whenever I was able to turn out at the time the regiment did, that is about half an hour before day (half-past three). After the regiment was dismissed I took a ride for two hours, which I found very pleasant, and was entertained with the wonderful vestiges of antiquity to be seen every yard I rode; such as ruins of ancient buildings, tombs, mosques, etc. etc., pieces of earthen vessels, pillars of granite, slabs of marble, etc. Near our encampment is conjectured to be about where old Alexandria stood; it is almost evident that the whole space we occupied, and which extended for more than two miles, had been built upon, as every yard indicated a relic of some building or other. One of our officers in his walk picked up a fine piece of antique sculpture; it was a nose in white marble broke off (perhaps ages go) from some fine statue.

31st.—General Finch and General Coote dined with me. They told me I had given them the best dinner they had seen in camp. Busby and I were fortunate in getting a woman of the regiment, who had been servant to Mrs. Colonel Wright, to cook for us, and she understood the thing well; add to which our poultry yard was well stocked and we fed our fowls well before we killed them. We had some good porter and good port wine, but scarce commodities in Egypt, of which our friends the generals partook with much glee.

August 1.—August the 1st a most memorable day; particularly in this part of the world, on account of Lord Nelson's action in Aboukir

Bay, (famous Battle of the Nile 1798); as also the Battle of Minden, (the Duke of Brunswick defeated the French 1759); three of the regiments that were in the action formed at present a part of this army, that is the 20th, 21st, and 25th. We displayed our colours, and gave our men an extra allowance of wine pour encourager. This day is a gala day with the Blue and Orange Society; all the members serving in this army dined with General Finch, who is of long standing in the order, and had a jolly day.

3rd.—Baron D'Urler, the Lieutenant-Colonel of De Roll's regiment, and Major Moore dined with us. (See *Diary of Sir John Moore*, edited by Major-General Sir J. F. Maurice, vol. ii.) The French pioneers from Rosetta taken at Cairo began to embark near Aboukir Bay, and General Hutchinson arrived on board Lord Keith's ship to settle with his lordship our future proceedings relating to the siege. A vessel arrived from Gibraltar with bad accounts respecting Sir J. Saumarez having been beat in an attack of some French ships in Algeciras Bay. (James Saumarez, Baron de Saumarez—1757-1836; admiral, made an unsuccessful attack on the French off Algeciras, but soon after defeated the French and Spanish and was made K.B. 1801).

The army of ———— (illegible) also arrived from Malta, 1600 strong, and likewise a company of artillery from Gibraltar, the latter much wanted here, and a great addition to the besiegers. As the commander-in-chief was arrived, we became anxious for the operations to commence, with a sincere hope of their being soon finished. The sickness increased in the regiment; all the same complaint; we lost three men and had near seventy in hospital.

6th.—Flag of truce from Alexandria; one of the French generals that had come down with the French Army from Cairo had asked permission to pay a visit to Menou, which was granted by our general, and the flag of truce was made on the occasion. We had accounts that the advanced guard of the army from India, under General Baird, was arrived at Cairo.

★★★★★★

Sir David Baird (1757-1829); commanded the Indian force in Egypt 1801-2; returned to India and received the command of the northern division of the Madras Army 1802.

★★★★★★

In taking my ride this morning before breakfast I saw two wild dogs; I was much surprised to see them, but I understand they are common in this country. I had seen two some mornings before, but I thought they were dogs belonging to some of the officers. They looked like white terriers, but with rather long tails; they were running about more like foxes than dogs, and I saw them get under the cover of some shrubs and coil themselves up just like a fox; they appeared very shy.

9th.—General Doyle's brigade, under the orders of my old acquaintance Colonel Spencer, arrived in camp from Cairo, consisting of the 30th, 50th, and 92nd regiments.

★★★★★★

Sir John Doyle (1750-1834); fought at Alexandria and Marabout. His brigade also contained, in addition to those mentioned by Dyott, the 89th regiment.

★★★★★★

Some of the Turkish gunboats came up into the lake, which is the first indication of any operations going forward since our arrival. The commander-in-chief still remains on board the *Foudroyant* with Lord Keith, but for what purpose he must know best; procrastination appears to we little ones as the order of the day; time will show.

12th.—General Hope, Colonel Graham, and Colonel Spencer, (mentioned frequently in the later years at Sir Brent Spencer), dined with me; they had all been on the expedition to Cairo, and gave a most melancholy account both of the wretchedness of that place, and the miserable state of the country on the banks of the Nile through which they had marched. They described the inhabitants as the dirtiest set of beings that nature ever formed; their villages a heap of mud walls and more like the worst kind of dwellings for pigs than habitations for human beings.

Cairo an immense place, very narrow streets, and so abominably dirty that they said it was wonderful the plague ever should get out of the town after it had once got in. The French that capitulated at Cairo were all embarked to the amount of upwards of 13,000 people, and sailed for Toulon in three divisions.

14th.—Orders for the brigade of Guards, General Ludlow's and Finch's brigades to be ready to embark for the westward. The 24th regiment was put into Finch's brigade instead of the Royals; the whole under the command of General Coote.

15th.—Received an account of Sir J. Saumarez having defeated a

131

Spanish fleet in or near Gibraltar Bay.

16th.—On the 16th, being Sunday, the three brigades paraded at three o'clock, and embarked in gunboats, flat-bottomed boats, and boats of all descriptions; the embarkation begun about six, and we were all on board by ten. At daybreak next morning we found ourselves about three miles to the westward of Alexandria, and about the same distance from the shore.

We pushed on six miles further, and landed without opposition; the enemy made some shew on the hills, when we first made the land, but did not interrupt us in our landing. The 25th regiment lead the column, and after we had got possession of the heights, we lay on our arms. The day was intensely hot, and as the men had four days' provisions to carry, as well as their ammunition and knapsacks, I expected to have seen many fall from fatigue. The ground we occupied (the 25th regiment) was an old quarry, from whence had been dug the stones of which ancient Alexandria was built. The position of the army was strong; our right flank was to the lake, where we landed, and our left to the Mediterranean.

The enemy had a battery on an island to our left, which in part commanded the entrance into the old harbour of Alexandria. This was attacked by our artillery the next day (17th), and the army advanced about one mile over sand and a continuation of the quarry. The weather very warm.

18th.—We were joined by a party of Lowenstein Yougers, or sharpshooters, as also by a detachment of the 26th Dragoons. The whole advanced, and we supposed we should have had some opposition, but we took up a position three miles in front without molestation. Our artillery kept up a constant fire against the enemy's work on our left called Marabout, and in the course of the day sunk two of their gunboats that were lying near the fort.

On the 19th several boats from our fleet, which was cruising off Alexandria, with a piece of ordnance in each boat, came into the harbour for the purpose of cutting off a communication by sea with Marabout They were attacked by the gunboats sent out by the enemy, but our boats beat them off. It engaged our attention very much seeing the attacks between the boats; our Johnnies appeared to have an evident advantage, both in courage and management of their boats.

21st.—Marabout surrendered, and in the evening several Turkish and English ships-of-war anchored in the old harbour. From the time of our landing we had depended chiefly on our salt rations for provisions, as nothing was to be had unless we got it from the camp to the eastward, except some coffee, sugar, and a small quantity of wine we brought with us. The day we left headquarters to the eastward, the army made an attack on the enemy's outworks on that side, which must have caused a considerable diversion in our favour for landing to the westward. They gained two of the enemy's advanced works, and immediately erected batteries, from whence they kept up a heavy cannonade and annoyed the French much.

22nd.—Our army was under arms at three o'clock, for the purpose of advancing and attacking the enemy, and to take up a position about three miles from the town. Lowenstein's sharp-shooters and our light companies were in front, followed by the first battalion 27th regiment as the advanced guard; then the artillery. The Guards in column on the right close to the lake, and flanked by gunboats; ours and General Finch's brigade in column on the left to the sea, flanked by the ships-of-war that had come into the bay the night before. We had not advanced half a mile when the enemy began to cannonade, and skirmishing also between the sharp-shooters. The enemy's artillery, consisting of four field-pieces (twelve-pounders) and four batteries, two on our right and two on our left, kept up an incessant fire for near three hours, during the time we were advancing.

Our loss was inconsiderable, amounting in the whole to not more than fifty men killed and wounded. An unlucky shot struck our regiment, shattered an officer's leg (Lieutenant Horking's), as also the thigh of a soldier, and wounded three others. Mr. Horking and the soldier were obliged to have their legs amputated in the field. At one time the shot fell very thick about the regiment, and I expected much mischief must have followed. Just as the cannonading began, a shot struck an officer, Howe, belonging to the staff, who was riding close to our regiment, and immediately afterwards another shot struck the ground within eight yards of our grenadiers, and bounced over the company.

The army took up a position about three miles from Alexandria upon strong ground, and secured on both flanks, with an extensive plain in our front. We did not sit down until near one o'clock and thoroughly fagged. The country we had marched over the most wretched it is possible to imagine; indeed it was all alike from the time we had landed, consisting of high steep hills composed of old mortar and rubbish, or deep sand, pits and sand-hills. The whole from where we left the quarries had evident marks of having been built over ages ago.

The ground appears to rise in a sort of gradual ascent from the sea on one side and from the lake on the other; to the former it is rocky, and to the latter sand. Just beyond where we landed the Desert of Lybia began. There was a very curious catacomb a little beyond the quarry at our first position; it consisted of vast chambers excavated in the rock, and sort of shelves for placing the coffins.

There was a beautiful large fig-tree at the entrance full of fruit, but it was soon plucked after our arrival. There was a heap of black-looking dust lying in the catacomb, which I remarked to an officer of the 54th regiment who was there at the time, and who appeared an intelligent man, and I found afterwards was an antiquarian. He said he believed it was human hair, which it was ascertained never decayed by time; he desired I would take a little of it in my hand and examine it, which I did accordingly and found a great deal of hair apparently mixed with the dust.

On the left of our new position and close to the sea, there were very extensive excavations in the rocks, and which were supposed to be the famous Cleopatra's Baths. Time had smoothed in a great measure many of the partition walls, but the traces of large apartments and every convenience for supplying the water and for keeping it cool, etc., were perfect. Near Cleopatra's Baths, a most extensive excavation was discovered into which many officers went, and which was supposed to have been the Temple of Isis; but as there was great difficulty in getting in, and much filth and dirt after you were in, and as I was no antiquarian, I did not examine the famous temple.

The business of the 22nd must have been a very fine sight to an unconcerned spectator; just as the sun made his appearance above the horizon, the cannonade began; on the right of the line the lake covered with gunboats displaying all their pennants, flags, etc., and keeping up a constant fire, shewed that flank all alive; on the left of the line, nine sail of men-of-war with colours flying and all sails set, also keeping up an incessant fire, had a most picturesque and fine appearance. The troops, after they were formed in line, extended nearly across from the sea to the lake, advancing regularly, and the skirmishers keeping up a continual fire of small arms, and the field artillery supporting a heavy cannonade.

The enemy's batteries, field artillery, and sharp-shooters opposing us with a constant roll of fire. I was on the heights about the centre of our line just as the business began. I remember General Ludlow saying to me it was a different scene 'to being by the side of Walton Wood finding a fox.' I was in great pain all the day from having been seized in the night with the ophthalmia in one of my eyes, and could scarcely hold up my head; indeed I would not have turned out on any other occasion. Unfortunately for me I was for duty in the evening as colonel of the day, and had to sleep out with the command of the piquets. We had found good water by digging in the sand, and close by our second position we had a regular made well lined with stone, which had been much used by the French.

23rd.—A corps of Mamalukes joined us under the orders of Islam Bey; they encamped four miles in rear of our line; they are a fierce warlike-looking people, clad in loose dresses made of a sort of silky cotton, and wear turbans; they are mounted on chargers from upper Egypt, and are most expert horsemen. Their weapons of defence are a sabre, a fusil, and some of them pistols; but what they most trust to is the sabre, in the use of which they are said to excel all European cavalry. Their sabres are very handsome, and some of them of great value; (Colonel Paget paid £100 for one); they are manufactured at Cairo, except the blades, which they procure from Persia.

They have amongst them some beautiful Arabian horses, particularly beautiful for the purpose of chargers, but I scarce saw one that could be called a useful horse at home. The saddle is made very high both behind and before, so that when you are once wedged in, it's difficult to lose your seat. They ride very short, and the stirrup is a flat piece of iron or brass about 18 inches long, and 10 broad, with sides raised about 4½ inches high, something like an immense fire-shovel, but open at both ends. This stirrup answers the purpose of spurs, with the corners of which their horses are all scored along their sides. They have a most astonishingly severe bridle, with a single rein, so sharp that you will see them put their horses into full speed and stop them as suddenly as if they were shot. They have very fine trappings for their saddles, and an uncommon display of ornament about their bridles, and wear the large Turkish slipper.

Egypt is divided into provinces or districts, over each of which a *bey* presides, who commands a corps of Mamalukes. The *bey* receives the revenue collected by the Turkish officers, and remits as much as he chooses to the Ottoman Government. The Port professes to have an authority over the *beys*, but I believe it is merely nominal, as the Turkish Government is glad to be content with whatever is remitted by the *beys* by way of revenue, well knowing the inefficiency they have to enforce obedience.

Every *bey* has a certain number of Mamalukes under his command. These are all originally slaves, and indeed so are the *beys*, who have all been Mamalukes; they are purchased when very young in upper Egypt, and come from Nubia and Abyssinia; they are early instructed to ride, and the use of the sabre. Each Mamaluke has an Arab to attend him to look after his horse, camel, etc. They have wives which they marry in the upper parts of Egypt, but I could not find out what became of their progeny, as the son of a Mamaluke cannot follow his father's way of life. All Mamalukes must have the same origin, and must all have been slaves. It sometimes happens that the *beys* are made shorter *by the head* from the intrigues of some of their Mamalukes; in this case, or in case of natural death, a successor is chosen from the whole, and who has a sort of approval from the Grand Sultan.

The Mamalukes were very powerful at the time the French first landed in Egypt, but they destroyed a vast number of them. At present their establishment is low, but I should imagine, if Great Britain has an interest in retaining any possessions in Egypt, it would be better to cultivate a good understanding with them than with the Turks. We were miserably in want of water at our new position, as we were obliged to send back to our last ground of encampment for water, near four miles; a brigade from the eastward under Colonel Spencer joined us.

On the 24th a frigate arrived in nine-and-twenty days from England; I was much disappointed in not receiving a single letter. The commander-in-chief, Sir John Hutchinson, paid us a visit from the eastward, to see how the business was going on on our side.

25th.—At daybreak we opened a battery consisting of four 24-pounders from a work that had been thrown up in the night, and threw shells from some mortars, but I believe we did little mischief. The enemy in consequence of our battery opening cannonaded our camp with shot and shells; many of both fell in the camp, but I heard of no execution having been done. A detachment of the Turkish Army joined us consisting of 1000 men; they must not be called soldiers, as they are little better than a wretched rabble. They have no uniformity either in clothing, arms, or appointments; I mean as to the colour of their clothing, which is blue, black, brown, red, etc.; every soldier has a gun of some sorts, which Turko carries as he likes best, either across his shoulder, over his arm, or under it.

They wear a kind of sash made of a sort of bunting, which passes half a dozen times round the body, and in which everything belonging to them is carried. All of them had a dirk, and a pair of large horse-pistols stuck in his sash, and they will any of them sell all or any part of their arms or appointments. When sentries they appear alert on their posts, but we never trusted them without having some of our own people with them. They are extremely filthy and dirty in their habits and manners, and their encampment not to be described for dirt. Their tents consist of a long piece of canvas without any walls, under which about thirty of these turbaned heroes are either stretched at full length or squat on their bums smoking.

They appear to have very few officers; the superior ones to be distinguished, but the generality of them were only marked from the men by a sort of large medal or button at the upper part of the waistcoat. The detachment we had was commanded by the Bashaw of Wedding, the greatest beast I ever saw. A Mamaluke sentry was constantly kept with one of our dragoon vedettes at our advanced line, and did their duty with much exactness and precision. A piquet of Mamalukes mounted with ours and remained on duty.

26th.—Our commander General Coote determined this evening to make our attack on the enemy's advanced piquet, which was posted in the sand-hills in front of our left. I was colonel of the day and was posted with our piquet on the left. As soon as the moon was up about eight o'clock, the 20th regiment advanced in column unperceived by the French, and without firing a shot or receiving more than half a dozen (they had only one man wounded) they succeeded in either killing or taking prisoners the whole piquet, and thereby gaining a position upwards of a mile in front of our battery.

Our piquets had remained at the battery and were ordered forward to take up the position gained by the 20th regiment. Our piquet consisted of two hundred rank and file; we had relieved the 20th and posted our sentries, etc., and the regiment had marched back to camp. Lord Cork, (general officer in the army; born 1767, succeeded his father 1798), who was the major-general of the day, was gone to visit the piquet of the right, and I had ordered the officer who commanded a small detachment of sharp-shooters belonging to the piquet to accompany me to visit the advanced sentry, when we discovered a column of the enemy advancing in force. I had no sooner observed the circumstance to the officer than our advanced sentry fired.

This brought on a general fire from our piquets, and as we had some men in front of the general line, I was afraid they would have been hit by our own people. I got back to the piquets as fast as my horse would go. The whole were then engaged, and our front attacked smartly. The firing continued without intermission for near two hours, when the French thought proper to retreat. I got up a part of the 54th regiment soon after we were attacked, and before it was over the 27th was sent to our support.

Our loss was four officers wounded, and about thirty men killed and wounded. The enemy threw shot and shells into our camp the whole time of the attack, and our battery cannonaded them, but very little mischief was done from the artillery on either sides. The 20th regiment and the piquets, etc., took near fifty prisoners, who all agreed in the same story, and from whom we learnt that Menou must surrender, as the soldiers would not fight, they were so completely worn out with fatigue, etc.

I never lay down for an instant the whole night, not being sure whether Monsieur Le Petit might not propose a second edition, but we were very quiet. This was much. the sharpest fire I had ever been in of musketry; the balls for some time were flying pretty thick about me; I own I was very happy when the firing ceased.

27th.—An *aide-de-camp* from Menou came to our outpost (where I remained) with a flag of truce, to say that a cessation of hostilities was agreed on between General Hutchinson and the French general for three days; I believed all parties rejoiced at the event, both besiegers and besieged.

29th.—Cessation continued. I rode to the Mamaluke camp; saw the *bey* at his breakfast attended by his slaves, etc. A fine-looking old man with a venerable beard half down his stomach. The Mamalukes occasionally ride on dromedaries, when they wish to rest their horses; they are similar to the camels, except not quite so tall, and equally docile. They have a ring passed through their nose, by which they are guided, and are saddled the same as a horse. When they want to mount or dismount, they make them lie down; at all times they lie down on their bellies with their legs doubled up under them.

31st.—On the next day Menou sent in his terms of surrender, which were agreed to the next day, 1st September. And on the day following, the 2nd, we took possession of one of the works of the town, and several of the sub-works. The ceremony of taking possession was very gratifying to a conquering army, and equally dismaying to the conquered. The grenadiers of the army under the command of the senior colonel, and a detachment of the Guards formed the party, the whole under the orders of the senior major-general. I rode into Alexandria, but not so as to be able to see anything except heaps of rubbish. I also rode to Pompey's Pillar, which for the immensity of its structure and the antiquity of its existence, must be the greatest wonder in the world.

3rd.—Despatches made up for England: I wrote to my brother. Sir Nigel Gresley, Lady Louisa, Lady Pitt, General Stevens, and Lady Donegal. Colonel Abercrombie, the adjutant-general, carried Sir John Hutchinson's despatches, and Sir Sydney Smith took the admiral's. (Sir Sidney Smith (1764-1840); entered navy 1777; defended Acre 1799; admiral 1821). Colonel Paget accompanied them; they sailed in the E.I. *Carmen.*

6th.—We had an arrival from Malta, which brought a report that Admiral Cornwallis had fallen in with the French fleet, and had taken twelve sail of the line; and also that the preliminaries for peace were signed.

★★★★★★

Sir William Cornwallis (1744-1819); entered the navy 1755; admiral 1799.
Peace concluded at Amiens, March 27, 1802.

★★★★★★

I rode to headquarters and was told by the deputy adjutant-general that our regiment was certainly not to remain in Egypt: this I considered as most glad tidings. Great scarcity in the market, and of course advance in the price of provisions. In my way to headquarters I rode through the French advanced line, which had been occupied by them previous to the surrender; found it very strong, and next to an impossibility to have stormed it. A part of the Turkish Army were encamped near headquarters; I went to see the Captain Pasha's tent. It consisted of four separate apartments, the one you enter much the largest, fitted up in the Turkish style with cushions, carpets, everything seemed calculated for voluptuous indolence.

The *pasha* was sitting on his bottom on a cushion, two slaves keeping the flies from incommoding him; an attendant brought him coffee, and went on his knees to present it; another attendant was in waiting with his pipe, and there were two *janissaries* on each side the entrance to the tent. The *pasha's* kitchen seemed to be the best thing about the camp; it appeared like an immense tent without walls, the centre of which was formed of stoves, etc., requisite to assist the culinary art, and at which there were at least thirty cooks at work. He sends daily twelve dishes to the commander-in-chief's table, but I am told the Turkish cooking is by no means palatable to an English taste.

The Turkish Government have sent most magnificent presents to the general and admiral, as also to all the generals and staff-officers of the army. It is said that Lord Keith and Sir John Hutchinson have received presents to the amount of at least ten thousand pounds each. Whenever an officer of rank was presented to the *pasha* or *grand vizier*, he got either a shawl or a snuff-box. I was never presented, and therefore did not obtain a Turkish favour.

The *grand vizier* was with the Turkish Army left at Cairo; I was told the detachment of the Ottoman troops under his orders were in a much inferior state of discipline to those under the Pasha; if so, they certainly should not be called soldiers, as nothing in that shape can be half so despicable as what I saw before Alexandria. I was told by General Hope, who is certainly a man of much information and had more opportunity of judging than any other person, that the Captain Pasha was a man of resolution and very good sound judgment, active in his disposition, and a superior being to the generality of the Turks. He had been originally a slave and raised himself by superior talent.

9th.—Southerly wind and clouds of insects whenever the wind blew from the south. We had intensely hot weather and most dreadfully tortured with flies and insects; of the former I have seen my breakfast and table in my tent, when the breakfast things have been set, completely covered black over with flies. On the left of our encampment along the seaside there were curious remains of extensive and splendid fine baths excavated from the rock, with the traces of a great variety of apartments. One of the largest was said to be the baths of the famed Queen Cleopatra; these baths must have been most luxurious in that hot climate. There are remains of them all the way along the shore from our camp to Alexandria. There are also on the plains between camp and the town wonderful remains of the catacombs of the ancient Egyptians, most of them excavated from the rock, consisting of numerous apartments with a great number of shelves or recesses for the coffins in each.

11th.—Ordered to prepare to embark on board our old ship the *Agincourt*, and part in the *Heroine* frigate. I obtained a passport from the general to go into Alexandria, with the sight of which I was much entertained. Not anything remains to trace out the ancient city built by the Great Alexander except two pillars of granite standing in heaps of rubbish which are said to have formed a part of one of the ancient palaces of the kings. Amongst the ruins surrounding these pillars are seen variety of marble pillars and highly finished capitals of the Corinthian order; as also traces of an immense building.

The present outer walls of the town are supposed to have been built by the Arabs from the ruins of the ancient city, which history reports to have been eighteen miles in circumference. The extent of the wall is nearly three miles and had one hundred square towers at nearly equal distances, many of them in ruins, but the wall has been repaired by the French. The ditch is of considerable depth and surrounds the wall. Far the greatest space within this wall is completely covered with rubbish of old buildings. The French have made a new wall and ditch taking in the present town, and extending from the head of the old to the head of the new harbour. This wall is a handsome piece of modern masonry.

Near the new harbour and without the new wall are the two curious emblems of antiquity called Cleopatra's Needles: one of them is standing, the other is complete, but almost buried in rubbish. Their shapes pyramidal, about fifty feet high and eight feet square at the base They are of granite, and covered with hieroglyphics on every side, and which are quite perfect. The streets of the modern Alexandria are very narrow, and the houses lofty and almost all alike. The inhabitants consist of Turks, Greeks, Jews, Arabs, etc., a filthy-looking collection. The women seldom appear, and when they do they have veils which entirely hide their faces, and have apertures made for their eyes.

The roofs of the houses are all flat, and the doors at all times shut. The shops have not been replenished since the French had first landed, so there was little to be seen in them. There were many coffee-houses which were curious, as the persons frequenting them, and they were very numerous, were all sitting on the tables like tailors, smoking their pipes and drinking coffee. The town was in a wretched filthy state from the numbers of dead camels and horses lying in the very streets.

The French had been greatly distressed for provisions, and had eaten an amazing number of horses and camels, but latterly flesh was only allowed to the hospitals. Rice was their chief food, of which they made very excellent bread. The only public buildings are the mosques, some of which were large, but not at all ornamented. Many parts of the modern Alexandria is in ruins. I saw little to afford entertainment except the novelty of the scene. The streets as well as the inhabitants are equally dirty, and whenever epidemic disease gets into the place the wonder is how it ever gets out again. A part of the French were encamped within the new walls, and the remainder between the new and old wall.

Menou, the French commander-in-chief, was in the former camp. I met him walking with his *aide-de-camp*; he appeared about sixty years of age, and really looked more like an English miller than a French general. The houses of modern Alexandria seem to have been built from the ruins of the old town like the walls, as there is not the smallest appearance of the grandeur that ornamented the more ancient buildings. The day was most suffocatingly hot, and as I rode about the place for three or four hours, I was perfectly fagged.

12th.—Paid another visit to Alexandria; there is no greater curiosity than the cisterns for supplying the place with water, which are filled at the rising of the Nile by means of the famous canal made by Alexander at the time the city was built. The intention of the canal was not only for supplying water, but was also for the purpose of navigation inland from the Nile. The cisterns are of immense extent, and inside have more the appearance of the inside of a very large cathedral than anything I could compare them to. They extend under the whole of the space within the old wall and are found in different places outside the walls, and no doubt the whole of the ancient town was supplied in like manner.

During the time we were besieging Alexandria, it was thought expedient to make a cut through the canal in order to inundate the country, by which means the usual supply of water for filling the cisterns was prevented reaching the place. The consequence was that they were become very low as the usual time (the overflowing of the Nile) for filling them was past. The canal of Alexandria had from the extreme indolence of the natives been used as an aqueduct for a vast number of years, and was consequently dry when the Nile resumes its bounds; the cutting through it therefore was a trifling labour, and admitted a salt-water lake to inundate the country on the opposite side of it.

The inhabitants of Alexandria lived entirely on rice and coffee.

I saw a number of mills grinding the rice, drawn by a horse, as also several windmills. Two or three of the gardens which used to supply the place with vegetables were preserved, many of them had been destroyed by the French for firewood and other purposes. The gardens are thickly planted with palm-trees, which makes a charming shade from the heat of the sun. There are one or more machines in each for raising water from the cisterns, which is performed by means of a wheel worked by an ox or asses, and the ground is laid out in squares with little channels in different directions for overflowing it.

There was little growing in the gardens at the time I was there except parsley and some salad. The owners of the gardens were not allowed to water them, and as the French soldiers entered them when they chose, the wretched proprietor had no encouragement to labour, as he received nought for his pains. The palm-trees were loaded with dates, the fruit, but not ripe; they distil brandy from them and also preserve them for exportation.

13th.—I again rode to Alexandria, and as the dockyard and Pharos were still in possession of the French, it was necessary to make an application to one of their generals for a passport to see them. I accordingly called on General Friant, the second in command, who was very civil and instantly gave me what I asked. The French had converted the dockyard store-houses into the hospitals for their sick, after using all the stores.

On one of the wharfs was lying a most extraordinary piece of sculpture that had been brought from the neighbourhood of Cairo, consisting of the hand of a colossal statue of granite; the hand was clenched, and I should imagine the breadth of it across the knuckles could not be less than four feet; what must the size of the statue have been of which this fist composed a part. In the dockyard there was also a curious stone coffin, brought likewise from a catacomb in the neighbourhood of Cairo. Both these antiques the French had intended to take to France, but General Hutchinson forbade it.

The French soldiers were miserably clothed, they had on amazingly large cocked hats, with the long cock in front made of polished leather or some composition that resembled it. A coat with very long skirts made of a sort of cotton or calico of the country, blue, white, brown, etc., but arranged as gypsies. I observed a number of wounded and maimed men in Alexandria, but I also saw a number of as fine-looking soldiers as ever were seen.

The French Army had suffered most materially from ophthalmia and had numbers blind in their hospital. They had had no plague in the town after the first year of their arrival, but had suffered very considerable loss every year at Cairo and up the country, I met Menou in full state, two *aides-de-camp* in front, a general officer on each side of him, four dragoons, and four Syrians that he had brought from upper Egypt and that he was taking to France, closed the procession. They were on horseback and I believe he was paying visits, I took off my hat to him and he of course returned the compliment.

The Syrians were habited like the Mamalukes except having scarlet mantles or cloaks. The Mamalukes have theirs of all colours, striped, etc. etc. The heat and the stink the devil. The men-of-war lying off the dockyard of which we had possession were three fine frigates, a corvette, with several other ships-of-war totally dismantled, as also a number of merchant ships but of little value. The Pharos is a strong fortification guarding the entrance to the harbour, and situated on an island to which there is a communication from the town by means of a causeway. The work is very strong and is supposed to have been built by the Moors or Arabs.

Buonaparte had improved the works and mounted some fine pieces of ordnance brought from Malta. There were also furnaces for heating red-hot shot. I observed in one of the buildings some fine marble pillars which in all probability had been a part of ancient Alexandria; the shaft fluted, and the marble very beautiful.

27th.—Orders for the regiment to embark the next day; seven companies on board the *Agincourt*, and three on board the *Thisbe*; never received an order with more pleasure or carried one into effect with more punctuality.

28th.—Struck tents at two o'clock and marched at three to Aboukir Bay, twelve miles, where the regiment embarked together with the two battalions of the 27th regiment. We had a smart shower of rain on the march. Owing to the obstinacy and stupidity of the sailors in one of the boats, in which were five-and-twenty men belonging to the regiment that had come sick from the hospital tent, she upset, by which unfortunate accident two men were drowned.

29th.—I went on board the Captain Pasha's ship lying in Aboukir Bay. He was on shore, but there was a vice-admiral on board. The ship a three-decker, and a very fine-looking man-of-war. The *pasha's* cabin most magnificently furnished; rich cushions of damask and satin finely embroidered with gold; splendid pier-glasses and fine Turkey carpets, and all the furniture to answer; very unlike the inside of a man-of-war. There was a writing apparatus entirely of gold, several of the articles ornamented with diamonds. On waiting on the vice-admiral we were presented with pipes. He and his attendants were seated on their cushions, chairs were set for us, and soon after sweetmeats and coffee were brought in on very handsome silver waiters; the sweetmeats excellent.

The ship was very clean, and in the centre of each deck there was a cistern filled with water from the sea with two cocks in each constantly running, for the purpose of the Turks washing themselves, which is a part of their religious ceremony. They have also a coffee-house on board, where the sailors can purchase coffee ready made at all hours; it was curious to see them assembled at the coffee-house and drinking their coffee, The decks had a number of mats and carpets lying about on which the sailors reposed themselves; they have no hammocks, nor any other bedding than their mats and carpets, and we saw them stretched and rolling about in all parts of the ship.

As their ships never go out of the Mediterranean Sea, it is not of much consequence their lying on the decks; but if they were to encounter gales of all wind and boisterous seas, they must change their customs. They have no place in the ship set apart for their sick, and I observed several apparently dying men mixed on the decks with those in health. The Turkish sailors don't go aloft, they have slaves on board expressly for that purpose. I observed in the fore part of the ship some men in irons, who were Europeans, and on enquiry found out they were French prisoners. It is a custom with the Turks not to exchange their prisoners, and they always keep those they make in a state of bondage.

We were on board at twelve o'clock, which is the hour they go to prayers. We could not imagine what was going on forward, when we heard two fellows halloaing and whooping all over the ship, until we discovered it was to call all persons to prayers; the ceremony was soon over. After we had seen the ship, we returned to the vice-admiral's cabin: pipes were again brought in, but we declined a second smoking. The surgeon of the ship fortunately had been in England and acted as an interpreter for us.

On taking our leave the admiral paid us many compliments to the British and particularly to Captain Ryves, who was of our party, respecting the superiority of the British navy. On my return on board the *Agincourt*, a very singular circumstance was reported to me relative to one of the unfortunate men who had been drowned alongside the *Thisbe* the day before. The poor fellow had on his greatcoat and accoutrements, in the pouches of which there were sixty pounds of ball cartridges, notwithstanding which, the body floated close to the ship, after being under water four-and-twenty hours, and although there was a very brisk wind the body continued floating near the ship for some time. The extraordinary thing is that the body should rise in the very spot where it went down, and with the weight that was attached to it. The poor creature was lying on his face on the water, and was known from the circumstance of his having a black handkerchief tied about his head, being sick.

October 1st.—Got under weigh and made sail from Aboukir Bay about eleven o'clock, exactly twelve weeks from the time we had anchored there. The two battalions of the Guards were in company with us. As the wind was not fair, we were off Rosetta in the afternoon; the appearance of the town like Alexandria, but not near so large. The Nile discharges one of its branches at Rosetta; we perceived the water quite muddy. The entrance of the Nile very dangerous in consequence of the bar of sand raised at the mouth of the river by the violence of the wind acting against the rapidity of the current.

9th.—Very unwell with pain in my bowels; I was become as thin as the sparest of all the thin Buckeridges.

13th.—The ship taken out of quarantine; we found Lord Keith with the fleet lying in Valetta. General Cradock and the troops under his command that had sailed from Egypt were landed. (Sir John Francis Caradoc or Cradock—1762-1839; first Baron Howden).

14th.—I went on shore, and waited on General Fox, who was appointed to command in chief in the Mediterranean, and had come from Minorca for the purpose of making the disposition of the troops from Egypt. (Henry Edward Fox—1755-1811; youngest son of the first Baron Holland; general in the Mediterranean 1801-3).

The general told me he should send us on to Gibraltar as soon as possible. General Villettes was commanding the troops in the island of Malta. (William Villettes—1754-1808; lieutenant-general; governor of Malta 1801-7). None of the ships that had sailed with us had arrived except the *Thisbe* with our three companies; dined on board.

16th.—Instead of going forward to Gibraltar, I received orders to land, in consequence of Lord Keith's not consenting to send on the ship; I took the liberty of calling on his lordship to pray him to let us continue as was first intended, and push on to Gibraltar; but he was stiff, obstinate, and a damned sullen old Scotchman.

20th.—A Maltese vessel brought in an account that she had spoke the *Lodi*, a French ship-of-war, who told her that she was going to Egypt with the official intelligence that peace had been signed in London on the 1st of the month. This news surprised everybody, and was not entirely credited. The regiment was very sickly, and on our landing we were obliged to send near seventy men to the general hospital at La Valette, mostly with sore eyes and dysentery. Dined with General Villettes.

22nd.—Went to see the town and church at Citta Vecchia, situated near the centre of the island, about six miles from La Valette. Tradition reports that Saint Paul was cast away on the shore of Malta in a bay called after his name near Citta Vecchia, and that the Saint founded a church which is dedicated to him there. The town is small, but built in the same style of neatness as La Valette. Adjoining it, situated on the same height, are the fortifications, containing the church, a palace for the bishop, a house for the grand master, now occupied as a barrack, two convents, and a college. The works are not extensive, though capable of making considerable resistance.

The church is not so large as St. John's at La Valette, but certainly more beautiful, as the paintings appear in a much higher state of preservation, the ceiling is lighter, and the mouldings and gildings of the church appear recently improved, the marble pillars, etc,, of the grand altar far surpassing anything I ever saw, and there are some paintings that must undoubtedly be of very great value. Monsieur Buonaparte also made free with a considerable quantity of the plate, etc., at this church as well as at St. John's.

We were shown the dresses, etc., that the bishop and his assistants wear at the celebration of High Mass. There was an immense wardrobe quite full; some of the robes were of the most splendid embroidery it is possible to imagine. Amongst other things of value were two mitres richly embroidered with gold, and completely studded over with rich and most rare precious stones and diamonds; in the centre of one in particular was a diamond full as large as a walnut (?). I could not help asking the priest that was showing us the church how all these valuables came to escape the vigilant eye of the great consul.

He said, 'Ah, sir, if he had seen or known of their being here, they would not have remained in possession of the Holy Church.'

From the upper window of the church you have a fine view of the whole island, which is picturesque and curious. The road from La Valette is but indifferent, as you may suppose from the island being an entire rock. The Malta carriages which ply in the streets are not very elegant; they are drawn by a mule, and go on two wheels; some of them hold two, some four, people. The driver runs by the side of the mule, and guides him with a sorry halter. It is astonishing how fast they go. I think we were little more than an hour going to Citta Vecchia and about the same returning. The town of La Valette is principally supplied with water by an aqueduct from Citta Vecchia.

The soil throughout the island is very shallow, being either brought or scraped from the rock, and mixed with compositions of manure. The tillage is therefore not laborious. They plough with a mule and a cow abreast. The plough is simply a light beam and a coulter that does not go more than three or four inches into the ground, and is changed at the end of lant (?) each time, the same as the Sussex ploughs. The chief produce of the island is cotton. They grow some barley and abundance of vegetables, but they are obliged to change the seed of their potatoes every year, or they would become sweet as in the West Indies.

28th.—The Guards, who had been disembarked, were again re-embarked. Received orders that we were now to go to Gibraltar directly, and not to Minorca. 'What have you got in your bag, Mr. Courier?'—'Orders, sir.' 'And what in the bag behind you, Mr. Courier?'—'Counter-orders, sir.'

31st.—Could not sail for want of wind; dined on shore, and went for the first time to the opera, which is performed five nights a week. The theatre is fitted up in proper style with boxes and pit; the orchestra very good; one of the women I thought sung very well, and there was a very excellent buffo. They have a curious custom on a benefit: the person whose night it is goes round between the acts with a silver waiter in his hand, preceded by two boys holding lights, and collects the donations of the audience who are inclined to contribute. The admission is only eightpence to all parts of the house. Cheap amusement!

November 9.—Calm in the morning, but the wind sprung up about noon, and we had a fine fresh breeze all night. To the surprise of our faculty, several new cases of ophthalmia appeared, which made the physical gentlemen determine that the disease was infectious. I don't believe they or any of the followers of Galen or Hippocrates have been able to account for the cause of the disorder.

13th.—A boisterous uncomfortable day; wind directly against us and the sea running very high. The *Ulysses* in sight; spoke an American brig in the afternoon; sent a boat on board her, and got a Gibraltar paper with a confirmation of the peace and articles of the treaty; accounts in the paper from England as late as the 16th October; all joy at home on account of peace.

18th.—Came to anchor in Gibraltar Bay by eight o'clock in the morning. Found the rear-admiral, Sir James Saumarez, and fleet at anchor, as also several troopships. The *pratique* master, an officer on purpose to board all ships coming into the bay, came on board our ship, and amongst other things told us the regiment was to form part of the garrison.

I went on shore as soon as I had breakfasted, and waited on the governor, who confirmed the *pratique* master's intelligence, and told me the regiment should land the next day. I went on board to dinner, and communicated the certain intelligence to the officers, 'that they were to remain at Gibraltar.' We were in general much disappointed, as I believe the greater part had made up their minds to go to England.

23rd.—*Bon mot* of a soldier. Two of them were carrying the allowance of bread for a week on a hand-barrow, and by some accident it broke. One of them immediately said, 'Well, I see bread's fallen.'

January 1, 1802.—The new year commenced with remarkable weather for the latitude of Gibraltar.

5th.—The *Narcissus* frigate came in from the Isle of Wight in seven days, a remarkable quick passage. She brought very few letters, and not a single line for poor I.

9th.—Heavy constant rain. I wrote by schooner to Lisbon to Lord George, (Lennox), to the agents, to Mr. Allen, and to my brother. Hard to say I have not received a line from Staffordshire since I left England.

15th.—Heavy rain at night, and strong *Levanter* in the morning. 26th regiment arrived.

The Jewish doctors have a fable concerning the etymology of the word Eve, which one would almost be tempted to say is realised in the French women. Eve, say they, comes from a word which signifies to talk, and she was so called because soon after the creation there fell from heaven twelve baskets full of chit-chat, and she picked up nine of them, while her husband was getting the other three.—*History of Women.*

18th.—Two mails arrived by way of Lisbon brought by the *Penelope* frigate. The *Phaeton* frigate came in at the same time. I received a letter from my brother and also one from Phil. Answered the former letter same day by the overland mail.

24th.—Strong gale of wind, or, as it is called, a *levanter* from the east. The wind blows very forcibly down the Mediterranean, and meeting with resistance from the Rock of Gibraltar, it is very curious to see the effect the wind has in the bay; after striking the rock it comes round each end with violence, one wind blowing strong down the bay and the other blowing with equal force up it; so that when they meet a kind of whirlwind is occasioned, which raises the water in the same manner that a whirlwind does the dust on land.

I dreamed last night that Maria Gresley was married, but I did not ascertain the happy man. Do dreams bode good or evil? Time must determine.

February 5.—I rode to San Roque, and from thence in a detour to Algeciras a distance of six or eight miles, but the way I took made the distance twelve. The country from San Roque to Algeciras thinly inhabited and the land poor and ill cultivated. Some orange groves in the valleys and some woods of the cork-tree were pretty. The Spaniards appear very poor farmers; their system of ploughing pretty much the same as at Malta, that is, with two cows or two asses, the plough a light beam and a small coulter, guided with one hand, and they don't plough more than three inches deep.

The soil in general very sandy and light. The habitations of the peasantry miserable hovels that would discredit an English farmyard as a pigsty. The town of Algeciras is neatly built, and the streets, though narrow, tolerably well paved. I waited on the governor and made a sad blunder, as I mistook His Excellency for his *valet de chambre.* He was a mean-looking fellow, and as he neither spoke English or French, I made him understand as well as I was able that it was *his master I wanted.*

They have a playhouse, and an opera performed every night. I did not stay the amusement, I understood it was a wretched performance. The church is large and neat, ornamented like all Catholic churches; no paintings worth looking at. The dress of the Virgin Mary quite shocked me. A wax figure as large as life; dressed out in a flowing, full-trimmed, sky-blue silk gown and petticoat; lace ruffles, hair powdered, and a full-dressed cap. By way of preserving the figure and guarding the sacred person, there was a fine crimson damask curtain drawn before it. There were two regiments of infantry and one of cavalry at Algeciras, half clothed and worse fed. I returned to the garrison by the beach around the bay; had two rivers to cross, at both of which there was a good horse ferry. These rivers I had crossed in going from San Roque over bridges four or five miles from the seaside.

14th.—A sloop-of-war from Plymouth arrived; my kind and excellent friend Lady Louisa Lennox wrote to me, and sent me newspapers, magazines. *Navy and Army* List, and an *almanack*; she is the best creature in the world.

25th.—At half-past seven in the morning died General O' Hara, the much-lamented governor of the garrison; he had been unwell for some months, but not seriously so until the day sennight before he died. He was a man that had possessed uncommon brilliancy of wit and humour. As an officer he was considered a strict disciplinarian, of undaunted courage and an able general. He was generous in the extreme, and though his censures were harsh, they were always merited, and he invariably gave credit where credit was due. The commanding officers of regiments had always his support in carrying on subordination and discipline; to sum up all, I don't think the garrison will ever look on his like again.

April 14th.—The *Maidstone* frigate arrived from England with the account of the defensive treaty being signed; in consequence of which I made a party to take an excursion into Spain. Our party consisted of Brigadier-General Wemyss, Colonel Willington, and self. We proceeded with a muleteer and guide to San Roque on the 18th April. Mr. Raleigh, the secretary to the Governor, had been so good to send to San Roque for horses, etc., for us for the expedition. We paid sixteen dollars for each horse to carry us to Cadiz. We had seven horses.

We reached San Roque by five o'clock and saw a bull-fight, but of a very inferior degree, as it was merely tormenting a bull in the market-place by shaking a cloak or a piece of white cloth in his face, darting a stick pierced with an iron dart into his neck, or striking a firebrand upon his head. The poor devil was fatigued with plague and torment and was deprived of resentment, as he had a long rope tied round his head and ten or a dozen stout fellows lugging at it. It happened to be Easter Sunday and the commencement of festivity for the Roman Catholics; there were, of course, a great number of people assembled to partake of the sports, male and female; the former in long cloaks and *monteros*, the latter in red petticoats (short), and showing in general a tidy good ankle. We called on the governor, who gave us a passport for Cadiz. The inn or posada at San Roque clean, reasonable, and good beds.

19th.—We started at five o'clock in the morning on the same horses we had had from Gibraltar—such saddles and bridles, the former like the Mamalukes with the same fire-shovels by way of stirrups; proceeded through an open champaign country with some cultivation, though bad farmers, eight miles to Los Barrios, a small neat village, but such a *posada* to eat our breakfast in, '*Oh Diable.*'

The room we were shown into was about ten feet square, up a dark dirty brick staircase; a window, but no glass; a brick floor; and the furniture consisted of bare walls covered with the juice of tobacco emitted from the foul mouths of the natives. What did duty for a table was in reality a stool about a foot and half square and a foot high, on which appeared remnants of tobacco and lees of wine. Two tattered rush-bottomed chairs of a stature to match the table made up the furniture of our breakfast-room. The utensils for our tea equipage surpassed everything I had ever seen; the teacups were made of the coarsest earthenware possible, and of such a shape as might represent a diminutive brown *pot de chambre*.

We had provided ourselves with tea and sugar; all we required from the hotel was hot water, milk, and bread; the two latter were excellent, the former was boiled in an earthen jar. The Spaniards never use tea; of course, a tea-kettle was an implement unknown. After making a hearty breakfast notwithstanding the diet, we remounted our steeds and proceeded through a forest of cork-trees with only a single path, following the leader about ten miles to a single house, where our horses were to be fed. The forage was nothing but straw with a small quantity of barley. The straw they give their horses has the appearance of the chopped straw they feed horses with in England, but the appearance of the straw is occasioned by the method they use to thrash the corn, which is done by mares kept solely for breeding and for that purpose.

In all their corn countries they have circular places with stones of about twenty feet diameter; the corn as it is cut down and gathered is spread out and trodden by the mares, who are blindfolded, until the corn is clear from the straw. The straw is taken away and the corn winnowed and carried home. They never stack the corn in-the straw at all. After feeding the horses we proceeded some way through the forest (and such a road as I ever saw) without seeing a living animal of any sort, until we came to a very extensive plain, a perfect level country far as the eye could reach, a few small houses at three or four miles asunder, with many hundred acres of wheat and barley looking rich and luxuriant, as also on parts of the plain large droves of oxen and mares with their foals.

We stopped for ten minutes at a farmhouse and ate some eggs. The farmer was also a baker, and like all his neighbours a smuggler. We continued the plain for a few miles and again entered a thick wood. Came to an open common and to a most romantic situation called Ballhaille (?). The town placed on the very pinnacle of a high hill with a deep and rapid river running at the foot of it, which we crossed over a stone bridge and halted on the other side at a miserable *posada*. The town was directly above the *posada*, but the hill so steep and the approach so winding that the distance was upwards of two miles. It was seven o'clock ere we reached our resting-place for the night. My companions were a good deal fatigued, having been on horseback so many hours. We got a good salad and some eggs, which, with some fried ham and cold fowls of our own, made a good repast. Straw bed on a brick floor; a quiet mind made it a bed of down.

One of our guides, a facetious fellow, as we were pacing on, jumped up behind me and began to smoke his cigar with all the *sang-froid* possible; I was a little surprised at the fellow's facetiousness, but as I supposed it was the custom of the country, I was perfectly contented and rather amused with my companion. He rode a mile or two and repeated it several times *sans cérémonie*.

20th.—Set forward at five o'clock in the morning; mounted a very steep hill, which brought us on a level with the town, and from whence we had a fine view of the river and a rich valley below us. Passed over a common on a tolerable good road until we came in sight of Chiclana, a town twenty miles from Cadiz, where we breakfasted on our own tea and sugar; rather a clean *posada*, but our breakfast utensils as uncouth as at Los Barrios; excellent bread and fresh eggs.

After walking about the town for half an hour we proceeded to Cadiz which, on approaching, had the appearance of being built on the sea. The road from Ysalet, a perfect flat or rather causeway raised from the sea, indeed six miles of the road is made on arches under which the tide flows occasionally. We were stopped at the gate of Cadiz and our baggage taken to the custom-house; a mere matter of ceremony, and to put two dollars into the pocket of a jack-in-office. The town on the land side is fortified by a double wall.

We went to a *posada* kept by a Frenchman called Baillies in the Calle de Pedro Conde; his wife an Englishwoman, and as it was five o'clock we were glad to prepare for a comfortable dinner, which the appearance of things foretold. After enjoying a clean, good dinner we retired to repose; found our beds and accommodation very good and somewhat English.

21st.—Sallied out as soon as we had breakfasted, in full uniform, which we constantly wore, to the consul's, who attended us to the governor-general's, a Don Itterrigunia, a stiff, starch, black, ugly, dirty Spaniard, who scarce condescended to make a bow to us. However, as it was proper to see him, we did our duty and were then at liberty to pursue our researches. Cadiz is a remarkable well-built, fine town, the streets are narrow but uncommonly clean, the fortifications in good order, more than three parts of them washed by the sea. The houses are all alike and all built on the same plan.

The Place of St. Antonio is a tolerable square with a fountain in the centre; the houses not regular, not so well built as those looking towards the bay and many other parts of the town. The Calle Anciera is the best street, and where all the principal shops are situated. The Town or Merchants' Hall is in this street, which is a fine building. The new church was begun in the year 1717 and is not near finished; the architecture is magnificent, the expenses for building it are collected from a duty imposed on all ships coming into the bay. This contribution has been very trifling during the war.

A merchant told me that the revenue was fully sufficient to have finished the church long ago, but that the stewards and receivers, who are the dignified clergy, had appropriated the sums to more *pious* purposes. There are several fine churches with some good pictures. The armoury is large but not well stored; the keeper seemed much delighted to show British officers three or four English muskets. The place for the bull-fights is an amphitheatre built of wood, the diameter of which is about one hundred and fifty feet.

The barracks are in the casements of the fortifications and will contain three thousand men; the soldiers are well lodged but miserably clothed; except the Turks, I never saw anything so bad. The Alameda or public walk is situated near the walls of the town overlooking the bay, and is formed by four rows of elms, the side rows are for carriages and the centre for people to walk.

The inhabitants dine at two, and at five o'clock everybody assembles on the Alameda, the men to smoke and the women to intrigue; the former is so general that you see numbers of boys with lighted slow matches for the purpose of the men setting fire to their tobacco. The women, when out of their houses, are all dressed in the same manner: a black hood that reaches below the waist and covers the head, and a black petticoat, so that it is not possible to distinguish Joan from my Lady. We dined at our hotel, promenaded the Alameda and went to the play; a very neat theatre, the *parterre* or pit appropriated entirely for men, and the upper tier of boxes solely for women.

The Spanish dance of the *bolero* was performed and extremely well; it is a sort of reel danced by a man and woman. The streets are well lighted and perfectly quiet at night. The police consists of a mayor and aldermen, but acting under the directions of the captain-general of the province. I remarked that all the ordnance mounted on the fortifications had the same mark that King's stores have in England. The town is uncommonly well supplied with vegetables and milk from the neighbouring towns of Chiclana and Picto. The meat, both beef and mutton, very bad, but bread excellent.

The horses used in the streets by the porters for the purpose of carrying goods from one part of the city to another are very fine, but the most curious saddles for fixing the load I ever saw; it is a sort of pack-saddle raised two feet above the back, of a broad flat surface. The drays are drawn by mules, and instead of the weight being suspended on the back it is on the neck, and drawn by the neck. The shops are small and but indifferent, the people very civil; we were conspicuous in consequence of our dress, but the civilians as well as military were always attentive.

There is no such thing as a garden or even backyard to any house in Cadiz, and the commode is always at the top of the house. There is no manufactory, except a trifling one of silk stockings. It is calculated the city has suffered a loss equal to one hundred million of dollars by the war. On the ringing of a bell at sunset everybody in the streets stops and the men pull off their hats: a similar custom is, I believe, general in all Roman Catholic countries.

22nd.—After breakfast paraded the town all morning, dined at our hotel and went to the play, not at all amused with the performance, except the *bolero*. The women vulgarly dressed and nothing strikingly handsome. We had a most facetious fellow, a waiter, at our hotel. He was a Frenchman, and amused us with a number of anecdotes relative to the French Army; amongst the rest he related the story of a soldier on the march from France towards Portugal, having halted at a small town in Spain, went to the market and at a stall of an old woman purchased some oranges for which he paid, but was to receive change; a dispute arose and the citizen upset the old woman's stall and scattered her fruit; she, irritated no doubt, drew a stiletto and was going to stab the soldier, but his comrade observing it drew his sabre and cut off the old woman's head at a blow, and then exclaimed '*qu'elle se signifie*' (*sic*).

23rd.—We hired a berlin and three horses to go to Ysalet for the purpose of endeavouring to get a sight of the dockyard. We called on the port admiral, Marino, who had commanded the Spanish fleet in Sir James Saumarez's action. He was also at Gibraltar during the siege. Found the admiral very civil, but he could not allow us to see the dockyard; he told us it was not in his power to admit a stranger, though it was requested by a Prince of the Blood.

As a proof of the contempt with which the French treat the Spaniards, our friend the waiter was one day quizzing the dons, when we remarked he would be hanged if he talked in that manner; he replied he did not care a farthing for the captain-general or any *grandee* in Spain, and running out of the room, he returned with an infinite degree of apparent consequence, holding up his hat, in which was the national cockade, and exclaiming, '*Monsieur, voilà ma protection.*'

24th.—Left Cadiz in the morning, and proceeded in one of the ferry-boats across the bay five leagues to Port St. Mary's, a neat town on the beach with a barracks for 2000 men. We hired *caleesas, alias* bad buggies, to carry us and baggage to Xeres (Shery), a large and populous town. The view of the harbour and town of Cadiz from the hill above Port St. Mary's very beautiful, the country to Xeres full of corn and vineyards. At Xeres we were treated with the greatest politeness possible by the Messieurs Houries, the great wine merchants, with whom we spent the day and passed the night.

Went to M. Hourie's wine cellars, which I fancy are as extensive as anything in the world. They consist of two lofty buildings, each 270 feet long by 144 feet wide, and will contain 7000 pipes of wine. The quantity of wine annually made averages 20,000 pipes. Messieurs Houries employ between three and four hundred workmen, some of whom earn 5s. per day, and the common labourers 3s. The vineyards are five and six miles from the town, cultivated by farmers, who make from two to three hundred pipes of wine each and bring it to the merchants for sale.

There is a large Carthusian Friary about three miles from Xeres, which we rode to see after dinner; it consists of forty friars, who have a great revenue. The chapel is very grand, and some fine pictures in the refectory. The stables are on a great scale, and the friars breed some fine horses. After our return from the Chartreuse, we had a card-party at Mr. Hourie's; several Spanish officers and a Mr. Mousley, a Staffordshire man, who is settled in the wine trade at Xeres. Mrs. Hourie a very pleasant Frenchwoman.

25th.—We hired a berlin with five horses at Xeres to carry us to Seville, for which we paid fifty-four Spanish dollars, the distance sixty miles.

26th.—After breakfast sallied forth to see the sights. We had a letter to a Mr. Kiddle, a merchant from Exeter, who is settled at Seville, whom we found very civil. The principal buildings are the great church, very magnificent, fine altar and some good pictures; a curious clock at the top of the church made by a friar, and the church is remarkable on account of its being the burying-place of the famous Columbus; in the middle aisle is a flat stone to commemorate his deeds. There is a regular inclined plane to the top of the church, which is of a singular construction, from whence there is a most beautiful view of the town and country adjacent.

The Exchange or Merchants' Hall is a new building, and not quite finished; all the business and all the records relative to the Spanish South American possessions is transacted in this building. Formerly the ships fitted out from Seville, but since the establishment of Cadiz, that port has been found not only more commodious, but in all respects more convenient. Curious old palace for the kings of Spain, as also formerly the residence of the Moorish kings. In the palace are shown a number of Roman antiques brought from Italica, a settlement of the Romans near Seville, where they had been found from time to time. Fine *jets d'eau* and water-works in the gardens, and curious figures set out in the myrtle hedges.

The convent of the Caridad has some beautiful paintings by Murillo, who was an inhabitant of Seville. Ten thousand guineas had been offered for six of the paintings a short time before by some Englishman on his travels, but His Most Catholic Majesty had an idea they might be admired in some of his palaces, and they were to be removed to Madrid. They are all scripture pieces.

The cannon foundry is on a great scale, saw some guns cast and some bored. Colonel Willington remarked they carried on the business in a slovenly manner. We dined at our hotel in the Spanish style. There was a *table d'hôte* at the hotel, but we did not choose to attend, as they dined at one o'clock. There were several Englishmen in the house, riders for different manufactories, amongst the rest a Mr. Richards, from the neighbourhood of Coleshill, who we found extremely useful in showing us the town, as he spoke Spanish.

Every part of Spain has the same dinner, that is, in the first place, an *olio*, consisting of *bouille* of pork, beef, mutton, fowls, and all kinds of vegetables hodged podged together, the rest all made dishes and dressed with oil. Spanish wine, all (except the sherry) bad, and they give you the *vin du pays* as the beverage with meals. We paid two dollars a day for everything, that is nine shillings sterling, wine included. They are prohibited sending wine from one province to another, in consequence we could not get sherry at Seville, although we were only sixty miles from the manufactory.

After dinner we walked to the public promenade, which is a most curious place, literally on a bridge of boats across the river, where all the *beau monde* promenades from five o'clock until dark. There are seats on each side the bridge, and their carriages are all drawn up at the end waiting for the Dons and the Dowagers. One would have thought it impossible for people to assemble on a filthy wooden bridge by way of walk, when they have an opportunity of enjoying as fine a walk as it is possible. Curious-looking carriages drawn by mules, sometimes drove by a postillion in a full-dress livery suit, cocked hat, and jack-boots. They have not opened the theatre at Seville since the epidemic raged there two years ago, which carried off 20,000 souls.

27th.—We again set out for sights. There is a good barrack for a regiment of cavalry. The regiment called the *Carbineers*; they had more the appearance of soldiers, were better clothed and mounted, than any I had seen. I observed, whenever the soldier found any difficulty with respect to his horse, he immediately seized the pommel of the saddle. The Franciscan convent has some good pictures, copies from Murillo. The streets are very narrow, shops all open in the front and but indifferently filled. Population supposed to exceed 100,000; lower class of people very civil and almost always dressed in parti-coloured jacket of brown, with red, yellow, etc., and Montero cap, *toujours* the long cloak.

The exportation of wool is considerable, all the Estremadura wool is exported from Seville; it is purchased from the different farmers by riders and generally sold again by commission. The duties on wines the same all over Spain, that is, 30s. per pipe for exportation, and about 13s. for home consumption.

28th.—I went at eight o'clock to Grand Mass in the cathedral; the organ but indifferent, some very good voices, but the whole very fine. The Spaniards have a good appearance of religion, but no morality. I never saw such a mockery of religion as the service of the Church in Spain. Nothing entertained me more than the old women at confession. The tobacco factory is an immense range of building, and employs daily 2000 hands and 400 mules. I am no mechanic, but the machinery appeared to me very clumsy; there was in one room near 500 men rolling tobacco to make *cigarros*.

The room where the snuff manufactory was carried on was suffocating; a constant cloud of snuff not possible to penetrate. No tobacco can come legally into Spain but what is intended for the Government stores at this factory; yet notwithstanding the utmost vigilance of the government, vast quantities are smuggled from Gibraltar. This contraband trade is carried on to such a pitch that the smugglers frequently resist the soldiers, and generally repulse them. The tobacco is all imported from the Havannah.

Obtained leave to see the archbishop's palace; it is situated near the cathedral, a large pile of building, ill furnished and as uncomfortable as the inside of a church. There are a few good pictures, and what surprised me most, a gambling-table, something like a billiard-table, but played differently. I was entertained with the equipage of one of the dignified clergy; it consisted of a chariot made some time in the sixteenth century, drawn by six mules; the coachman clad in a blue coat, waistcoat and breeches, deep cuffs, and waistcoat pockets with a double row of broad worsted lace, large cocked hat, long queue and jack-boots. He drove as postillion the wheelers, and the pole-end mules he drove with reins, the leaders were drove by a postillion, the epitome of the coachman. The three off-mules had only one blinker to the bridles, and to my astonishment it was on the inside.

There were two footmen behind the carriage in the same livery except having on filthy white stockings instead of boots. The carriages in general execrable, and all drawn by mules. They have a mint at Seville for coining dollars; it had not been worked since the war, and the machinery appeared very clumsy. The quicksilver stores are of great extent; great quantities are used in working the mines in South America, but on account of the war they have an overabundance at Seville. It is procured from mines in some mountains sixty miles from Seville, and sent in leather bags on mules. It undergoes a sort of inspection at the stores in Seville, and is weighed out into specified quantities, packed again in leather bags, and then stowed into small deal boxes.

There was a large marble basin filled with it, from whence they weighed it out. I was surprised to see a brass weight of a quarter of a hundred thrown into the basin, and float about like so much cork on water. The reason is that the specific weight of quicksilver is heavier than either brass or lead. There are a number of fine statues, fountains, and public buildings in Seville, particularly convents, and the place for the bullfights is built of stone, and on a much larger scale than at Cadiz. We were hurried for time, and therefore left Seville next morning.

29th.—Proceeded in a coach and six mules; such an equipage, such mules, and such a coach; two *mulattoes* sit on a seat a very little raised over the fore-wheels; one of them drives the wheel mules, the other four are left to themselves; the mules are driven forward by holloaing and shouting, but if that does not answer, one of the *mulattoes* jumps off his seat, and lays a long stick pretty severely on the mules' sides. We paid 85 dollars for the coach to Granada, that is, about £19. 3s. sterling.

30th.—To Osuna, twenty miles, a plain all the way; some corn and large groves of olives. As our travelling was nearly the same rate as a London waggon, I always walked one half of the way. Osuna is a large town; during the time of the Moors must have been strongly fortified, of which there are curious remains; a fine cathedral, and three or four convents, but nothing worth noticing. A most astonishing extensive view from the top of one of the towers over all the adjoining country, which is a plain. Saw some droves of sheep of a small kind, but neat and very fair wool; wretched-looking peasantry.

The shepherds and all the horsemen you meet carry guns for their protection against a set of rascals that frequent all parts of Spain, and rob when they think they may make the attempt with impunity. From Osuna sixteen miles to a miserable village called Pedrera; saw a large flock of sheep going to Malaga for the use of the troops; they were small, two years old, and cost sixteen shillings each.

May 1.—Started at five o'clock; lost our way from the ingenuity of the *mulattoes*; we found the road after some countermarching, and reached Alameda to breakfast, twenty miles.

2nd.—Delicious weather, and we intended to have got under weigh at an early hour, but our *mulattoes*, being Sunday, were run away to offer their devotion to the Virgin, and did not return to us until six o'clock, when Mass was finished. We breakfasted at a single house called La Venta de Archidona, about two miles from the town. The difference between a *venta* and a *posada* is that at the former you may have lodging and accommodation for horses; at the latter you can only have your *own* provisions cooked and lodging for your *beasts*.

At the *venta* we met a coach from Granada loaded with no fewer than six fat greasy friars going to Seville. Their huge carcasses were the least heavy part of the cargo, for such a quantity of provisions, meat and drink, I never saw.

The approach to Loja very beautiful, the town situated in a fine rich valley well cultivated and enclosed with a deep winding river, much the prettiest spot I had seen in Spain. It was Sunday, crowds of people in the market-place, all the men in long cloaks, pretty-looking women. I saw several parties dancing the *bolero* with *castinettes*, and their music a *mandoline* (like a guitar). Shops all open, and instead of Sunday being a day of prayer, it is a day of the greatest rejoicings. I walked into the town long before our carriage, and purchased a very curious bird from a peasant, which he called a *ceison*; we had it cooked for dinner. The *venta* very good, deserves to be called a *Hôtel d'Angleterre*. The evergreen oak and cork trees, which look very like oaks, had a fine appearance in parts of the road, and gave a parkish look to the country.

3rd.—Left Loja at five o'clock, and continued the fine valley for four miles, and then a miserable country for twelve miles to a miserable *venta* at La Hache. From La Hache eighteen miles over a flat country to Granada, the last eight miles through a most highly cultivated valley, well watered by artificial canals. Passed a small village with an immense pile of building—'To the Spanish Minister.'

Abolish all convents, the first and greatest evil.
And pack off your friars and nuns to the devil.
Much improvement you'll find it, if to Seville you there go.
When the cloak is forbid and the cap of Montero.

Reached Granada at three o'clock; the approach to the town remarkably good, but the streets extremely narrow, quite Moorish; went to a very good *fonda, alias* hotel, kept by an Italian. The *fonda* is superior to either the *venta* or the *posada*, as the former provides everything. We were fagged, and did not move out after our arrival.

4th.—As usual, after breakfast, set forward to see sights. The cathedral a superb building, in my opinion superior to Seville, but it is not generally considered so. There are very fine pictures in it and some fine pieces of sculpture. We waited on the captain-general of the province, who resides at Seville; found him most perfectly civil and well bred; he invited us to dinner, which we of course accepted. He is a major-general in the Spanish service, his name Don Vasco. A very good dinner *à l'Espagnole, Olio,* etc. Bad wines, sat about half an hour after dinner, and to coffee.

There were about twelve Spanish officers at dinner, but their names I can neither write nor read. After coffee we walked with his Excellency to the Alameda, and accompanied him to his box at the play; no amusement in the *Comadie*, but the dancing excellent. We expressed a wish to see the *bolero* danced; the general sent immediately, and ordered it to be performed. He keeps up great state, and has always two dragoons before his carriage when he goes out. (The playhouse bad; they are building a new one.)

The Alhambra, as it is called, or the palace, formerly inhabited by the Moorish kings when the country was in their possession, is reckoned the finest remains of that sort of antique grandeur in the world. It is situated on an eminence adjoining the town, and from the walls you have a magnificent view of the town and all the adjoining country. The castle contains a vast range of apartments, with evident traces of their former splendour. Curious Moorish work on the walls and ceilings; vast variety of tiles with different patterns and colours.

They show an extraordinary method the queens of those days had of being perfumed after coming out of the bath. A large marble slab perforated with twenty or thirty holes is fixed in the floor of a small room; the perfumes are prepared underneath, and the fumes arise through the holes in the marble, on which the lady places herself. Several baths on a scale of magnificent splendour, and the walks, etc., in the garden, must have been cultivated to enjoy at all hours that climate; in short, everything seemed formed for the highest luxury and sensual pleasures.

Notwithstanding the height of the Alhambra, the number of water-works, fountains, etc., is astonishing. In the front of the Alhambra is a magnificent palace built according to modern architecture, but not finished. It was begun by Charles V., but not finished, and had remained in the state he left it ever since.

6th.—Hired mules to carry us across the mountains to Malaga. Left Granada at eight o'clock and travelled over an indifferent country and bad roads twenty-eight miles to Alhama, formerly a Moorish station, with the most miserable, wretched, dirty posada on earth, and the most idle-looking inhabitants I ever saw, I observed the dress of the women was changed from black to white, but made after the usual fashion. The country women when at work with their needle have a large cushion on their knee to which they occasionally fasten their work. The snow was lying on the Granada mountains within five miles of us, but notwithstanding the sun was most extremely hot. The natives at Alhama amused us all night with most discordant music; it was the eve of some saint and the *religieuse* were welcoming the happy day.

7th.—Left the stinking *posada* at six and proceeded over such precipices and along such roads as nothing but mules could have passed in safety. Here and there a patch of corn and a few olive-trees, with a miserable hut, at one of which we breakfasted, having carried with us all the requisites to provide a repast. Arrived at Velez Malaga at three o'clock, twenty-six miles from Alhama, the latter part of the road very good, through vineyards and groves of oranges and fig-trees. Great appearance of industry on approaching Velez Malaga, and vines cultivated to the very tops of the highest mountains in the neighbourhood. Some very picturesque views as we approached Velez, a neat, clean town with a very good *posada* kept by a Frenchman. A very curious castle in ruins, from whence there is a fine view of the adjoining country.

The road passes by the seaside almost all the way and through corn and vineyards, orange groves and fig-trees. Great appearance of industry in the country, people working in their vineyards. The approach to Malaga is close to the shore; you arc stopped at a sort of guard-house belonging to the custom-house, but only questioned. Went to the *Auberge Française*, a filthy, dirty hotel. Called on Mr. Laird, the English Consul, whom I had known at Gibraltar; he dined with us and we walked in the evening. Malaga is a large town, the greater part modern built; the population said to be 80,000. Fine building the new custom-house, and a fine pier and good mole.

An English sloop-of-war, the *Racoon*, was lying in the pier. Good vegetable and fish market; beef and mutton execrable. The police fix a maximum on the price of meat, and consequently no attention is paid to fattening. Observed in the poulterers' shops fowls divided and quarters hung up for sale. Streets narrow and abominably dirty. The shops pretty good. Went to the play; theatre a very good one, and the *bolero* well danced. The farce produced one of our countrymen, whose character was distinguished by his bluntness, as he never exceeded the two monosyllables of yes and no. The Frenchman characterised in the same farce by a short-cropped black head of hair, *à la Brutus*.

9th.—The great church is built after the model of the cathedral of Granada, but did not strike me as being near so fine; it is scarcely finished and has very few paintings. We called on the governor and were invited to dine. From the old castle, a Moorish edifice, you have a fine view of the town and adjacent country, the latter a fine valley, rich in corn, wine, and oils, etc. The great staple is wine, of which they export upwards of 40,000 pipes annually, chiefly to the Spanish-American settlements. They have attempted an imitation of the sherry, in my opinion quite equal to it. They should not call it an imitation, as nobody will choose an *imitation* when he can procure the *real*.

They export a great quantity of dried fruits such as figs, raisins, etc. Import their sugar from the Havannah, which was very high during the war, 40s. per hhd., now only 15s. Labourer's wages about 2s. 3d. per day. Overseers of works have 4s. 6d. The lower class of people live almost entirely on vegetables (salads), oil, and bread, the latter most excellent all over Spain. Very high duties on all English goods imported, amounting almost to a prohibition.

11th.—Left Malaga at five o'clock on horseback, a horrid road, and through a wild uncultivated country forty miles to Marbella; kept along the coast almost the whole way; got to a most filthy, dirty *posada*, but having a letter from the American Consul to one of the natives, he gave us beds. Marbella a poor fishing town.

12th.—Set out at four o'clock with an intention of reaching Gibraltar; got as far as Estapona, twenty miles, a small fishing town on the coast; the road tolerably good, some vineyards, and abundance of rhododendra and myrtles growing by the roadside. At Estapona we found a boat sailing for Gibraltar, and as my companions were pretty well *done*, we embarked at eleven o'clock and reached Gibraltar by seven. On our arrival we found His Royal Highness the Duke of Kent had taken possession of his new government. (Edward Augustus, Duke of Kent and Strathearn—1767-1820; fourth son of George III.; governor of Gibraltar 1802-3).

We had hurried and plagued ourselves from the time we left Gibraltar in order that we might get back to the garrison before the duke arrived, but we had not succeeded, and therefore, if my advice had been taken, we should have made our excursion more at our leisure.

24th.—Left Gibraltar in the *Pomone*, Captain Gower.

The Duke of Kent had expressed his wish to have seen the regiment, and would have reviewed us the next day, but the Admiral, Lord Keith would not allow the *Pomone* to wait, and it was so good an opportunity to get up the Mediterranean I did not resist it. Mr. Thompson embarked with me as *compagnon de voyage*. Sailed from Gibraltar Bay at half-past seven in the evening, with a fine breeze which continued all night.

28th.—Delightful weather; saw the island of Majorca in the morning of the 29th by five o'clock. Anchored in Mahon Bay, Minorca; breakfasted with Sir James Saumarez, the admiral, on board the *Caesar*, and went afterwards on shore to Mahon. Quite a Spanish town, narrow streets and neat, clean houses. The dress of the inhabitants very curious, particularly the women, who have remarkable long black hair, which they wear queued down their backs.

The Government House occupied by Major-General Clephane, who commanded. The harbour of Mahon reckoned one of the best and finest in the world, but in my opinion not equal to Malta. Preparations were making to evacuate the island, as the Spaniards were to take possession on the 14th June. Fort George, which defends the entrance of the harbour, had been repaired by the English and apparently at a great expense. Gower and I dined with Captain Younge on board the *Picque* frigate.

30th.—Gower and myself began a tour of the island. General Clephane was so good to lend us horses and to procure us a guide. We set out from Mahon about ten o'clock and proceeded along the great public road, which was made by the English formerly and extends the whole length of the island, near six miles, and took a cross road to Mount Touro, the highest spot in the island and on the top of which is a convent inhabited by eight or ten friars, fine, jolly-looking fellows.

From Mount Touro a complete view of the island, the whole of which is naturally poor and barren, but from the extreme industry and indefatigable labour of the inhabitants it is well cultivated and every inch of it made the most of. Dined at Alayor (a small town with four companies of the 36th regiment quartered) with Colonel Hart. After dinner rode eight miles, dreadful bad road, to Foutadonis, a neat house belonging to one of the natives living at Mahon, but who had sent orders to his servants to accommodate us by General Clephane's desire. Excellent beds, etc.

31st.—Breakfasted at Ferrerias (six miles) with the priest and schoolmaster, a fine, talking old Minorceen; spoke French, and re-membered the 25th regiment being quartered in Minorca. The friar gave us a famous breakfast, that is, bread, butter, and eggs; the tea and sugar we carried with us. I was quite delighted with the priest, and he appeared much gratified with our visit.

Proceeded through what is called the Great Boranco, a deep valley in which are all the nicest gardens possible, full of oranges, lemons, etc. etc., and on each side perpendicular rocks with variety of shrubs of all descriptions; the descent into the Boranco is almost like going down steps, but after you reach the valley the perfume and the view is charming. Rode on to Ceudadella to dinner, a regular fortification but not of considerable strength. The Spaniards always made it the capital of the island, and all the old *dons* and *noblesse* still live there and have an attachment to the Spaniards, much stronger than any other of the islanders.

The country but very indifferent about Ceudadella, the town much more regular than Mahon; a very narrow channel comes up to the town, only accessible by small craft, and no roadstead for shipping. We slept in the Government House, where General Fox had put up two or three beds, etc., for his own convenience.

June 2nd.—Dined at General Clephane's, and in the afternoon paid a visit to an old *don* and his wife, the father and mother of Mrs. (Billy)

Boothby, as also a sister of hers; much rejoiced to see a gentleman who had known their daughter and seen her family. (The daughter of Signor Miguel del Gado, of Mahon in Minorca; married William Boothby, who succeeded as eighth baronet in 1824). They spoke French and were more particular in their inquiries about young Billy than any other of the family.

3rd.—Captain Gower gave a dinner to some friends on board the *Pomone*; took a passage in an American ship bound to Leghorn. It struck me with wonder and astonishment to see the enormous expenditure of public money that was squandered away in the most lavish manner on the fortifications of Minorca. Permanent fine stone-works erected in various parts of the island, for what? To make a present to the Spaniards, as the island must to a certainty be restored to that nation on a peace, and therefore I cannot conceive why General Fox should have squandered away the public money to erect permanent works for the advantage of our enemies.

If fortifications were necessary, let them be made, but let them be erected at the lowest expense and, of course, not of durable materials. I was astonished to see a fine stone pillar erected by General Fox to commemorate *his* having made the new road across the island, with a pompous inscription and panegyric on the British Government, concluding with a well-turned eulogium to the merits of the general. It is reasonable to suppose that one of the first acts of the Spaniards, on their recovering possession of the island, will be to overturn a pillar that blazons the conquest of the island by their enemies and, of course, records their disgrace.

4th.—Early in the morning I sailed from Mahon on board an American ship.

6th.—Made the island of Corsica, but the master of the ship was at a loss to know what part of the island it was; but at twelve o'clock we got an observation, and by that means ascertained our situation; in the afternoon we saw the land on the continent, supposed some part of Savoy.

8th.—Fair wind, blowing fresh; made the Bay of Leghorn in the morning, and got into the harbour by twelve o'clock. The ship did not anchor in the bay but ran immediately in for the quay, which required good *coachmanships* as it was a very narrow passage and blowing hard. A boat came alongside and put the ship into quarantine, a most unpleasant event; but what can't be cured must be endured.

9th.—Captain Hope of the *Leda* frigate lying in the bay called upon me in his boat; I entreated him to use his exertions to get us out of quarantine. There is no harbour at Leghorn, it is quite an open bay, and the merchant ships are obliged all to lie alongside the quay.

10th.—My friend Hope obtained a mitigation of the period of our quarantine, and I landed about nine o'clock; the entrance into the town through a handsome gateway of the fortifications and into a narrow but well-built street (which are all paved with flagstones). Called on the deputy-consul, a Mr. Grant, to whom I had a letter from Captain Gower, and then waited on the governor (a Tuscan), a very fine, gentleman-looking old soldier.

The garrison consisted of French and Tuscan troops, but I did not think it necessary to call on the French general. The town is large, regular, and well built; the principal street wide and commodious, with very fine shops, particularly for statuary, etc., and jewellery. The fortifications are in good repair. I should imagine the population is as great in the suburbs, outside the fortifications, as within the body of the works. The theatre very neat, nothing very capital as to singers at the opera; and the ballet was performed by children, and very amusing; the reason they have no grown-up dancers is on account of their having discarded all French dancers from the stage, a strong proof the great nation was not in favour at Leghorn. I dined with a Mr. Littledale, the partner of Mr. Grant, a very good English dinner; other performers all English.

11th.—There is an extensive coral manufactory belonging to a Jew; the process of transmuting the coral rock into a fluid state is performed by fire, and from the fluid the coral beads are cast. There are most wonderful extensive magazines for oil, which is one of the great exports and which brings in a certain revenue to the state. The church is plain, with some paintings, but nothing curious. The Jews' synagogue is very large. I went to see the service performed, but I was soon satisfied, as the whole consisted of horrid yells by way of singing; the congregation was entirely of men. The *rabbi* was a venerable-looking man, whose occupation was the giving out the staves to be sung. The coffee-rooms, of which there are five or six in the main street, are crowded at night with ladies and gentlemen for ices and ice-water. Chairs and seats are placed in the street near the coffee-houses for accommodating the idlers.

12th.—The hotel at Leghorn where I lodged is kept by two brothers of the name of Passini; they had lived much in England as *valets de chambre*; an excellent house with every possible accommodation. I dined with Mr. Grant; a magnificent dinner and every description of wines, and all sorts of luxuries. I was advised by Mr. Grant to purchase a carriage, which I accordingly did, from Passini, a sort of low phaeton or rather barouche, as it was constructed to shut up close for night travelling. I gave thirty pounds for it. The weather very warm, and they were just beginning the harvest. I left Leghorn about eight o'clock, after being well supplied with eating and drinking from my friend the deputy-consul.

I had intended to have gone from Leghorn to Genoa, and through Nice to Marseilles, but I was advised rather to take the route to Florence, Bologna, and across Mount Cenis to Lyons, to which I agreed, and proceeded from Leghorn to Pisa, fourteen miles, through a flat, fine country and arrived at an indifferent hotel about ten o'clock. The road excellent.

13th.—The situation of Pisa is extremely pretty, divided by the river Arno, over which there are two bridges; fine quays on each side, and regular, well-built houses.

Some good paintings in the great church, which is a fine building, as is also the baptistery and burying-place. The leaning tower is a great curiosity, being a very stupendous building, but erected intentionally (?) fifteen feet out of the perpendicular; from the top you have a fine view of the town and the adjacent country. Went to see some fine paintings of pictures at a house belonging to one of the noblesse. Much amused.

The French in their excursions to and from Leghorn had robbed all the churches, etc., of everything valuable. The opera house very handsome; and as it was Sunday, a crowded company and good singing. The scenery and decorations of the ballet very beautiful, and charming dancing. The principal dancer's name. Madam Favian. Pisa is a place that has been much frequented by English on account of the salubrity of the air and medicinal qualities of the wells in the neighbourhood.

14th.—Left Pisa at six o'clock; beautiful country and good road to Lucca. The enclosures by the roadside small and divided only by poplar-trees, by the side of which are planted vines that extend their branches from tree to tree and hang in the most beautiful festoons possible to describe; the enclosures filled with luxuriant corn. Lucca is a large old town and famous for oil; streets narrow, good-looking houses. Saw for the first time the tree of liberty with the tri-coloured flag. The great church is a fine old Gothic building with some paintings by old masters, but nothing curious. The town is fortified, and we were stopped for our passports at the gate. The streets are paved with flagstones, and there is a very tolerable, inn, at least for a breakfast. From Lucca fourteen and a half miles to Borgo (*illegible*) indifferent road, beautiful views and highly cultivated country, full of corn, wine, and oil.

The Apennine mountains in front and others less lofty, but covered with olive-trees to the very summit. Passed several very good-looking houses, but they wanted English neatness. Just as we stopped to change horses my servant discovered that one of the wheels of the carriage was nearly off. One turn more and we should have been on the *pavé*; the *voiture* was soon repaired. The next stage was nine miles, good road to Pistoja through a fine rich country; it is a large town, but we only stopped to change horses, and proceeded nine miles on a good road and fine country to Prato; large town, but nothing curious to see except a manufactory of woollen cloths; from thence ten miles through a beautiful country and fine road to Florence.

The environs for ten miles round Florence the most picturesque and highly beautiful of anything I ever saw, and the adjoining hills covered with houses of the nobility and people of fortune. Reached Florence about seven o'clock, stopped at the gates to show the passport. Drove to the Hôtel de Schneiderf, or rather Hôtel d'Angleterre. It is kept by a man whose name it bears, and who was servant to Mr. Windham, the British Envoy at the Court of Florence; he had also lived with the Duchess of Devonshire and had been much in England. (Georgiana Cavendish, Duchess of Devonshire—1757-1806; eldest daughter of the first Earl Spencer; married, 1774, fifth Duke of Devonshire).

It was by far the best house I ever was at in any country, and as reasonable. An excellent good sleeping room, large well furnished dining-room; breakfast, two courses at dinner and a bottle of wine, all for two crowns per day. As we entered Florence we met two men on horseback, dressed *à l'Anglais* and mounted on very English-looking horses, which we concluded must be from old England. As we had been travelling from an early hour in the morning we were glad to get to dinner, and did not move out in the evening.

15th.—Having been given to understand that the French *chargé d'affaires* was particularly attentive to the English who called upon him, and had also more influence at Florence than any other person, the first thing I did in the morning was to wait on him. He was unwell and I did not see him. It was also necessary to call on him in order to obtain a passport to travel through France. The town is very handsome and situated in a valley, through which the river Arno runs, and has three fine bridges; one in particular, the arches of which are elliptical, is the most beautiful thing of the kind I ever saw; the streets are rather narrow and all paved with flagstones.

Many parts of the town are ornamented with fine statues and sculpture. The palace of the *ci-devant* Grand Duke, now of the King of Etruria, is a very magnificent thing and inhabited by His Majesty, but the great nation, when they first entered Florence, carried off almost all the valuables, such as pictures, glasses, tables, damask, furniture, etc. Some of the apartments are still very grand, parts of the furniture having been left.

At two miles from Florence is what is called the Casino, a sort of ornamental farm or gardens belonging to the Royal Family, where the king and queen go in state every evening at seven o'clock. All the *beau monde* attend, and it is a sort of Corso or public place, where people drive about in their carriages or walk, as they choose. Before the French were at Florence and in the grand duke's time the gardens and pleasure-grounds were full of game, such as hares, partridges, etc. I saw the King of Etruria and his queen and princess in an open carriage; His Majesty is but rather a mean-looking man.

From the Casino people go to the play; the Royal Family there every evening. They have a box overlooking the stage on one side. Very little ceremony observed on their coming into the theatre. The house small, but very handsome; the performance a *burletta*, and as I did not understand the language, found it rather stupid. The price of admission only one shilling. The theatre is called Pergola. The boxes quite dark, and therefore I could not judge of the people.

16th.—Walked in the morning to see the guard relieved at the palace. The king and queen with one of their children were listening to the music. Very poor troops the Tuscan soldiers, a tolerable good band. The anatomical gallery of waxwork figures extremely curious, and particularly interesting to gentlemen of the Faculty. In the same building there is a most extensive assortment of natural curiosities;

birds, fishes, marbles, minerals, etc., all exposed for public view every day. The Grand Gallery of Florence was certainly before the French Revolution the finest collection in the whole world; it is still in a high state of preservation, and although the French seized on almost everything wherever they went, they must have the credit of not having made any seizures from the Florence Gallery.

The collections of paintings, statues, and busts, extremely numerous, and of the first masters, in a high state of preservation, and open to the public every day. A few of the best pictures were sent to Sicily, on the first visit of the French, by way of safety. The Boboli Gardens, adjoining to the Palais de Pitti, very extensive in the old-fashioned Dutch taste, long walks, and numerous statues and figures. Very beautiful view from the upper part of the gardens commanding all the town and the surrounding country; the hills covered with corn, olive-trees, and vineyards, and very closely inhabited. In the evening the opera, beautiful scenery and excellent ballet; the first dancer very capital, her name Decairo. The king and queen were there, but the house was not full.

17th.—There was a grand religious procession, being Holy Thursday. All the orders belonging to the different convents, churches, and other places of worship marched in procession through the streets, which were strewed with flowers and in many parts had canopies hung across for the purpose of keeping off the sun.

18th.—All the morning in the gallery, visited several churches with some fine paintings in them. There is a room adjoining the gallery filled entirely with portraits of the greatest masters, painted by themselves. Amongst them there is one of Sir Joshua Reynolds much admired. Very good markets for meat, poultry, and vegetables; beef sixpence per pound, very fine.

19th.—Went to see the Chapel de' Medici; it is an octagon of about thirty feet diameter, entirely lined with marble, and enriched with most magnificent tombs, finely sculptured in marble, granite, etc. etc., of the Medici family. In the old palace of the grand duke there are some fine rooms and some finely painted ceilings. The costume of the country women in the neighbourhood of Florence is very curious. They wear stiff silk gowns with an abundance of silver lace and fringe; immense hips and long stays; the hair rolled up from before and behind at the top of the head; a large chip hat ornamented with ribbons, silver and lace fringe, etc., stuck upon the bundle of hair at the top of the head; very high-heeled shoes, and every woman has a fan. Numbers of the lower class of the women at Florence beautiful, and the finest figures in the world.

As I intended to leave Florence this day, it was necessary to send to General Clark for a passport to travel to France. The general was unwell, but sent his secretary; he gave me an invitation to dinner, but I was engaged. Quitted Florence at ten o'clock in the evening after the opera and proceeded with a passport from General Clark to Bologna, eight posts, between sixty and seventy miles, mountainous and very indifferent road, travelled in the night in consequence of the warmth of the weather; some wild, picturesque, fine views, but no town of any note; reached Bologna about three o'clock the next day.

20th,—The approach and entrance to the town very good; it is a very large old place and had a garrison of two thousand French troops; the tree of liberty in the square. Went to the opera, a dirty filthy theatre, and the most filthy performance I ever saw. The opera a squall; the ballet an obscene, bawdy display of naked women, at least they might as well have had no covering as the dress they had on. The company a most vulgar collection, a number of French officers in the parterre; shocking ruffians. Bologna is a part of the Cisalpine Republic; all the Bolognese wear the Republican cockade, green, white, and red instead of blue; found a tolerable good inn. The convents turned into barracks.

Very fine paintings at the palace of Sampieri by Raphael. At the institution there is a fine library and a numerous suite of rooms filled with arts and science, but like every part of Italy, marked with the depredations of the French, who had carried off numbers of the best pictures, bronzes, sculptures, etc. This academy must have been on a great scale. In the Church of Madonna there is a beautiful picture of Ecce Homo by Caracci, who was a native of Bologna. The palaces and houses of the great citizens are on a large scale, but an evident appearance of poverty amongst the people; still the French have a number of friends. There are two leaning towers, but not curious after seeing that at Pisa. There is a remarkable phosphoric stone they sell at the institution; it is found in the neighbourhood and undergoes a chemical preparation. The wine at Bologna very bad indeed.

Proceeded at five o'clock for Modena.

Arrived at Modena between nine and ten on 21st, a clean good-looking town, full of French troops. Arcades in most of the streets for people to walk under; the palace of the duke a vast pile of building, but not inhabited. Quantities of cherries, pears, and plums in the market, as also abundance of vegetables. There are some very good-looking houses and barracks. Left Modena after breakfast and passed through a most beautiful rich country, thirty-two miles, to Parma, changed horses four times; the only town on the road is Reggio, large and ill built. The road all the way from Modena excellent.

Spanish troops in Modena, rather good looking; streets wide and houses good. Curious black net over the mourner's head, something like what the lower class of the Spaniard wear with the *montero*. Parma an excessive neat pretty town. Spanish troops in garrison; the palace has been immense, but is in ruins; palace and garden of the duke adjoining the town very good. All confusion; numbers of carriages and livery servants; academy; gallery of sculptures and pictures adjoining the theatre, no good ones except a curious antique of a woman.

23rd.—Left Parma at four o'clock and arrived at Milan by half-past six, eighty miles; breakfasted at Piacenza. Four posts from Parma. It is a large town, long narrow streets, in the centre of which there are flagstones for the wheels of the carriages. The square or *piazza* has two fine equestrian statues in bronze. Leaving Piacenza, across the Po in a ferry, from thence to Milan, the finest road I ever travelled. Passed through Lodi, a neat town, remarkable for the famous action fought at the bridge, (Buonaparte crossed the Po and Adder at Lodi, occupied Milan and besieged Mantua in 1796). Country from Piacenza to Lodi rich with corn and vineyards, from Lodi with meadows and full of cattle for making the famous Parmesan cheese (very good at the hotel of Parma).

All the country about Lodi and to Milan full of water, and they have means of covering all the fields every week; entrance to Milan very fine, and the very finest road I ever saw. Stopped at the gate for our passport; curious mode the women at Lodi have of putting up their hair behind with a thing of this shape o——o run through the hair on the upper part of the back of the head, and the hair all plaited and twisted round it. Went to the opera; beautiful theatre, larger than the King's or the Haymarket, very good opera and beautiful ballet. Boxes have an anteroom to each for servants; large rooms on the second flight for card-playing and all sorts of gambling. Parterre very large and only half of it seated; orchestra excellent, upwards of sixty performers.

24th.—Went to see sights; streets narrow and ill built, flagstones in the middle for the carriage wheels; shops good, but not equal to Leghorn. *Duomo* or cathedral, fine building, lined inside and out with white marble, but not half finished; great numbers of statues, no paintings, Ambrosian Library large, but nothing like the institution at Bologna Gallery. All the paintings and sculpture carried away to Paris.

★★★★★★

In May 1796 the members of the Directory wrote to Buonaparte, 'Leave nothing in Italy which will be useful to us, and which the political situation will allow you to remove.' The people of Milan were therefore asked for twenty million francs and a selection from the paintings in their churches and galleries.

★★★★★★

Ducal palace, nothing fine in the building; but the rooms must have been magnificent, particularly the ballroom; at present the habitation of the chief director of the Cisalpine Republic. Platform for the guillotine; citadel, fortifications in ruins, large barracks. Troops at drill; soldierlike-looking, but very dirty and ill clothed; cavalry, good horses, but ill rode; apparent idleness in the people, much gambling and singing. Provisions dear, meat tenpence per pound. Took a box for the opera, much delighted with the ballet; paid near ten shillings for the box.

25th.—Got up early to see the guard mount; poor business and bad band; cavalry very dirty; wrote to my brother.

26th.—In consequence of a quarrel with the postmaster respecting the charge for posting, called on the commandant to refer the business to him.

Did not reach Turin until nine o'clock owing to delays of different sorts, several rivers to pass, quarrels with the postmen, carriage broke down, etc. The country from Milan a perfect flat; fine corn and some grass land; roads to Vercelli good, from thence very, very stony; the distance from Milan to Turin ninety-five miles; some of the rivers very rapid; hotel at Turin pretty good, L'Auberge Royale.

28th.—Two French *demi*-brigades marched into Turin. Agreed with a *voiturino* to take us to Lyons; we were to pay him fifteen *louis d'or*, and he to find us and to pay all expenses. Went to see a very curious and most ingenious manufactory of sculpture in wood; as far as I could judge it was excellent. Wrote to my brother. The shops at Turin very inferior to either Milan or Florence. I observed there was scarce a good house in Turin that had not a French sentinel at the door, and was, of course, occupied either as a quarter for a general officer or for some public military purpose.

The *auberge* we were at had sixteen officers billeted, who did not pay one farthing for their rooms, and probably would not spend sixpence in the house; *liberté et égalité*. I have taken notice that in many of the towns in Italy the public clocks and church clocks strike the hours twice, about a minute between. Left Turin at five o'clock in the afternoon, a flat road eight miles to Rivoli (through a rich country), a palace of the Duke of Aosta now in decay; from thence the road but indifferent to St. Antonio, ten miles further.

The women of the country all wear an immense straw hat, a good thing in the burning sun out in the fields. Idleness of the lower class of people in Turin, playing cards in the streets; the porters, when not employed, sit down on their baskets and get out their cards; three men were guillotined the morning we reached Turin. Water running down the middle of all the principal streets; tri-coloured flag and cap of liberty in all the principal squares.

Proceeded from St. Antonio at four o'clock; passed along a vale between two very high mountains, most picturesque views and waterfalls, to Novalesa to breakfast, distance twenty miles; saw the fortifications of De la Brunette close to the village Susa; all destroyed by the French; carriage taken to pieces at Novalesa and carried by mules; very expeditious in taking the carriage to pieces; steep ascent; paved; waterfalls; precipices; nude state of the people; plain at the top; droves of cattle; make the Gruyere cheese; lakes; fine trout; ugly women; curious petticoat, all plaited to make large hips and a *derrière*; convent; Buonaparte conspicuous by a memento on a stone over the door; goitres, saw several; fine rich pasture; abundance of snow; our coachman, a violent anti-revolutionist, told us half the people in Turin of the same way.

Small villages, all the tree of liberty and soldiers quartered upon them. The descent from Mount Cenis not so long as on the other side. Arrived at Lasnebourg at four o'clock; beautiful valley; fine view of Mount Blanc; glacier; all snow; wretched poor village; got excellent trout and good Gruyère cheese and also good wine; the distance from Novalesa to Lasnebourg fourteen miles.

30th.—Set out at five; a most uncommon cold morning.

July 1.—Left La Chambre at five and breakfasted at Aiguebelle, distance fifteen miles; the same valley and most beautiful views; the village in a vale with mountains rising on every side to the clouds, either highly cultivated or towering great trees almost perpendicular; very good road; numbers of vineyards; shocking ugly people; to Montmelian, the same beautiful valley and fine road; crossed the Ache and quitted its wandering banks; drove through a well-cultivated, fine plain.

Excellent road to Chambéry, where we arrived at four o'clock and got a good dinner; it is the capital of Savoy, narrow streets, and a dirty-looking old town; sad devastation made by the French; the palace burnt, all the gardens, etc., destroyed; everything Frenchified according to the true *bon patriot* system; observed *citoyen* wrote up in several streets; all the people with the national cockade, but from what I could learn they are wisely sick of *liberté*; the convents all destroyed; several fine houses deserted or appropriated for the use of the troops; very good wine at the hotel *à la poste*, and as Montmelian was famous we got a bottle of that; it is a sort of Burgundy; sound full wine, but not so high-flavoured; as also a sort of excellent Gruyère cream cheese; and charming fine strawberries all through the Alps. The Alps begin to decrease at Aiguebelle; the situation of Chambery most beautiful in a vale highly cultivated with views of rocks, mountains, woods, *châteaux*, villages, etc.

2nd.—Did not set out until after breakfast and went to Bourgoin; some of the most romantic views I ever saw; fine waterfall near one hundred yards high; quit the Alps; near is the famous road called La Grotte, made through a mountain more than a century ago; it is extremely curious.

Between Aiguebelle and Pont de Beauvoisin is a most extraordinary precipice by the side of which the road passes; a river runs between; two perpendicular mountains; the height one thousand yards at least, and on the side of one of them is the road made; there is just space between the mountains at the bottom for the river, and gradually widens at the top; the distance may be one hundred yards; the sides of the mountain covered with wood and shrubs, and the road winds along it for a mile.

At Pont Beauvoisin enter France; a small river marks the division from Savoy; we dined at a wretched dirty place; did not see any national cockades; from Beauvoisin to Bourgoin a good road and fine country, but a melancholy appearance of the war; every decent-looking house untenanted; land ill cultivated; not half inhabited; the people in the fields more than half of them women and the rest old men; large vine-yards; no national cockades; sullen melancholy look; the general appearance of the country very different from what we had seen; fences; large trees, and looking very like England; people civil; country people pulling off their hats; unusual, never saw it in Italy; Bourgoin, a dirty poor town; troops at parade at Beauvoisin; sergeant taking snuff from the captain's box; privates accosting the officers, '*citoyen*.'

3rd.—Set out from Bourgoin at five; had some young potatoes and excellent butter for supper; execrable roads; had been left all the war, and were recently repaired with large round stones; breakfasted at a wretched spot they called L'Hôtel, an odd dirty house halfway to Lyons; fine country, but worn out for want of proper cultivation; poor crops, and nothing but women, old men, and children at work; gathering the harvest, looking melancholy, no national cockades; several *ci-devant* good houses, all demolished; price of meat where we breakfasted, butter 9 pence, bread 3 pence, meat 3½ pence per pound; flat country to Lyons; corn looking thin; approach to Lyons good; entrance through the suburbs very bad; arrived at the Hôtel des Ambassadeurs at twelve; melancholy appearance of the place in consequence of the disasters that befell the city by the Revolution.

Mr. Jacquier, the banker, told me he thought Buonaparte would repudiate his wife and marry a princess of some European power and make the consulship hereditary. (Napoleon divorced Josephine on December 15, 1809, and married Marie Louise of Austria on April 2, 1810).

Houses demolished; convents all made barracks; three thousand troops in garrison; streets narrow and full of people; town house fine building; Hôtel de Dieu on a tablet; *liberté et égalité*; playhouse very poor after the Italian theatres; performance good; people all stood in the pit.

5th.—Wrote to Lady Louisa; silk stockings bad and dear; left Lyons at four o'clock; long hill from the town; beautiful country and fine harvest; passed through Ville Franche; wretched old town; slept at a small town called St. George; dirty *auberge*.

6th.—Proceeded from St. George and breakfasted at Mâcon; a small old town on the banks of the Saone; the country, vines, and corn looking very well; tolerable good crops; mostly women at work in the fields and old men; several good-looking houses; the roads all repaired and in good order; Mâcon is close on the banks of the Saône, with a handsome bridge across it. Leaving Mâcon, a handsome house on the left; formerly the property of Monsieur Perigord, and given to his daughter, whose husband emigrated, and who Robespierre wished to have married; the house in ruins; fine country to Châlons, where we dined; very good town close to the Saône; handsome bridge.

7th.—Beautiful country; full of vines and fine corn to Dijon.

From Dijon hilly and very open country to Villeux (?), where we slept. Corn country and latterly some vines; parts of the road bad and stony; saw few people in the fields, and mostly women at work in the vineyards.

8th.—Left Villeux (?) at four o'clock. Fine-looking; excellent road from thence to Joigny, where we slept; fine triumphal arch on the bridge for Buonaparte, as he returned from Lyons.

9th.—Proceeded at seven; fine country; large good-looking *château* of a *ci-devant* noble near Villeneuve, formerly Treasurer of France; guillotined at the Revolution; good road on the bank of the Yonne to Sens; curious rafts of wood on the river; over the gate at Sens, Caesar's motto of *Veni, Vidi, Vici,* in compliment to the consul on his return from Lyons; wretched poor town; archbishop's palace made public offices; churches destroyed; before the Revolution there were fourteen churches and as many convents; the latter all in ruins, the former only four remaining; one of the churches is made into a meat market and a flour magazine.

Poor discontented at the price of bread; drawing comparisons between the price before the Revolution and the present time; corn and vines all the way from Auxerre; no enclosures; trees planted by the roadside; curious stage-coaches; much heavier than a London waggon; six horses drove by one man, riding as postillion the wheel horses. After passing Villeneuve saw a good-looking house of the President of Paris; at the Revolution he was arrested, but made his escape. To the right a *château* of the Duke of Châtille, he was guillotined; house now inhabited by farmer; it stands low, and no appearance of pleasure-ground or park; country all open for miles and some small plantations of trees; road uncommon fine; planted on each side and paved in the middle.

Entering Moret, another *château* of the Duke of Châtille; now inhabited by some of his descendants; smaller house than the one to the right; after passing Moret, enter the forest of Fontainebleau; paved road all the way; *château*; flew to look at it immediately. Oh! what a falling off; my heart ached when I entered the court; but when the unfortunate Antoinette's *boudoir* and bedchamber were shown, it almost rent one's heart. The only room that is not completely demolished is the *boudoir*; it is most elegant; glasses, fine ceiling, and fine doors are all that remains. The king and queen's apartments, the Council Chamber, and the *salle à manger* one may imagine; all the rest is a ruin. Many places the utmost pains have been taken to erase Royalty, in others the crown and other regal emblems remain. The palace itself is an extensive range of old buildings; nothing princely; nothing regular; the stables are large, but not what I expected; the regiment of *Chasseurs* occupied them.

By the bye, the woman that showed the palace as drunk as Newgate. The chapel in the palace totally destroyed; gardens very extensive; quite in ruins. Much furniture at the *auberge* we were at must have been from the palace at the time all were sold; the nicest chairs, beds, tables, looking-glasses, etc., possible; two famous arc chairs. Large town Fontainebleau; very old and looked as dismal as a churchyard.

10th.—Fine road to Paris; *château* of the Duke of Orleans; now inhabited by some female; looking ruinous. *Château* of the Duchess of Bourbon and Princess Lamballe; now the property of a banker at Paris; snug-looking place; saw nothing like an English place. Entrance to Paris very poor; got to the Hôtel de Vendôme; devilish dear; four *louis d'or* a week; went to the *Opéra Comique*; neat house but small; men vulgar and women more,

24th.—Set out at six o'clock; five posts to Rouen to breakfast; a fine large old town; view of the river beautiful (the Seine), navigable for vessels of two hundred tons; trade totally at a stand during the war. Excellent road from thence to Dieppe; poor town; fishermen; corn country all the way from Paris.

25th.—Embarked at six o'clock in the *Lark* packet, and landed at seven the next morning the 26th at Brighton; very glad to find myself in England again; proceeded to Stoke to dinner.

September 24.—The review on Ashford Common; my friend Addisbrooke lent me a horse. The A.D.C.'s attending were Lord Craven, (William, seventh Baron Craven—1770-1825; major-general in the army and lord-lieutenant of Berkshire; created Earl Craven 1801),

Colonels Bligh, Witham, Gower, and Dyott.

Went in a chaise and breakfasted at Belfont. Returned to town and dined with Wynyard.

December 6.—Went to London per mail and paid my duty to His Majesty at the *levée* on the 8th, and on the 9th was presented to Her Majesty at the drawing-room to kiss hands on being appointed A.D.C. to the king.

11th.—Left London and returned to Freeford on the 12th.

January 4, 1803.—The third subscription assembly under the patronage of Mrs. Sneyd (Brickly Lodge). The weather remarkably open and mild until the 11th, when it set in to freeze for the first time during the winter.

14th.—Dined at the Swan, a farmer's dinner, to partake of a round of the immense ox that had been fed by my brother.

20th.—Dined with Hankey and went in the evening to a masquerade at Ranelagh, rather a—s rakish (?) collection; lost my hat and greatcoat, both stolen out of the carriage.

26th.—Received a letter to my utter astonishment from the adjutant-general to say, that in consequence of what had happened at Gibraltar, I was by the duke's order to join the regiment immediately. It seems there had been a spirit of mutiny which had shown itself in the garrison, in which the 25th took part.

I left Freeford per mail the 28th, and got to town next morning. Waited on the adjutant-general, who told me I was to go out with Sir Thomas Trigge.

The 2nd February I was at the *levée*, the king very gracious, but not a word about the regiment. Frost and snow and very cold weather until the 13th, when it rained and continued all day the 14th. Was kept in London, and could neither have my orders to embark for Gibraltar, nor would they say I might return to the country. Tired to death of London, and a great deal of rainy weather made it still more tiresome. Received great kindness and attention from General Stevens and also from Mr. Greville. The Duke of Kent's secretary arrived on the 22nd, and brought as satisfactory accounts of our regiment as I could possibly expect to receive. He told me the regiment was in a better state of discipline than any regiment in the garrison, and had been so ever since the unfortunate event.

On the 2nd March I was released from my suspense by Calvert telling me I was not to go to Gibraltar.

On the 6th I took my departure from town, to my great joy, and returned to Freeford on the 7th.

26th.—A county meeting at Stafford to address the king on his escape from the brute Despard. (Edward Marcus Despard—1751-1803; an officer in the colonial service, devised in London a plot against the government 1802; executed for high treason at Newington). The address moved by my brother. Went in the afternoon to Keel; remained there until the 30th, and returned to Freeford. The first fortnight in April remarkable hot weather, and the forwardest spring almost ever remembered.

On the 13th and 14th the thermometer was on the former day in the shade at 62° and in the sun at 96°, and on the latter day in the shade at 68° and in the sun 96°.

The month May remarkably dry; cold northerly winds until the 25th, when there was fine rain.

Accounts arrived in the country on the 21st that the long negotiation that had been pending between this country and France was at an end, and war was the consequence. (War was declared against France on May 18, 1803).

On Sunday, the 29th May, I went to London; on my arrival I found the regiment was ordered direct from Gibraltar to the West Indies. June On the 1st June attended the *levée*, and in the evening was at the grand ball at Ranelagh given by the Knights of the Bath; by far the most magnificent thing I ever saw.

June 4.—Drawing-room in honour of His Majesty's birthday. I dined afterwards with the Duke of Clarence. In the *Gazette* of this day my name appeared as a brigadier-general in the West Indies.

24th.—Went on a visit for three nights to Windsor to see my friend Colonel Sneyd, and on the 28th I left London, and returned to Freeford to wait until an opportunity presented itself for my going to the West Indies. On my arrival at Freeford I found my brother very unwell with a gathering under his ear. He suffered very much, and was obliged to undergo two operations by Ward of Stafford.

All the months of July, August, and September in a state of the greatest uncertainty, expecting daily orders to embark, but on the 3rd September I received a letter from September Wynyard to say I was placed as brigadier-general on the Irish staff. This was in consequence of the regiment having arrived at home, and sent to Ireland. The order that was sent to Gibraltar for the regiment to proceed to the West Indies did not arrive until after the regiment had sailed. Lichfield races, the 13th September, very little turf sport and very little company. A new stand opened for the occasion.

On the 3rd October I went to London to make arrangements for going to Ireland. Applied for my nephew, Thurston Dale, to accompany me as Major of Brigade, which was granted.

On the 7th I dined at Mr. Greenwood's; met the Duke of York, very gracious.

Embarked at Holyhead at eight o'clock in the evening of Monday the 24th, and was on shore in Dublin at seven the next morning. Waited on the commander-in-chief, (William, first Earl Cathcart—1755-1843; in Ireland 1803-5), he had left Dublin on a tour. I was informed by the adjutant-general I was to be stationed at Cork. I had the honour of an audience of the Lord-Lieutenant, Lord Hardwicke. (Philip Yorke, third Earl Hardwicke—1757-1834; lord-lieutenant of Ireland 1801-1806).

Left Dublin on the 26th, and reached Kilkenny about eleven o'clock.

The next morning at seven o'clock I had an express to say my station was changed, and instead of Cork I was to go to Waterford, for which place I proceeded, and arrived at six o'clock in the evening of the 27th. A most detestable road from Kilkenny to Waterford. Curious sign on the way. Two Pats sitting at a table drinking whisky: underneath is written, 'Fear God and Man, and drink as hard as you can.'

On the 7th November I went to Curraghmore for two days on a visit to the Marquis Waterford, who had called on me. (Henry-de-la-Poer, second marquis—1772-1826; privy councillor in Ireland; colonel of the Waterford militia).

A very fine place, but the house indifferent: the style of living very inferior to an English nobleman.

27th.—Mail was robbed by a bandit six miles from Waterford in the county Kilkenny. I was ordered, in consequence, to a small village (Mullinava), to make every inquiry into the robbery, and attended there, as also on the two following days; met Lord Ormond and the magistrates of the county Kilkenny. December Went to Curraghmore on the 11th December, and was ordered to Kilkenny on the 13th to attend a meeting respecting the mail robbery.

January 8 1804.—Went to Clonmell to see the 25th regiment as they were ordered to Cork; never saw the regiment in higher order. Snowed all day, and rained all the next as I returned. Dreadful rain all the month of January and beginning of February. The latter end of the month the finest weather possible.

February 20.—Accounts arrived of the serious indisposition of his Majesty, to the great dismay of all his subjects.

June 27th.—Went across the Waterford Harbour from Dunmore to Loftus Hall, a seat of Lord Ely's on the county of Wexford side, (John, second Marquis of Ely—1770-1845; privy councillor in Ireland; colonel of the Wexford militia).

A curious place situated on a peninsula, not half a mile across from sea to sea. The house very indifferent, and has not been inhabited since the Irish Rebellion 1798, of which the neighbourhood was the grand depot. Picked up two or three most uncommon-sized mushrooms, full as large in circumference as the upper part of the crown of a man's hat, and as blooming and fresh as a small one of a night old.

28th.—Went to Curraghmore to pass a few days at Lord Waterford's. A large party in the house and very pleasant.

August 29th.—To my very great surprise I received orders to attend the king as one of His Majesty's A.-D.-C.'s during the royal visit at Weymouth; the consequence of which was that I left Curraghmore and the party at eleven o'clock at night, and posted off to Waterford. No packet sailed until the 30th, when I took my departure (with some regret from Waterford, where I had met with much kindness and attention) on board the *Earl of Leicester* packet. Sailed about ten at night, and landed about twelve the next day, the 1st September, at Milford. Proceeded immediately September in my own carriage to Bristol by way of Haverford West, Narbeth, Saint Clears, Caermarthen, Llanon, Pyle, Cowbridge, Cardiff, Newport, New Passage, Bristol, Old Down Inn, Cannards Grove, Sherborne, Dorchester, Weymouth. Arrived at twelve o'clock Tuesday, the 4th September 1804.

Met with a most flattering and gracious reception from His Majesty and the Royal Family, and fixed myself for the Weymouth campaign. Found the Stafford Militia and the two Somersets, as also a part of the Hanoverian German Legion.

Wednesday, 5th.—Attended His Majesty on board the yacht: all the Royal Family went on board, *viz.* the Queen; Dukes Gloster, Cumberland, Cambridge, Kent; Princesses Augusta, Sophia, Elizabeth, Mary, and Amelia. The attendants Lord Paulet (Lord-in-waiting), General Garth, Fitzroy, Maningham, Cartwright; *Aides-de-camp* Dyott, Stewart, Campbell; Ladies-in-waiting, Ilchester, Matilda Wynyard, Elizabeth Thynne. The fleet consisted of three yachts and the *Eolus* and *Crescent* frigates.

The king dined alone at one o'clock, the queen and females at two, and we soon after; a very good dinner. Came on shore at five o'clock. The king attended the piquet mounting, and then to the theatre.

6th.—Cruising again, but no females.

7th.—All on board, and in the evening at the queen's house; three card-tables; all round games.

8th.—His Majesty gave a grand *fête* in honour of their wedding day; two hundred people dined at the hotel; dancing after dinner and to the play in the evening.

Saturday, 15th.—Review of the Hanoverian Dragoons; dined with the Duke of Cambridge, and the play.

October.—A continuation of fine weather with not more than one bad day to prevent His Majesty sailing until the 1804 29th October. *Fêtes*, balls, plays, etc., as also reviews and sham fights; His Majesty daily improving in health and strength.

On Saturday evening the 27th after the play, I took my departure from Weymouth in order to attend the king at Cuttnells (?), for which place His Majesty was to set out on the 29th. I decamped on the 27th for the purpose of securing post horses, and paid a visit at Lymington to my old friend and master General Stevens. Stayed there the 28th, and on the 29th went to Cuttnells to meet the Royal Family, who arrived at four o'clock at Mr, Rose's at Cuttnells. The attendants were lodged in the king's house at Lyndhurst. We dined with the Royal Family, and in the evening cards. I had the honour to play at their Majesty's table.

30th.—All went to a Mr. Drummond's, a beautiful place in the New Forest; a most splendid magnificent knife-and-fork breakfast at two o'clock and returned in the evening to Cuttnells. The king rode.

31st.—To Lymington to visit Sir Harry Burrard Neale, (second baronet;—1765-1840; admiral; M.P. for Lymington for forty years). On the way through Lymington the Royal Family stopped at the

Town Hall to receive the address from the Corporation; dined at Sir Harry's, and returned to Cuttnells about six; cards in the evening.

November 1.—To Southampton. The King, Princesses Sophia and Amelia rode; the latter's horse fell down and the princess hurt, but not very materially. The Corporation presented an address. Returned about one o'clock, dressed, and went to dine at Mr. Burklay's in the Forest.

2nd.—The Royal Family left Cuttnells for Windsor, and I went to Stoke; found poor Lord George Lennox in a very bad way; never saw a man so altered. Remained at Stoke until the 5th and went to Highfield; stayed with Sir W. Pitt until the 8th and then to Windsor to pay my duty to their Majesties, the king having been pleased to give me an invitation; nothing could be so flattering as the gracious reception I met with from their Majesties. I was lodged in the queen's lodge. In the evening a grand assembly at the queen's apartments in honour of Princess Augusta's birthday. I was honoured by being called to play at the queen's table at cards.

9th.—Rode out with the King, Princesses Sophia and Amelia; returned about two o'clock, and in the evening the Queen's assembly.

January 2, 1805.—On the 2nd went to Leicester and returned on the 4th.

13th—Went in company with Swinfen to London.

Attended Her Majesty's birthday on the 18th, and on the 19th went by the king's command to Windsor and remained until the 23rd; returned to town and left London the 24th and reached Freeford the 25th.

Took my departure for Ireland on the 28th. Slept at Wrexham and proceeded early next morning by Llangollin to Bangor ferry. Travelled a new road by Capelcarrig, and was very near being upset in consequence of a hill covered with ice and the horses not being turned up.

Left Bangor early on Wednesday; called on Lady Uxbndge at Plasnewydd, (Caroline Elizabeth, daughter of the fourth Earl of Jersey and first wife of the Earl of Uxbndge, first Marquis of Anglesey).

Embarked at Holyhead about ten at night. Did not reach Dublin until twelve o'clock the next night, the 1st February. Waited on the commander of the forces, and was directed to proceed without loss of time to Waterford in consequence of a report of the enemy's fleet being off the coast.

The report of the enemy's fleet all a false alarm. Nothing will equal the kindness and attention I experienced from every person at Waterford; there was no necessity for my being at any expense for keep, as I was constantly invited out to dinner.

On the 10th I received official information to move to Dublin on my being relieved by Brigadier-General Peter, who did not arrive at Waterford until the 26th.

March 1.—Waited on Lord Cathcart, the commander of the forces, who I found extremely civil. I was ordered to take the command not only of the garrison, but also of the east district, consisting of the three neighbouring counties to Dublin. My quarters were in the barracks, and the garrison consisted of the 3rd and 12th Dragoons; a light infantry battalion of the line and the 9th, 36th, 53rd, 72nd regiments; Tyrone and Armagh Militias. Rather singular that I should have been quartered in Dublin just twenty years before, Adjutant to the 4th regiment.

On the 5th I had an audience of his Excellency, the Lord-Lieutenant Lord Hardwicke, presented by Lord Cathcart. Nothing was ever equal to the shameful and scandalous state of the streets of this city from dirt and infamous paving. I never saw anything like it, nor did I suppose it was possible for the streets of a great city to be in such a state. I took up my abode in the barracks on the 12th, and occupied the quarters my lieutenant-colonel had done when I was quartered in Dublin twenty years before.

On the 14th a drawing-room at the castle (they are in the evening). Was presented to the lady-lieutenant, and on the 27th was presented in form at the *levée* to my lord-lieutenant.

On the 21st a grand ball and supper at the castle in honour of St. Patrick.

22nd.—I dined at the lord-lieutenant's, a most splendid and magnificent big-wig dinner; no ladies. Twenty-four at dinner, consisting of lords, judges, bishops, and generals. A long continuation this month of cold, dry easterly winds. All the month April dry, cold easterly winds, with hail and snow.

On the 23rd the lord-lieutenant gave a great dinner in honour of St. George and also to celebrate the installation of the Knights of the Garter, of which Lord Hardwicke was a companion, and which took place with great magnificence on this day at Windsor. Lieut.-General

Sir Charles Asgill arrived from England and took the command of the district. The infantry regiments in the garrison reported to me, and the cavalry to General Cotton.

★★★★★★

Sir Charles Asgill (1763?-1823); colonel of the 6th Foot; commander of Dublin 1800; general 1814.

Sir Stapleton Cotton, Viscount Combermere (1773-1865); lieutenant of foot 1790; served in Flanders 1793-4; at Cape Town 1795; against Tippoo Sahib 1799; major-general 1805; succeeded as sixth baronet of Combermere 1809; served in the Peninsular war; created Baron Combermere 1814; commander-in-chief in Ireland 1822-5; commander-in-chief in India 1825-30; created Viscount Combermere 1827; field-marshal 1855. (*The Golden Lion*, The early life and military career of Stapleton Cotton, by Mary Combermere, W. W. Knollys & Alexander Innes Shand is also published by Leonaur).

★★★★★★

In the middle of April the field days began in the Park by brigades. I was well paid. Lord Cathcart extremely hasty in the field, but very clever and thoroughly master of the business. The field days continued all the month of May. Dry cold weather.

On the 4th June the Yeomanry paraded in the Park, the regulars on their several parades and fired in honour of the day. The lord-lieutenant gave a sumptuous entertainment in the Park at the Vice-Regal Lodge. No appearance of summer; all the month of June dry cold weather.

July.—Hard at work three times a week; the whole July of the infantry out. Very little warm weather and very little like summer.

August 1.—The camp on the Curragh consisting of twenty battalions infantry, the 3rd and 5th Dragoon Guards, two squadrons of the 18th and two of the 23rd Light Dragoons; a fine sight to see the whole take the field, which they did at the same time, the different columns having been regulated so as to arrive at the same hour on the verge of the common. Very rainy and uncomfortable weather almost the whole month.

I was ordered to march four regiments from Dublin, the 9th, 36th, 63rd, and 82nd, to a common ten miles on the road towards the Curragh, there to meet three regiments from that post and to encamp the whole for the night, and to return with the three regiments the next day to Dublin; rather a pleasant excursion as the weather was fine.

The 4th back to Dublin, after having a pleasant excursion, and seeing some fine wild scenery. I forgot to mention from Arklow we went to see the famous Wicklow goldmines. Did not observe anything very curious. A number of labourers were digging gravel out of the bed of a small river and washing it in order to discover a few small particles of gold which were scattered amongst it The mine, as it is called, has been taken possession of by government, and the result of their labour is said to amount to nearly three guineas a week clear, a paltry concern.

The accommodation at the inns of Wicklow, Rathdrum, and Newtown tolerably good, but in a very inferior and humble style to that sort of entertainment in England. The new garrison of Dublin, which was changed on the breaking up of the Curragh camp, consisted of the second battalions of the 26th, 28th, 30th, and 48th regiments, and of the Cavan, the Donegal, and Wexford Militias. An abundance of rain all the middle of October.

On the 20th Lord Cathcart received the appointment of Ambassador to Russia and was to proceed immediately to England, but owing to the constant prevalence of gales of wind from east, he did not leave Dublin until the 30th. Lord Harrington named to succeed him. (Charles Stanhope, third Earl of Harrington (1753-182 9); commander-in-chief in Ireland 1805-12).

Some regiments ordered to embark, *viz*. 8th, 9th, 20th, 30th, 36th, 89th.

In the beginning of November I dined with an old Waterford acquaintance. Major Godfrey of the Kerry Militia, and met there some relations of his (Mrs. Thompson and her two nieces), rather smart-looking women and great fortunes. A few days after I invited them to breakfast at my quarters in the barracks and gave them music, etc. I was a little smitten with the second, Miss Eleanor.

Lieut.-General Floyd ordered to take the command of the forces as Lord Harrington was employed on a diplomatic expedition to Berlin. (Sir John Floyd—1748-1818; lieutenant-general 1801; general 1812; created baronet 1816).

December.—I had frequent opportunities of seeing the Thompsons, and felt a very considerable increase of inclination for Miss Eleanor, who I could not help flattering myself did not quite disapprove my attention to her. Mrs. Long, the wife to the Chief Secretary, (Charles Long, first Baron Farnborough—1761-1838; raised to the peerage 1820), gave a grand ball at the castle.

I danced with Miss Eleanor and in the evening proposed for her and to my great joy was accepted. The marriage ceremony did not take place until the 11th January, when it was performed at Leeches Hotel (where Mrs. Thompson was staying), by my friend Dr. Batson, the Bishop of Clonfert, about eight o'clock in the evening. No person was present but just her own family.

January 1806.—We remained at Leeches Hotel until the 27th, when we took possession of my quarters in the barracks *en familles* and I was as happy a man as any in the world.

About the middle of February I applied to General Floyd for leave to go to England on the 1st March, to which he consented, and accordingly on Saturday the 1st we sailed in the *Duke of Montrose* packet about eight in the evening and arrived at Holyhead at five next morning after a fine passage. We went to bed for a few hours and proceeded to Conway, where we slept, and the next night at Chester. Did not set out from Chester until eleven on Tuesday and reached Freeford about ten. Found my brother and his wife quite well.

The next day saw my mother, etc., and was rejoiced to find her so well.

Left Freeford on the 22nd of March and arrived in London on the 23rd; went to Windsor for two nights on the 2nd April; most graciously and kindly received by my Royal Master; was delighted to find His Majesty so well in health, though his sight very defective. Left London on the 24th.

On the 8th May went to Wicklow to inspect the Clare regiment of militia.

June.—His Majesty's birthday celebrated in the usual manner; a grand dinner at the Vice-Regal Lodge in the Park.

Constant drills and field days all the month of July. The beginning of August Lord Harrington arrived to take the command of the army. His lordship had been appointed to succeed Lord Cathcart, but had been prevented reaching Ireland by his employment in the diplomatic line.

On the 8th I embarked with my darling wife for Holyhead in consequence of her having been unwell since our return. She had been recommended by Dr. Beislie to try Cheltenham. We had a long passage; did not reach the Head until five o'clock on the evening of the 9th. Slept at Gwyder and the next day I accompanied her to

Capelcarrig, where we stayed all night, and she was to proceed next morning on her route, and I returned to Holyhead and embarked in the evening for Dublin; had a long passage and did not land until next afternoon at (*illegible*) at five o'clock.

In the beginning of September I received the joyful account that I was to be moved to the English staff and to be stationed in Sussex.

On the 15th September I went in the mail coach by way of Drogheda, Newry, Hillsborough to Lisburn, and from thence to pay a visit to Mr. Robert Thompson at Greenmount, a beautiful situation overlooking Lough Neagh and Thanes Castle. I remained with him until the 28th and went to Cromore, Mr. Crombie's, by way of Portglenone, where Mrs. Dyott's father left an estate. From Cromore I visited the famous natural curiosity of the Giant's Causeway, a most stupendous and wonderful effort of nature.

Returned to Mr. Thompson's on the 22nd and left Greenmount on the 23rd on my way back to Dublin. Took the route of Belfast on my return, which I consider the most prosperous and flourishing town in Ireland.

I reached Dublin at an early hour on the 25th and embarked on the 26th for Holyhead, and breakfasted at Freeford on the 28th. Stopped there for a week's shooting, and on the 8th October rode to Tewkesbury, where I met my carriage and arrived at Cheltenham rejoiced to find my wife in excellent health and much recovered. Mrs. Thompson and the Misses were there. I rode over to Cirencester to Lord Bathurst's to see Lady Louisa and Miss Lennox. (Henry Bathurst, third Earl Bathurst—1762-1834; Tory statesman; master of the mint 1804).

The 20th October Mrs. Dyott and I went to Bath for two nights.

On the 23rd we left Cheltenham and went to Leamington near Warwick, a watering-place similar to Cheltenham. Remained there until the 27th and proceeded to London, where we stayed until the 21st November, to have my future station finally settled, which was fixed for Hastings in Sussex, to which place we proceeded, having slept at Tunbridge Wells, on the 21st, and reached Hastings to dinner next day.

January 1807.—On the 16th I went with Mrs. Dyott to town for the purpose of her accouchement and also to pay my duty to Her Majesty at the drawing-room on her birthday; the Court not very crowded.

191

ELEANOR DYOTT, *NÉE* THOMPSON,
WIFE OF GENERAL DYOTT

On the 15th February I rode to town in the day on purpose to see my dear wife; had quite an uncomfortable ride from the extreme warmth of the season; stayed in town next day and returned on the 17th, the most severe cold day I almost ever felt. The transition from heat to cold very wonderful. Snow on the ground and a very severe frost and hard gale of wind. *March 18th.*—I went to town to attend my little daughter's christening. We had fine weather for the last fortnight, though rather cold for the season.

Returned from London on the 1st May, remarkably sultry and hot weather.

I went to Leamington on the 27th April to speak to my brother (in consequence of the dissolution of Parliament) respecting any chance I might have if I offered myself as a candidate for the city; we agreed it would not do, and therefore I returned to London.

On the 3rd of May I received a letter from my brother with a requisition from a number of the inhabitants of Lichfield to desire I would go and offer myself for the city. I accordingly set out immediately and travelled post; reached Freeford very early on the morning of the 5th; but after making every inquiry and calculation, it was found advisable not to stand an opposition, and I therefore set out on my way back next morning, and arrived at Hastings on the 8th. Nothing, I suppose, ever could have equalled the zeal and anxiety of all description of people at Lichfield on my account; the most flattering attention that could have happened to any man, and which I never can forget.

On the 2nd June, Eleanor and I went to town, I to pay my duty to His Majesty at St. James'; a most crowded Court. We returned to our quarters on the 6th. The end of the month I went over to Brighton, merely to call upon Lord Charles Somerset who was appointed to command the district.

July.—On the 25th left my house at Hastings and July took a small house (Hollington Lodge) three miles from the town of Hastings for three months; extraordinary dry weather from the beginning of June, and at times very hot.

On the 29th Lord and Lady Warwick; the two Ladies Greville; Lord and Lady Lovaine; Lord Amherst; Sir Js. and Lady Burgiss dined with us at our cottage, which we find a much more comfortable dwelling than the house in Hastings.

★★★★★★

George, second Earl of Brooke and Warwick (1746-1816) mar-

193

ried secondly in 1776 Henrietta, daughter of Richard Vernon. Ladies Greville daughters of Lord and Lady Warwick.

George, eldest son of the first Earl of Beverley and second Baron Lovaine; born 1778; married Louisa Harcourt, third daughter of the Hon. James Archibald Stuart Wortley.

★★★★★★

On the 5th October I rode to London to meet Mr. Burnaby for the purpose of placing his son Richard at the Academy at Woolwich. We went there together on the 6th and the boy was admitted a cadet.

On the 27th November I went to London in my way to Windsor to pay my duty to His Majesty for a few days. The 28th I dined in Grosvenor Square and on the 29th (Sunday) I started at seven in the morning and reached Windsor in time to make my bow to the Royal Family as they stepped out of the carriages to church. I was most graciously received by the king, as well as by all the princesses. The weather was so cold the Royal Family did not go to Frogmore, and therefore were not seen until the evening at music. His Majesty did me the honour to talk to me for some time, and Her Majesty very gracious.

Monday morning.—Attended the king to chapel; afterwards the weather continuing cold, His Majesty did not ride. Princesses Augusta and Amelia took a short ride in the Park. In the evening cards; I played at Princess Elizabeth's table.

December Tuesday.—Attended chapel. His Majesty would not ride, though the weather was much less severe; since the king's sight has been so bad, he has quite given up any enjoyment from riding exercise, and in consequence gets corpulent from the sedentary life he leads, as His Majesty plays backgammon all morning with General Fitzroy. (Lord Charles Fitzroy—1764-1829; general; son of the third Duke of Grafton; *aide-de-camp* to George III. 1795).

In the evening the usual party; I played at Princess Elizabeth's table.

Wednesday.—At chapel, and though the day was tolerable, the king did not ride. Princesses Augusta and Amelia took a long ride; only Colonel Disbrowe and myself of the party. In the evening I had the honour of playing with their Majesties at commerce. The good king's sight very defective; however he managed to play his cards, and was in high good spirits and appeared most perfect in health.

Thursday morning after chapel I took my leave and never experienced more flattering condescension than on this visit.

Friday.—I had a good deal of business to do in the city, and in consequence of the advice of my friend General Spencer, I called upon the adjutant-general to express my anxiety and readiness to be employed on any active service whenever it should please His Royal Highness the Commander-in-Chief to think proper to call upon me. General Calvert was very kind, and promised to take a good opportunity to make known my wish and offer to the duke.

★★★★★★

Sir Brent Spencer (1760-1828); served in the West Indies 1779-82; at Alexandria 1801; equerry of George III,; served in the Peninsular War.

Sir Harry Calvert (1763?-1826); entered the army 1778; *aide-de-camp* to the Duke of York 1793-4; adjutant-general of the forces 1799-1818; general 1821.

★★★★★★

Saturday.—I left town; did not get away until two o'clock and reached home by half-past ten, and to my great joy found my dear wife and little girl quite well; it was unusual, so long an absence.

January 1808.—The season mild and good weather. Early in this month I received a letter from General Calvert, the adjutant-general, to say it was very probable I should be appointed to a brigade of the line, whose headquarters might for the present be Hastings. I obtained two months' leave of absence, and on the 14th January set out from Hastings, with wife, bairn, and domestics, and slept at Seven Oakes.

On Saturday the 16th April to my great surprise, I received a letter from General Wynyard to say I should be ordered on service immediately to the Mediterranean. This put me into some confusion, particularly on my wife's account, as she expected to be confined soon. However, I lost no time and proceeded to town on Monday the 18th; called next morning on the adjutant-general, and was informed I was to serve under the orders of General Spencer then at Gibraltar, but in what part of the world was not known, nor was I told when I was to embark.

I left town the next morning to attend my wife to Freeford, where we arrived on the 21st. Such weather never was known for the season; the snow between Towchester and Daventry was a foot deep, and I never saw it snow faster than as we travelled the road between those places. I remained with my wife at my brother's at Whittington until the 1st May, when I took a sorrowful leave of her and my friends, and set out in the mail for London. I never suffered more in my life or felt so much real grief as on quitting my family. Uncommon fine weather after a long and severe winter.

I reached town on the and, and was busily employed in preparations for embarking. I was to go out in an ordnance transport, but the time of sailing undetermined.

On the 4th May I received a letter from the adjutant-general to desire to speak to me; on seeing him, he proposed to me (in consequence of the situation of my wife, who was near her time) to change my destination for the Mediterranean by employing another officer on that service. The offer was too great a temptation to withstand, and I answered by saying if the Duke of York was quite satisfied that I had made no effort to shun service, I was content; to which the adjutant-general replied that was not possible, as the arrangement originated with him. I saw the duke the next day and found him most gracious, and approving the arrangement that had been made.

On the 8th I went to Windsor to pay my duty to His Majesty. The king as usual quite kind, and appeared pleased I was not to leave my family. I remained at Windsor until the 10th, when I returned to town, and left London on the 11th for Staffordshire, for a few days to see how my dear wife was going on, where I arrived on the 12th at Whittington to dinner and found all quite well. My brother and Mrs. Dyott of Freeford were at Leamington. I remained with my dear wife enjoying the peaceful abode of my good mother until the 18th, when I went in my curricle to Leamington to see my brother. Stayed all night and proceeded in the curricle to Daventry, and took the Liverpool mail to town, and arrived at the usual hour on the morning of the 20th.

I called upon Lord Charles Somerset to see whether it was decided where I was to be stationed. He recommended my going to Hastings for the present, and that he would endeavour to find out if I was to be permanent there or to move. Accordingly I proceeded from London in the afternoon of the 21st and slept at Seven Oakes, and set out early next morning for my old quarters, where I found myself exactly the day five weeks I had left them. I did not venture to take the house I had at Hollington on account of the uncertainty of my sojourn, but went into a small lodging in the town of Hastings.

On the 26th (*a move again*) I received a letter from Lord Charles

Somerset to request, as there was not one general officer in the district but myself, that I would repair to Brighton as headquarters and to remain until I was relieved. Major-General M'Kenzie, the second in command, was gone to London on some particular business. I accordingly proceeded in the afternoon as far as Horsebridge, where I slept, and reached Brighton to breakfast the next morning. I did not find there was anything material to be done. I took up my quarters at the Castle Inn. Very little company at Brighton, and nobody I knew except Major and Mrs. Arkborn, formerly Mrs. Norbury.

I went over to Horsham, twenty miles from Brighton, on the 30th, to look at a house belonging to Lord Francis Hertford, (second Marquis of Hertford—1743-1822), as I had some expectation I might be stationed there, but after inquiries I found the furniture in the house did not belong to his lordship, and consequently was not to be let furnished. I had intended to have gone to London for the birthday, but could not as there was no general officer in the district.

On the 28th May, to my very great surprise, I received a letter from my sister Mary to inform me that my dear wife had been safely delivered of a son on the 26th; it was very unexpected, as she did not reckon on the event happening until June.

On the 8th June Brigadier-General Houston arrived at Brighton to serve in Sussex. (Sir William Houston—1766-1 842; served in Flanders, Minorca, and Egypt; in the Walcheren expedition 1809; in the Peninsular War 1811-12; created baronet 1836).

As I was particularly anxious to see my wife, I left Brighton next day and went to London, and on the 11th proceeded to Whittington to my mother's, where my wife had been confined. I found her uncommonly well and the little boy tolerably so; he was not a stout child, and had been complaining. I remained with my dear wife only until the 15th, and left her and her little boy pretty well.

Arrived in London per mail next morning, and set out on horseback on the 17th for Hastings, and arrived next morning at my old quarters at Hollington, which I had again engaged as my residence.

On the 29th Lord Charles Somerset inspected my brigade in Crowhurst Park, and I dined afterwards (to meet him) with the Leicester Militia by an invitation from the colonel, the Duke of Portland. (William Henry Cavendish, third Duke of Portland—1738-1809; a distinguished statesman and twice prime minister).

August 1.—I set out on horseback in the afternoon to Tonbridge on my way to London, where I arrived the next morning, and on the 3rd paid my duty to the king at the *levée* on account of my promotion as Major-General, having had no opportunity of paying my respects sooner. I found His Majesty as usual very gracious, and I was rejoiced to see the good king in such good health.

I left town again in the afternoon of the 3rd; rode to Tonbridge, and home the next morning. The weather was very warm, but nothing to what it had been on my late journey.

11th.—Went to Brighton to attend the Prince of Wales' birthday. On my arrival I was going to the Pavilion and met His Royal Highness at the gate. He was uncommonly gracious, invited me to dinner that day, and added, of *course* on the next. Music in the evening.

★★★★★★

Cobbet wrote of the Pavilion: 'Take a square box, the sides of which are three feet and a half, and the height a foot and a half. Take a large Norfolk turnip, cut off the green of the leaves, leave the stalks nine inches long, tie these round with a string three inches from the top, and put the turnip on the middle of the top of the box. Then take four turnips of half the size, treat them in the same way, and put them on the corners of the box. Then take a considerable number of bulbs of the crown-imperial, the narcissus, the hyacinth, the tulip, the crocus and others; let the leaves of each have sprouted to about an inch, more or less according to the size of the bulb; put all these, pretty promiscuously, but pretty thickly, on the top of the box. Then stand off and look at your architecture.' Such was the residence of H.R.H. the Prince of Wales.

★★★★★★

On the 12th a review of all the troops in the district. Most of the infantry had been collected and encamped for the purpose, and consisted of the following regiments:—North and South Gloster, Renfrew, West Essex; Berks; Bucks; Montgomery, South Hants, Sussex, Northumberland, Nottingham, East Middlesex, a troop horse artillery, the 3rd Dragoon Guards, the 10th Dragoons, and two squadrons of the Bays. The prince was received near the centre, then passed along the front, after which a *feu de joie* from right to left of the front rank and from left to right of the rear.

The whole then marched past His Royal Highness in slow time; it was a beautiful day and a very fine sight. The prince gave a most mag-

nificent dinner to about one hundred and thirty people. His Royal
Highness was in high spirits, and we passed a very jolly day. In the
evening everybody went to a ball at the castle, such a crowd I scarce
ever saw.

★★★★★★

Mr. W. H. Wilkins, in *Mrs, Fitzherbert and George IV.,* vol. ii.,
writes: 'In 1808 the prince also kept his birthday at Brighton,
and celebrated it with his brothers by a grand review on the
Brighton Downs. The prince was in Hussar uniform as colonel of the 10th Light Dragoons: his sabre was of the richest
description, and the sabretache and saddlecloth were of scarlet,
superbly embroidered and nearly covered with gold . . . this
was the last of the prince's birthday celebrations in which Mrs.
Fitzherbert took part.'

★★★★★★

13th.—The 10th Dragoons was to have been reviewed by the
Duke of York, but on account of the rain it was put off. The prince
gave a ball and supper at the Pavilion; there was upwards of three
hundred people, and, of course, a splendid entertainment. All the royal
dukes, except the Duke of Clarence attended the prince's birthday,
and he was prevented by sickness. Every room in the Pavilion is fitted
up in the Chinese style, very elegant and very beautiful.

I returned to Hollington on the 14th. The weather in the beginning of September tolerably fine for two or three days; afterwards until
the 12th constant rain so as to prevent any diversion shooting.

On the 11th I set out for Freeford for the purpose of partaking of
some shooting. I rode to Tonbridge in the afternoon and into London next morning; proceeded by the mail that evening and arrived at
Freeford on the 12th. It was Lichfield races, but I did not enjoy that
rural sport as I had formerly done. I met Colonel Sneyd and Mr. William Sneyd at Freeford. The partridges were in great plenty and I had
famous sport. I remained at Freeford until the 21st and returned per
mail to London, stayed in town the next day and rode on the 23rd to
Tonbridge, and arrived at home on the 24th. Was happy to find my
dear wife and her two darlings quite well. The weather during my
stay in Staffordshire was very fine, and continued until the end of the
month although cold for the season.

On the 6th December I received a private communication from
General Wynyard, deputy adjutant general, to say I was named for the
command of a brigade upon service in Spain and to embark almost

immediately. This news threw a gloom over my fireside; however I set to work and packed up to prepare for a start.

Unfavourable accounts arrived from Spain and I was kept in a state of constant suspense as to the time of my departure, until the 25th, Christmas Day, when I received a letter from my friend General Wynyard to say I was placed on the staff of the army under Sir J. Moore from the 25th. I in consequence lost no time to finish my packing up, and proceeded from Hollington on the 27th with my wife and children to Seven Oakes and the next day to town. The weather had been uncommonly severe, snow and extreme hard frost until the morning of the 27th, when a gentle thaw and mild rain came on; notwithstanding which the travelling was very good as the roads were not broke up; reached London by one o'clock on the 28th. On my arrival in town I learnt from the adjutant general I was to proceed to Corunna with Major-General Fergusson. It was intended I should have gone with General Sherbrooke, but in consequence of the illness of Major-General Spencer, Sherbrooke was appointed to his command.

★★★★★★

Sir John Moore (1761-1809); ensign 1776; at St. Lucia 1796; in Holland 1799; in Egypt 1801; under Sir Harry Burrard 1808; killed at Corunna 1809.

Sir John Coape Sherbrooke (1764-1830); at Seringapatam 1799; Wellesley's second in command in the Peninsular campaign 1809; governor-general of Canada 1816-18.

★★★★★★

On the 3rd January (1809) I attended the Duke of York's *levée*, and on the 4th paid my duty to the king at his *levée* and was graciously received.

8th.—I left London for the purpose of embarking to join the army in Spain. My wife and dear children left town at the same time to go to Brighton, where she intended to remain during my absence. Her sisters were at Brighton and had invited her to stay with them, but her visit was not to be very long at their house. The parting from my dear wife and sweet babes is too much even for me to describe. She, poor soul, had a bad sore throat and was far from well, and our little boy had been vaccinated and was otherwise a little peevish on account of his health.

The day was as dismal as possible from incessant rain; the *tout ensemble* made me as miserable a being as ever existed. We parted at

Hyde Park Turnpikes, my wife proceeded to Ryegate to sleep, and I, with melancholy wretchedness as my companion, took the road for Portsmouth, where I arrived between eleven and twelve at night. I was hurried away from town at a short notice, not having been made acquainted to a certainty until the day before, *how* or *where* I was to go from. The commander-in-chief's secretary wrote to me to say an application was made to the Admiralty for a passage for me to Corunna, but I heard no further until I called two or three days after upon Captain Hope, (Sir William Johnstone Hope—1766-1831), one of the Lords of the Admiralty, (1807-9), who told me an order was sent to Portsmouth for to carry me out with Major-General Fergusson at the time the troops (then embarked) proceeded under the orders of Major-General Sherbrooke.

But I had no further communication from the commander-in-chief's office on the subject, although Hope told me an answer had been sent to the secretary the day the application was made, and that office was surely the proper channel through which I ought to have received my information. Captain Hope told me on Saturday I had no time to lose as the convoy was ordered to sail immediately and the frigate I was to go on board was one of the convoy, and therefore, as I before mentioned, I took my departure the following day.

On my arrival at Portsmouth I learnt the news of Sir John Moore having been obliged to retreat, and on the Monday morning the 9th instructions arrived with the post admiral at Portsmouth to delay the sailing of the fleet. Major-General Sherbrooke was in command of the expedition then embarked, which consisted of a brigade of Guards under the orders of Brigadier-General Campbell and a brigade of the line under Major-General Tilson; and the arrangement was made for my embarking in the *Isis*, a fifty gun ship, with Generals Tilson and Campbell, and General Fergusson was to embark with General Sherbrooke in the *Niobe* frigate. No instructions were sent to General Sherbrooke respecting the delay on sailing. We formed a mess of the general officers and established an ordinary at the George Inn.

On the 11th the agent of transports received a letter from his board to say the fleet *was to sail immediately*, and the admiral by the same post received instructions still *to delay it*; and at the same time an order came from the transport board to disembark three hundred artillery horses that had only been embarked two days before.

This made many people imagine it was a previous step to the disembarkation of the whole. In this state of suspense we continued until the afternoon of the 13th, Friday, when a messenger arrived for all the light transports and those with recruits for the several corps in Spain to proceed instantly, under the convoy of the *Fisguard* frigate, on board of which General Fergusson and myself were to embark, and the troops under convoy of the *Isis* to proceed at the same time under sealed orders; however Lord Castlereagh's instructions to General Sherbrooke were so curious and apparently so confused, that the general was under the necessity of sending back to the Secretary of State for an *explanatory;* his Lordship having in the first instance desired the general to proceed *immediately*, taking with him a company of artillery that had arrived that morning; but on the general inquiring if the transports were ready to receive the artillery, he was told the ships could not possibly be in a state to receive the men *until the 17th.*

General Sherbrooke was therefore obliged to send to Lord Castlereagh to know whether he was to wait for the artillery. Our convoy was settled and as the wind was fine, we were hurried off and sent on board at ten o'clock on the 14th in the morning, and the fuss and the impetuousness of the admiral (Montagu), was such that he would scarce give us time to put our baggage on board.

★★★★★★

Robert Stewart, Viscount Castlereagh (1769-1822); statesman; second Marquis of Londonderry.

Sir George Montagu (1750-1829); commander-in-chief at Portsmouth 1803.

★★★★★★

The party embarked on board the *Fisguard* consisted of Major-General Fergusson and his two *aides-de-camp*, Captain Mellish and Count Grimaldi; the former the celebrated man of that name, who after squandering away a vast fortune with the Prince of Wales, turned his attention to a military life, and at the request of the prince, General Fergusson took him as an extra *aide-de-camp.* The latter, the count, was a nephew of one of the French princes, and was another extra *aide-de-camp* given Fergusson by Lord Norris (?). My *aide-de-camp* was my nephew and former *aide-de-camp* Thurstan Dale. We sailed from Spithead about two o'clock with a fair wind and proceeded through the Needles, the light transports following; it was night and dark before we cleared the Needles, when the captain of the frigate (Boulton) lay too and waited for the convoy.

However the next morning not a single ship was to be seen, notwithstanding we waited until two o'clock in the day. As the wind was fair and blew fresh, the captain determined to make sail, concluding that the convoy was ahead of us. We accordingly stood on down Channel without anything particular occurring. It was singular to reflect on the situation and change of Captain Mellish's condition, from having lived in a style of high life, considered a first rate Buck of the age, racing for more money than any other individual of his day, the *companion* and friend of H.R.H. the Prince of Wales; now become the companion of a *cabin* and humble attendant on a *Major-General* as *aide-de-camp*.

Monday the 16th.—We were supposed to have cleared the Channel, but no appearance of our convoy. I could not help feeling particularly anxious on their account as my horses were on board one of the ships. In the hurry of our sailing from Portsmouth my horses and those of General Fergusson's were ordered to be taken out of the ship in which they had been embarked and put into another transport, and this ceremony was to take place at Spithead. However, the *transhipping* took place without any accident.

19th.—Very fine morning; spoke a transport brig from Corunna that gave us sad and melancholy news; he said the troops had been nearly cut to pieces, and that very few had embarked; that all the fleet had sailed from the bay, but did not mention their destination. This intelligence was most unwelcome. The master of the brig said he was bound to England and had sailed the evening before under convoy of a gun brig. Our anxiety to fall in with the fleet and to gain further information was great, and for which purpose the captain of the frigate altered his course as the more probable means of meeting some of the vessels. Felt a most visible change of climate since we sailed from England; the weather today as mild as a fine April.

Friday 20th.—Nothing could be more perplexing than our state of anxiety respecting the unfavourable news we had received from the brig yesterday, and most arduously did we look out for a strange sail. The morning was fine, and the wind had shifted in our favour, but as we had got considerably low down into the Bay of Biscay, we were supposed out of the track of anything homeward bound, and not sufficiently near the coast to fall in with any of our cruisers. The wind in the evening increased and blew hard, but unfortunately the wrong way and instead of gaining we lost distance.

The waves might certainly be said to be mountains high, for when the brig was very nearly close to us, she at times totally disappeared from our view. It is a great satisfaction being on board a man-of-war in a gale of wind comparatively speaking with a merchant ship, as you feel so much greater security in the former. The weather was violent, and the rain so incessant I did not go upon deck the whole day. It was singular that the subject of the psalm for the morning service of the day, should have applied so peculiarly to our situation in a gale of wind. Captain Boulton mentioned a curious circumstance respecting the quantity of canvas that might be used when all sails were set in the ship. He said he had calculated the quantity, and that it amounted to 11,050 square yards. We all dined today in the gun-room with the officers of the ship. It is the custom on board men-of-war for the captain to dine with the officers on a Sunday, and as we soldiers were the captain's guests, we of course were invited.

23rd.—At four o'clock in the morning of the 23rd land was discovered, which proved to be Cape Ortegal on the coast of Spain. We were pretty close in when we got up and saw a brig to windward. The gale had very much abated in the night, and we had great hopes of speaking the brig and obtaining some information respecting the army; but our hopes were frustrated, and our anxiety was still kept alive with dismal apprehensions for the events we were to receive. The weather became very fine, but the wind against us. The season felt as mild as the month of April in England.

Never was suspense more uncomfortable than ours, and the conjecture of what had really occurred to Sir John Moore's army was as desponding as possible. (The Battle of Corunna, in which Moore was killed, took place on January 16, after which Soult occupied Oporto).

In the afternoon it blew very fresh; saw a strange sail, and made a signal to speak her. She had troops on board, and said she had been blown out of Vigo, and was going to Corunna. It was Captain Boulton's intention to have sent a boat on board her for one of the officers belonging to the troops, for the purpose of obtaining some information respecting Sir John Moore, but a most unfortunate accident occurred in the attempt to lower a boat.

Five sailors had got into the boat; by the neglect of the boatswain, the boat upset, and the unfortunate men were all precipitated into the sea. Two of them clung to the boat, and were hauled on board; two more got hold of oars that floated from the boat, and after being in the sea for half an hour (during which time a second boat was sent to their assistance), they were miraculously saved, as the sea at the time ran very high with a heavy swell; the fifth man, melancholy to say, was not seen after the boat upset alongside. This sad accident threw a gloom over us, and prevented any further attempt to speak the brig, or to send on board her. We also felt much disappointment in being again prevented obtaining any intelligence from the army. Casualties of this nature in large societies like a ship's company are soon forgot, and the loss of a companion did not in the smallest degree affect the common detail, and the poor man was no sooner gone from this world, than his memory seemed obliterated from the minds of his associates.

The boat was entirely lost, and as a top-gallant mast had been washed over the day before, I could not help feeling a certain sensation that an occurrence of this nature might occasion alarm, should the boat and top-mast be picked up at sea, and known to belong to the *Fisguard*. How many untoward stories have originated from less probable circumstances? We stood for the land in the evening.

24th.—In the night another gale of wind came on, and it blew extremely hard the next morning. We were sitting at breakfast in the cabin, when a wave struck the ship, and in consequence of our all clinging to the table hands and feet, the lashings gave way, and coffee, tea, ham, biscuits, generals, *aides-de-camp,* sailors, etc., were sprawling on the floor, paddling away in different fluids, some with a slice of ham plaistered to his cheek, others with his eye closed by a pat of butter: it was the most ridiculous scene possible.

Very fortunately nobody was hurt either from hot tea or broken tea-cups. The gale lulled towards the afternoon, and we had fine weather in the evening. It was the first night I had slept with any degree of comfort since we had been at sea. The ship had been so incessantly agitated and tossed about, it was quite impossible for a landsman, and that from an inland country, to get any repose. It was nearly calm most of the night and the next morning. Delightful and mild weather like midsummer in England, and with the little wind there was, tolerably fair.

26th.—Thick hazy weather, but to our great astonishment about twelve o'clock, through the haze, we saw a large man-of-war close alongside of us, and soon afterwards observed a fleet. On exchanging signals, the man-of-war was the *Alfred* of 74. Captain Boulton went on board of her, having first hailed her, and learning she was convoying to England the sad and last remains of Sir John Moore's army. Soon after

Captain Boulton had arrived on board the *Alfred*, a signal was made to express that the general officers on board the *Fisguard* were to go on board the *Alfred* to return to England.

This summons we considered as a most fortunate event, for had we not by the merest accident fallen in with this fleet, we could not conjecture what was to have become of us, the French being in possession of Corunna, Vigo, Oporto, and probably of Lisbon and Cadiz: and as the *Fisguard* was under particular sealed orders to proceed, after landing us at Corunna, it is not possible to conjecture what we could have done under such circumstances.

On arriving on board the *Alfred*, we found General Craufurd, and General Alten, the latter of the King's German Legion: each of them had the command of a brigade embarked in the fleets and which had gone on board at Vigo, having been detached by General Moore from Astorga when he began his retreat. We learned that they had received intelligence at sea the day after they sailed from Vigo, that a severe action had taken place at Corunna, in which Sir J. Moore had been killed and Sir D. Baird lost an arm, but no further particulars excepting that the loss on the part of the British was dreadful. The captain of the *Alfred* (Hay) had no positive intelligence as to where the fleet under Admirals De Courcy and Sir Samuel Hood had sailed for.

******

Robert Craufurd (1764-1812); lieutenant-colonel 1797; served against the Irish rebels 1798; killed at Ciudad Rodrigo 1812.

Sir Charles, Count von Alten (1764-1840); of a Protestant Hanoverian family; served in Hanoverian Army 1781-1803; joined the British army 1803; held command 1805-15.

Sir Samuel Hood (1762-1814); created baronet after Corunna 1809; vice-admiral 1811.

******

Captain Hay was to receive his orders from a ship that was to speak him off Cape Finisterre; but not having fallen in with her, he decided to proceed for England, The *Alfred* was crowded at the time we were added to the crew, having on board a great part of the 95th regiment with a detachment of the 43rd. We were thirteen officers in the cabin; however, we managed to stow away very comfortably. After we had been in bed about an hour, there was an alarm that an enemy's line-of-battle ship was in sight, and in consequence everybody was called to quarters, and the necessary preparations made for battle. I began to regret having left the frigate, not wishing to partake of a sea-fight. On the enemy coming near us, she was discovered to be the companion of our voyage, and proved the *Hindostan* of fifty guns, which ship was convoy with the *Alfred*.

It was quite ridiculous to see the effect occasioned by the alarm, and if His Majesty's ships are all in the like state of confusion when going into action, I can't understand how they come off triumphant. General Fergusson's *aide-de-camp*, Le Comte Grimaldi, said the alarm had one good effect, 'it made them clean their cannon.' We had a most delightful wind, going seven and eight knots.

27th, Friday.—Fine day and fine wind, though getting perceptibly colder.

28th.—I was much amused with the accounts of the campaign, and found General Craufurd a most intelligent and pleasant man. The wind continuing fair and the fleet all in sight. We expect to make the land early tomorrow morning. How little did I suppose, on leaving England, that my first letter to my dear Eleanor would be from *England*. How uncertain are all the expectations of this world; instead of being on shore as was determined, it came on very thick weather in the night, which continued the next day and blew very strong.

29th.—We were fearful of approaching the shore on account of the very hazy state of the weather. However, about five o'clock in the evening, we got sight of land and which was conjectured to be somewhere off Exmouth. Although there was a chaplain on board we had no service on Sunday, on account of the blowing state of the weather.

30th.—The next morning at daylight we made sail (having lain too all night after making the land), soon after it came to blow, and so thick and hazy there was no seeing a mile. It increased towards noon to a perfect hurricane, and the master assured us, though he had been at sea twenty-five years, he never experienced so violent a gale of wind. Our situation became extremely alarming as the wind was dead on shore, and no certainty as to our situation.

We could carry no sail, and merely drifted away before the wind. Very fortunately the wind shifted in our favour about two o'clock, and we were able to keep clear of the land. Still the gale continued, and it appeared as if the ship would have been blown out of the water. I must own I felt a good deal alarmed, and a tear started when I thought on my dear wife and sweet children. As night came on our situation became more awful, although it was fortunately full moon. Still the thought of driving away before the wind, uncertain as to where we were going and not knowing whether we might not every instant go on shore, occasioned sensations to arise better imagined than I can relate.

We all lay down about nine o'clock, though with little prospect of sleep; but it was not possible to keep our feet in the cabin or sit upon a chair, necessity compelled us to go to bed. Divine Providence protected us, and the gale began to lull about eleven o'clock and cleared up for a fine evening. As to dinner or even sitting at a table it was quite out of the question. The scenes of confusion and uproar in the cabin, occasioned by the violence of the sea, was sometimes ridiculous. The rudder-head was unshipped in the after-cabin, and everything upon it, consisting of boots, boxes, baskets, decanters of wine, glasses, etc. etc., all went smash in a heap on the cabin floor. I shall never forget the day and nights, or the very awful sentiments the occasion imposed. God Almighty in his infinite mercy protected us, and I humbly offered my thanks to the Divine Providence for His goodness. The next morning the weather was as calm as possible, and like a May morning.

31st.—As soon as it was light we made the land, which we found to be the Isle of Wight. There was very little or no wind all the morning, and we did not reach St. Helen's until six o'clock. Two line-of-battle ships were lying there. Our captain went on board one of them and brought us a newspaper, from which we learnt the accounts of the proceedings at Corunna as also the melancholy fate of the *Primrose* brig, that was intended to have been companion to the *Fisguard* and formed part of our convoy.

She sailed from Portsmouth at the time we did, but got aground off Lymington and remained a few days with the transports. In going down Channel she was totally lost off Plymouth, and every soul on board perished. The gale we had encountered on the 30th had made sad havoc in Portsmouth harbour, sixteen transports having been driven on shore. Several of the *Alfred's* convoy had not arrived, and for whose fate serious apprehensions were entertained.

February 1.—I landed the next morning, after the ship had moved up to Spithead. It is impossible to imagine anything at all like the streets of Portsmouth from the crowds of officers, soldiers, dragoons, and dragoon horses; as the greater part of the troops from Corunna were disembarking; such miserable, tattered beings I never saw, so wan and worn out, both with respect to drapery and general appearance, was never before exhibited. I remained in Portsmouth no longer than was necessary to land my baggage, and proceeded to Godalming, where I enjoyed the comforts of a fireside and a good bed once more in old England. I never saw anything like the roads from the incessant rain; and in consequence of the great run, the horses were all done up.

2nd.—I did not reach town the next day until near four o'clock. Went immediately to the Horse Guards and reported myself to the adjutant-general. On my way along Pall Mall I found my agent's house (Mr. Bruce's) had been burnt down that morning. I was under alarm, for some property of mine was lodged there, plate, etc., to the amount of near £1000, but it was fortunately saved. My nephew, Thurstan, and I took a comfortable dinner *tête-à-tête* at the Blenheim coffee house.

8th.—Went next day to Windsor to pay my duty to their Majesties, and never was anything so very gracious as both the king and queen. His Majesty did not return from London until nine o'clock, when the gentlemen in attendance were sent for up. I was immediately called to their Majesties, and kept in conversation until they went to supper.

9th.—The next morning, Tuesday, attended His Majesty to chapel, and afterwards to ride in the park. I was much rejoiced to find the king's sight so well. In every other respect I never saw His Majesty better. The king returned about twelve, and the princesses rode an hour longer. In the evening I had the honour to play Commerce at their Majesties' table. The king requires great assistance to make out the cards; however he gets through it and it appears to amuse him. His Majesty won the pool.

March 20.—Remained at Brighton with my family until the middle of the month when, having received orders to be placed on the Home Staff and to be stationed at Winchester, I quitted Brighton, bag and baggage, slept at Havant and set up my standard the next day, 21st, at Winchester, having previously taken a house belonging to one of the prebends of the cathedral.

May 2.—Went to Sir William Pitt's for a night; found poor Sir William getting very old and infirm, but otherwise tolerably well for a man at eighty-four. Lady Pitt uncommonly well. The next morning proceeded to London on horseback for the purpose of paying my duty at the drawing-room on the 4th. Her Majesty had been unwell and had not had a drawing-room for a very long time. The queen very gracious, and I was invited by the Princess Mary to the queen's house in the evening; not a large party. His Majesty uncommonly well and very gracious. I had the honour of playing Commerce and instructing the Princess Charlotte Augusta of Wales in the mysteries of the game, (1796-1817, only child of George IV). She is a lively, fine girl and promises to be handsome.

28th.—Went with my wife to Hartford Bridge in our way to London for the purpose of paying our duty at Court on the king's birthday. Arrived in town by three o'clock on the *29th*. The drawing-room was crowded to a degree seldom known. Mrs. Dyott went with the Marchioness Donegal. I was invited to the queen's house on the 6th June.

We left town on the 9th; slept at Hartford Bridge, and arrived at Winton early next day, and rejoiced to find our children quite well. I was told by the adjutant-general in London, that I was to be moved from Winton, as it was intended to withdraw all the troops in consequence of the barracks not being safe for their accommodation.

The move from Winchester turned out what I little expected, as on the 24th I received a letter from adjutant-general to say I probably should be immediately appointed to the command of a brigade for service, and accordingly on the 1st July I had a further communication to inform me I was July to go without delay to the Isle of Thanet, to take the command of a brigade consisting of the 6th, 50th, and 91st regiments, and to report myself to Lieutenant-General the Marquis of Huntley, who was to command the 2nd division of the army preparing to embark under the orders of Lord Chatham.

★★★★★★

George Gordon, Marquis of Huntly and fifth Duke of Gordon (1770-1836); lieutenant-general 1808; general 1819.

John Pitt, second Earl of Chatham (1756-1835); master of the ordnance 1801-6; commanded the Walcheren Expedition 1809; general 1812; governor of Gibraltar 1820-35.

★★★★★★

This deranged my domestic tranquillity pretty considerably, and I was again to undergo the sad task of separation from my dear wife and sweet children, a task not easily to be described, and scarcely to be endured. I have had to experience this dismal trial no less than three times in the last year and a half; I do most sincerely hope this may be the finish to all the melancholy scenes of this nature.

11th.—I called next morning on Lieutenant-General Sir John Hope, who was commanding at Canterbury, and a very old acquaintance. He pressed me to stay to dinner, which I could not refuse, and in consequence I took the opportunity of walking out to call upon my old acquaintance Mrs. Fawcitt, who looked as well as I ever saw her. After a pleasant dinner with my friend Hope, I proceeded in the evening to Ramsgate.

12th.—My brigadier-major (Captain Colclough) had arrived two or three days before, and taken a lodging for me. The next morning I received a letter from my dear wife with most comfortable accounts both of her and my sweet children. I found the 6th and 50th regiments at Ramsgate, and the 91st quartered at Margate. I saw the 50th regiment paraded on the sands in the afternoon, a very fine battalion; and dined at the tavern.

13th.—Inspected the Sixth regiment on Thursday, and the 91st on Friday, 14th; the latter regiment not so strong in numbers as either of the others. Lieutenant-General the Marquis of Huntley arrived in the evening of Thursday. I called upon him next morning, and like his manner and appearance very much. I dined with Lieutenant-Colonel Walker commanding the 50th regiment. He had his family with him, and I could not help commiserating their situation.

15th.—I had ordered all my brigade to parade Saturday morning at seven o'clock, and was in the act of forming the line when Lord Huntley came to tell me he had received orders for immediate embarkation. This, of course, put an end to our parade, and the troops returned to their quarters to pack up finally for their berths on board ship. All was hurry and bustle. I was at breakfast at nine o'clock and received a message from the marquis to say the first intention was changed; the men were not to embark on board men of war as originally proposed, but to go on board transports. *Orders and counter orders.*

At twelve it was discovered that no orders positive had been received for the embarkation to take place, and this was not discovered until Lord Huntly had taken his departure for Deal to visit the admiral, when all former orders were suspended and a consultation held as to whether the communication received amounted to orders for embarking. I decided it did not, and therefore the embarking was postponed until Lord Huntley's return from his interview with the admiral at Deal.

I had a letter from my dear Eleanor on Thursday, and a small parcel this morning, containing two shirts in addition to my stock which I thought it advisable to send for, and by the opportunity I heard again from my darling dears at Winchester. My brigade was embarked, as a further order arrived in the afternoon for that purpose. The three regiments were soon on board, and sailed into the Downs in the course of the night. I dined with Lord Huntley.

16th.—The 38th regiment from Deal arrived and embarked. I attended Divine Service in the afternoon, and dined with Mr. Marsden, an old Dublin acquaintance. All the week passed in preparation of embarking troops, stores, etc. etc. If the object to be gained equals the extent employed, it must prove of great magnitude to England.

22nd.—The wind was easterly, which prevented the division embarked at Portsmouth from going in the Downs. I experienced great civility and kindness from Mr. Marsden, who with the family were residing at Ramsgate for the summer. He was under-secretary to the Irish Government, when I was quartered in Dublin, and a sensible intelligent good sort of man. He invited me to dinner almost every day, and I accepted his kindness pretty often and found it highly preferable to the noise and bustle of the tavern, which was daily crowded to excess. Saturday the 22nd I dined with Lord Chatham; not a very comfortable feast, as we were thirteen crowded into a small room, and did not dine until seven o'clock, as his lordship had been to Deal.

23rd.—Thurston and I attended Divine Service at the Parish Church. I received a letter as usual (daily) from my dear Eleanor with comfortable accounts of her and sweet babies. Hearing of them and writing to Eleanor was the only comfort I had. We were kept in hourly suspense, expecting hourly to go on board, but the unfavourable state of the wind prevented the Portsmouth division of ships reaching the Downs until the 27th, on which day the Marquis Huntley, Brigadier-General Montressor, and myself embarked in a yacht of Sir William Curtis's, and after partaking of a good dinner I was put on board the *Hussar* frigate in the Downs (Captain Skene), and Lord Huntley on board Commodore Owen, the naval officer to superintend the Marquis Huntley's division.

★★★★★★

Later General Montressor is mentioned as Sir Henry Montressor.

Sir William Curtis (1752-1829); lord mayor of London 1795; created a baronet 1802; friend of George IV.

Sir Edward Campbell Owen (1771-1849); admiral 1846.

★★★★★★

So powerful an expedition was never assembled by Great Britain. It consisted of 2000 cavalry; 2000 artillery men; 34,000 infantry; and on the morning of the 28th at six o'clock the first division sailed for its intended destination, with the wind at SW.

30th-31st.—Just before the evening closed we saw the land on the Flanders Coast, and were then satisfied our destination was the Scheldt. The fleet anchored for the night, and got under weigh at daylight the next morning and stood in for the land.

August.—The main body of the army under Lord Chatham had proceeded to the attack of the island of 1809 Walcheren at the entrance of the Scheldt; and Lord Huntley's division was to have made a landing on the island of Cadsand for the purpose of taking possession of the batteries that guard the entrance of the Scheldt opposite the island of Walcheren; but on our anchoring near Cadsand we found our means not equal to the attempt, as the Commodore (Owen) could not land more than six hundred men at one time, there not being boats for more. But notwithstanding, we were kept in a state of hourly suspense from the 29th July until the 4th August, when the commodore received instructions from the admiral commanding the fleet, Sir Richard Strachan, to say we were to join the headquarters of the army at Walcheren.

★★★★★★

Sir Richard Strachan (1760-1824); fourth baronet; naval commander of the ill-fated Walcheren Expedition 1809.

The Earl of Chatham, with sword drawn
Stood waiting for Sir Richard Strachan;
Sir Richard, longing to be at 'em,
Stood waiting for the Earl of Chatham.

★★★★★★

The constant state of suspense we had been kept in was irksome in the extreme. Three or four times we had made every preparation to land, the boats alongside, and the troops all prepared; but as the enemy appeared in great force, and were strongly defended by cannon and works, it was fortunate we did not attempt to get on shore, as in all probability the six hundred men we embarked would have been sacrificed.

5th.—It was a singular circumstance that during the whole time we were detached, our Lieutenant-General Lord Huntley should have received no communication whatever from Lord Chatham, and that every proceeding was under the direction of the navy. On the 4th we experienced a very heavy gale of wind, which continued until twelve o'clock at night. We were at anchor with a shoal sand-bank on one side of us, and the enemy's coast on the other. We had two anchors out, but dragged notwithstanding; however, we rode out the gale.

6th.—And on the 5th anchored near the line-of-battle ships with the fleet on the side of the island of Walcheren, near Campvere. In the night it blew a tremendous gale of wind. In coming in we got aground, as had several of the line-of-battle ships. There never was such a sea, or such a navigation.

7th.—I went on shore and walked to Middleburg, the headquarters and largest town in the island of Walcheren. It is uncommonly well built, clean, and a remarkable handsome place. The left wing of the army, under Lieutenant-General Sir Eyre Coote, effected a landing without opposition on the island of Walcheren on the 31st July and proceeded to the attack of Tarvere or Campvere, a fortified place on the north side of the island, which surrendered the next day, as did the town of Middleburg in the centre after sending out a deputation from the inhabitants.

A division of the army was immediately pushed on for the attack of Flushing, a large town and strongly fortified both to the land and sea, and where the French had a numerous garrison and showed every determination to defend the place to all extremity. All the island of Walcheren had belonged to the Dutch until the French Revolution, when Flushing was taken possession of by Buonaparte, he leaving all the other part of the island to the King of Holland. (General Pichegru conquered Holland, December 1794). Flushing held out with great obstinacy until the 15th, when it surrendered conditionally.

8th.—On the 8th Lord Huntley's division disembarked on the island of South Beveland, which is divided by the Scheldt from Walcheren, and where the division of the army under Lieutenant-General Sir John Hope, had been landed without opposition when Sir Eyre Coote landed on Walcheren. Beveland is a part of the province of Zeeland, and like Holland, a perfect flat, highly cultivated, and the soil as rich as it is possible for the earth to be, full of dykes, ditches, and drains, and, of course, at particular seasons extremely unhealthy. The island is intersected by high banks that have been originally formed to keep out the sea, and that are in general planted.

The small towers and all the habitations are as clean and neat as can be. The people are very industrious, civil, and obliging. The horses are very fine and all alike; a strong, handsome draught horse with long tails, and so docile that children drive them. My brigade moved to some small villages on the south side the island near the Scheldt. I was quartered at a village called Borasland, and was put up in a large house tolerably comfortable.

10th.—I received orders to be president of a general court-martial to assemble at Tar-Vere in Walcheren, to which place I returned on the 11th and expected to be away two days, and was kept seven.

13th.—On the 13th I went to Middleburg to see the batteries open against Flushing. I went to the top of the church at Middleburg, from whence I could observe everything that was going forward. It was a tremendous sight to see the dreadful ingenuity of man exerted in the destruction of his fellow creatures. We had sixty pieces of heavy ordnance opened at once, besides the ships of war, and a new species of warlike annoyance consisting of fire rockets, which are discharged and thrown into a town or elsewhere, and which set fire to whatever they come in contact with. Flushing had near one hundred pieces of ordnance to resist all this. The fire from the besieging army and from the besieged was most awful.

14th.—On the next day eight line-of-battle ships moved up close to the town and began a heavy cannonade; notwithstanding, and although the town was on fire in many places, Monnet, the French general, held out until the 15th in the evening, when on being summoned, he agreed after some time of hesitation to surrender and the terms were concluded in the evening. Our loss amounted to upwards of eight hundred men killed and wounded, with a proportion of officers. The French lost nearly double.

16th.—The next day I went into Flushing and so sad a spectacle I never saw. There was not a house that had not been shot through and through, many battered to dust, and many others burnt to ashes. The large church and town house, both vast piles of buildings, were consumed by fire, and it was supposed between five and six hundred inhabitants perished in the various ruins. It is utterly impossible to describe the horror and dismay exhibited in the countenances of the poor, miserable, wretched beings observable in the streets, who remained to lament the loss of their family and friends.

18th.—On Friday the 18th, the garrison of Flushing, consisting of near six thousand men, marched out according to the terms of the capitulation and laid down their arms. The whole were embarked on board the men of war that had brought out part of our troops, and proceeded immediately for England. I went to see the ceremony of the garrison laying down their arms.

Lord Chatham and all the general officers belonging to the part of the army in Walcheren were present, as the whole was under arms and formed a line from the gates of Flushing to the spot appointed, where the arms were to be piled. Lord Chatham took a station and the French marched past him.

General Monnet, the governor, was by Lord Chatham during the ceremony. Some of the regiments were as fine looking men as I ever saw; but all very dirty and miserably dressed. Immediately after the ceremony was over I returned to Middleburg, and as the general court-martial was concluded and approved by Lord Chatham, I proceeded on to my brigade in South Beveland and arrived at Borasland to dinner.

I was obliged to travel fifteen miles in a Dutch waggon and was tolerably well jumbled. The German Light Brigade and General Grosvenor's division of the army were ordered to North Beveland, and we concluded that directions would be given for our moving on nearer the scene of our ulterior object at Antwerp. (Thomas Grosvenor— 1764-1851; commanded brigades in Copenhagen 1807; and in Walcheren Expedition 1809; general 1819; field-marshal 1846).

19th.—I rode to call upon Lord Huntley and afterwards to the town of Ter Goes, the capital of the island. It is not so large as Middleburg, but like it as to good buildings and clean streets. The weather has been constantly since our arrival stormy, wet, and very unsettled, though at times intensely hot.

20th, Sunday.—And sorry to remark, no appearance of the Sabbath as we had no chaplain, nor either prayer-book or bible. Admiral Lord Gardner with four sail of the line was anchored in the Scheldt near my quarters at Borasland. (Alan Gardner, first Baron Gardner—1742-1809; lord of the admiralty 1790-5; created a baronet 1794; peer of the United Kingdom 1806).

21st.—I endeavoured to persuade him to come on shore to take a ride. His Lordship; Captain Codrington, his captain; and Captain Legge took a ride on my horses. I did not attend them, as I went to Barsland to see the 91st regiment, and dined afterwards at Montressor's quarters with the General. Lord Chatham arrived in the island from Walcheren and made the headquarters of the army at Ter Goes.

22nd.—I dined on Tuesday with Lord Huntley.

23rd.—And next day gave a dinner to all the field officers of my brigade. We dined ten; pretty well for a campaign dinner. My *aide-de-camp*, Thurstan, assisted in the kitchen, and our cookery under his directions and the execution of a butcher of the 8th regiment, we made out very well. Lord Chatham again moved headquarters to the advance of the army to a place called Crabbersdyh.

26th.—Great sickness prevailed in the army; it broke out very suddenly, and made its appearance in all the corps. Fevers in general, and some dysenteries. We had a great deal of rain and very unsettled weather.

27th.—I wrote to my dear Eleanor, having received two letters from her of the 15th and 20th. A council of the lieutenant-generals was assembled at headquarters, when it was decided that all operations against Antwerp were impracticable in consequence of the force it was known the French had collected (from the long delay that had taken place in our proceedings in the island of Walcheren), 35,000 men. They had also erected batteries in all directions, and to effectually stop our proceedings, they had inundated all the neighbouring country.

28th.—This decision occasioned orders for the army in South Beveland to break up. Some brigades were ordered to England, and the whole of the cavalry which had not disembarked were to return home immediately. I with my brigade was unfortunately ordered to remain to garrison the island of Walcheren, much against my inclination on account of my dear wife's confinement, which was to be expected the beginning of October and at which we had both promised ourselves to be together.

30th.—My brigade marched from Borasland on the 30th and crossed the Scheldt and arrived at Middleburg. The sickness had increased very considerably and the arrangements made to accommodate them were most shameful; when the sick arrived on the Walcheren side and were taken out of the boats there was no means for many hours of conveying them to Walcheren, nor did waggons arrive for the purpose for ten hours after they landed.

31st.—We found very considerable sickness in all the corps at Middleburg and increasing to an alarming degree. To me there appeared much want of exertion to meet the difficulty arising from crowded hospitals and the shocking places allotted as barracks for the troops.

September 1.—Generals Grosvenor, Lord Paget, Houston, Disney, Graham, and Picton gone home on account of sickness; and notwithstanding the alarming increase of the malady no steps of any consequence taken either for the removal of the sick or for their better accommodation.

★★★★★★

Sir Moore Disney (1766?-184.6); fought in the Peninsular War; major-general 1809; commanded 1st brigade of Guards in Walcheren.

Thomas Graham, Baron Lynedoch (1748-1843); Sir J. Moore's *aide-de-camp* in the Corunna campaign; commanded brigade in Walcheren Expedition; created a peer 1814.

Sir Thomas Picton (1758-1815) 1 lieutenant-general; took part in siege and capture of Flushing; appointed governor of Flushing; invalided home.

★★★★★★

7th.—In my brigade, which consisted of 2400 men, I had 1024 sick. The 6th regiment in my brigade, 900 strong, had 501 sick, and the 23rd regiment had not one man to do duty. The mortality had not hitherto been considerable in proportion to the number of patients. But from the state of the hospitals great losses must be expected. I never (thanks be to Divine Providence), was in better health in my life.

8th.—My *aide-de-camp*, Thurstan Dale, was seized with the fever of the country and was very unwell. He was much alarmed, and I never saw a man so low spirited or apparently more frightened in my life. I was quite satisfied home was the only place to cure him, and therefore I lost no time in acquainting him with my intentions to send him to England.

13th.—And accordingly on the 13th I obtained a passage for him with Lord Amelius Beauclerk, (1771-1846; admiral), to Portsmouth. The sickness continued to a great degree amongst the troops and the mortality great. In the army left in Walcheren consisting of about 14,000, there were near 8000 sick.

14th.—On the 14th Lord Chatham at last embarked for England. He had been detained by contrary winds for several days. I should imagine his lordship's feelings must be uncomfortable, as the newspapers had been most liberal in their abuse of him. The weather for some days had been cool and comfortable. Sir Eyre Coote was left commander-in-chief on Lord Chatham's departure and I was second in command. Sir Eyre took me from my brigade and appointed me to superintend all the troops in the island. The sickness amongst the troops became most alarming.

18th.—On the 18th my brigade-major (Colclough) was so unwell I was obliged to send him to England, which left me without a staff officer. I attended Sir Eyre Coote to visit all the hospitals in the island on the 16th and 17th, and a more wretched melancholy duty no man ever performed; indeed I don't suppose it ever fell to the lot of a British officer to visit in the course of three days the sick chambers of nearly 8000 unfortunate men in fevers; and the miserable, dirty, stinking holes some of the troops were from necessity crammed into, was more shocking than it is possible to express. The sick of the army on the 17th was:—

> 235 officers,
> 379 sergeants,
> 140 drummers,
> 8141 rank and file,
> ———
> 8895

and daily increasing.

20th.—On the 20th Sir Eyre Coote sent an *aide-de-camp* to England, to report in person the serious situation we were in.

24th.—I visited the hospitals in Middleburg, and never did I behold such shocking objects as the various wards exhibited. We had constant gales of wind and with violent rain. The admiral, Sir Richard Strachan, had been embarked for some days with the expectation of sailing for England, but could not move on account of the violence of the weather.

On the 24th the sick amounted to:—

191 officers,
377 sergeants,
145 drummers,
7813 rank and file,

——

8526

The deaths in the previous week had amounted to 287.

29th.—Dreadful weather for the season of the year; rain, gales of wind, thunder and violent hailstorms. Thanks to ;the all ruling Providence, I kept my health amidst all the dreadful scenes of disease and death, not having experienced a moment's sickness since I came to Holland.

October.—The month of October began with fine weather; frosty mornings, and easterly wind on the 3rd. One thousand of our unfortunate sick were embarked for England. I made an inspection of the barracks at Flushing. I was distressed to see in what miserable places the soldiers were put up. In one house I found fifteen men belonging to the 5th regiment in a room scarce twelve feet square and with twelve of the men sick, and nothing but a couple of blankets to lie down upon.

8th.—Looking forward with great anxiety for the arrival of the packet, in hopes of hearing that I should have leave to return to my dear family.

The packet arrived, but no leave. Instead of it a letter from the adjutant-general to say my application must be made through the officer commanding this army. Accordingly I had to write to Sir Eyre Coote, who was kind enough to forward an application recommending that I should have leave, particularly as Major-General Moncrief had arrived. Near three thousand sick were sent to England, and notwithstanding the fineness of the weather, the disease did not abate in the manner expected, and the convalescents did not gain strength, and such as were obliged to return to the hospitals did not recover.

22nd.—Major-General Lord Dalhousie arrived, and therefore I looked forward with great hope that the answer to Sir Eyre Coote's application would be favourable. (George, ninth Earl of Dalhousie—1770-1838; distinguished himself at Waterloo; created a peer of the United Kingdom 1815).

24th.—On the 24th Lieutenant-General Don arrived to relieve Sir Eyre Coote. (Sir George Don—1754-1832; lieutenant-governor of Gibraltar 1814).

25th.—All the troops in Middleburg attended Divine Service to commemorate the day, his Majesty having entered the fiftieth year of his reign. The brigades had not paraded since the sickness commenced. What a melancholy and dreadful falling off in their appearance; from being six as fine regiments as ever paraded, they were reduced to a handful, and those looking sickly, pale, and wretched. The weather uncommonly fine during the whole month of October.

29th.—By the packet which arrived on the 29th, I expected to receive my leave to return to England, and was grievously disappointed. However, General Don very good-humouredly (as he had not the power to grant me leave) made an excuse to send me home with despatches, and I accordingly to my great joy took my departure from Walcheren on Tuesday the 31st by the packet, having slept on Monday night on board the *Revenge*, Captain Charles Paget, lying off Flushing. (Sir Charles Paget—1778-1839; fifth son of the ninth Baron Paget and brother of the first Marquis of Anglesey).

November 1.—Landed at Harwich the next morning and reached London in the evening and delivered my despatches. . I was kept in town to see Lord Liverpool, the Secretary of State, as also the commander-in-chief until the 5th, (Robert Banks Jenkinson, second earl of Liverpool—1770-1828; succeeded his father in 1808; secretary for war and the colonies 1809-12; premier 1812-27).

Proceeded for Winchester by way of Windsor, where I called to pay my duty to the king for half an hour and reached home to dinner, and made most happy to find my dear wife and sweet children quite well. My little girl Eleanor knew me directly, but little Dickey had forgot me.

7th.—On the 7th I went to town by the mail to pay my duty to His Majesty at the *levée* on the 8th, and returned to Winchester next day.

13th.—On the 13th I was seized with an attack of the Walcheren fever, which continued fourteen days. The same day my dear wife was safely delivered of a boy, our third child. She had a very good time, and soon recovered her health; the poor baby caught cold the day after its birth, which settled in its eyes and was very troublesome for some time.

28th.—I went to Windsor on a visit to their Majesties, and was most graciously received,

December 2.—Stayed there until the 2nd December and returned to Winchester. I had a present of a frock, cap and coral from the queen and princesses for our new born babe. His Majesty was uncommonly well and his sight not worse than when I was at Windsor in January.

January 16.—On the 16th January I went to London for the purpose of paying my duty at the drawing-room in honour of Her Majesty's birthday. To my very great surprise I received a communication the next day from the adjutant-general specifying my being ordered to join the army in Portugal under Lord Wellington, (Arthur Wellesley, Duke of Wellington—1769-1852).

But from the situation of my private affairs and having so recently been separated from my family, I asked permission to decline the staff altogether, which was agreed to, and for the first time after twenty-nine years service, I found myself a gentleman at large.

22nd.—On the 22nd I left Winchester with my family March to pass some time at Leamington in Warwickshire (an edition of Cheltenham). We travelled self, wife, three children, and two maid-servants in our own carriage with a pair of post-horses as leaders. Slept first night at Ilsley, the next at North Aston and to our cottage at Leamington the third. Delightful weather for our journey and with the exception of one stage, from Banbury to Southam, found the roads remarkably good.

April 28.—On the 28th we received a melancholy account of the serious indisposition of our dear good mother, who had been seized at Butt House, where she had gone on the 23rd, to make a visit to the Lees. My brother Phillip came from Butt House on the 29th, and brought the sad tidings that my poor mother could not recover. She remained with her usual sweetness of disposition, serenity, and composure until the 3rd May, when she was called by an all-ruling Providence to a better world at the great age of eighty-six. The world never contained a more amiable, more moral, or more religious woman, or a more kind parent, or more affectionate wife. Her happiness consisted in contributing all in her power to afford comfort and happiness to those about her, and certainly no mother was ever more beloved by affectionate and dutiful children than she was.

May 16th.—On the 16th I rode to Freeford, and stayed two nights;

returned to Leamington on the 18th, and on the 20th I went by the Coventry coach to London with an intention of proceeding to Windsor to pay my duty to their Majesties, but in consequence of the dangerous state of the Princess Amelia's health, (a confirmed invalid for two years), which I learned on my arrival in town, I put off my visit.

I had a communication from the adjutant-general to say I was to be placed on the staff for a short time with eight other general officers for the purpose of inspecting the local militia, and was to be attached to the Severn district. I accordingly made an application to General Ward commanding the district for my orders, and found I was to have the inspection of the regiments in South Wales.

24th.—I left town on the 24th, and got to Leamington next morning, where I only remained one night, and proceeded by way of Stratford-on-Avon, Alcester, Evesham, Tewkesbury, Gloster, Ross, Monmouth, Usk, and Newport to Cardiff to inspect the East Glamorgan Battalion on the 28th. Returned that day to Newport, and inspected the Monmouth West Battalion, and proceeded in the afternoon by Pontypool and Abergavenny to Brecon to inspect the East Brecon, which took place next morning.

29th.—In the afternoon I went by Abergavenny to Monmouth, and inspected the 30th, the West Monmouth Battalions. Found the regiment commanded by an old friend, Lieut.-Colonel Molyneux, who had been a shipmate with me when I went to America. I left Monmouth in the evening, and went as far as Ledbury by way of Ross, and proceeded next morning to Worcester, Alcester, Stratford, and to Leamington.

June 4.—On the 4th we broke up our camp at Leamington, and in consequence of my sister Mary having offered us the use of my poor mother's house at Whittington, we took possession bag and baggage. We found the old mansion most comfortable, but I frequently felt the loss of my dear good mother, who had been the mistress and worthy inhabitant so many years.

July 17.—I stayed in London the 17th, and went to Windsor next day; was graciously received by the king and queen and by all the Royal Family. Had the honour of playing at their Majesties' table at Commerce in the evening. I was sorry to find our good king's sight become so indifferent. He was obliged to be led about, and could merely distinguish light from dark. I never saw His Majesty's general health better or in better spirits. He rides every morning, but his horse is led, or he has a person riding on each side of him. I remained at Windsor a week, and never experienced more gracious attention than all the time of my visit. Lady Louisa Lennox, Lord and Lady Markhen (?), and Lord and Lady Bathurst were staying at Lord Harcourt's in the neighbourhood of Windsor.

★★★★★★

Henry, third Earl of Bathurst (1762-1834); married Georgiana, third daughter of Lord George Henry Lennox.
William Harcourt, third Earl Harcourt (1743-1830); succeeded his brother 1809; general 1796; field-marshal 1820.

★★★★★★

I dined at Lord Harcourt's one of the days, and returned to walk the Terrace at Windsor in the afternoon. The king and two of the princesses walked the terrace every evening. His Majesty was conducted by his two daughters, an afflicting sight, and seemed to have an impression on everybody. Numbers of people most evenings, but on Sunday a concourse.

August.—I called upon the adjutant-general in London, who asked me if I wished to be put on the home staff. I told him I should be very glad, provided I was not to be called upon suddenly for foreign service. I was surprised and much gratified to find in a few days after I returned to Whittington to receive a notification to say I was appointed to succeed Lieut.-General Craufurd in the command of the Ireland district, and to have my headquarters at Lichfield; this was an hour of gratification I little expected.

In consequence, I took the house in Lichfield belonging to Mr. Carey, adjoining the old Vicar's Hall, but remained in the old mansion at Whittington until September, having previously sent for my goods and chattels which I had left at Winchester.

20th.—The weather was uncommon warm in September, which prevented good shooting; however, I enjoyed myself much, not having had an opportunity of being in Staffordshire at this season for many years. The races took place at the usual period, and were tolerably well attended, but nothing like what they were formerly. They did me the honour to appoint me Steward with Sir Oswald Mosley for the next year.

January 1811.—A great deal of frost and cold weather in January; shooting most days with tolerable success. I went to Beaudesert for a day's shooting with Lord Paget, (first Marquis of Anglesey), and never saw so much game in so short a time. We were not out more than three hours, and killed twenty-five pheasants, seven hares, and four rabbits. His lordship slayed far the greater part. We went to Wichnor to stay two nights with Thomas Levett.

March.—On the 4th I entertained the corporation of the city at dinner to commemorate the day our ancestor killed Lord Brooke during the Siege of Lichfield Cathedral. All very jolly and sociable.

✶✶✶✶✶✶

Shaw, in his *History and Antiquities of Staffordshire*, i., writes: 'Clarendon says it was a common soldier; but others say it was Dumb Dyott, so called because he was deaf and dumb; and no doubt, he was one of that loyal family, and most probably one of the six sons of Sir Richard. . . . His eldest son Anthony was major of a regiment of foot in the army of Charles I. Mathew, his third son, was a captain of horse, . . . and Michael, sixth son, a captain also. . . . Uniform tradition has handed down the fact of its being a gentleman of the name of Dyott who killed Lord Brooke; and the late Mr. Green . . . caused a marble tablet to be set up against the wall of the small house in Dam-street, with the following inscription:

> March 2, 1643, Lord Brooke, a general of the parliament forces, preparing to besiege the close of Lichfield, garrisoned for King Charles I., received his death-wound on the spot beneath this inscription, by a shot in the forehead from Mr. Dyott, a gentleman who had placed himself on the battlements of the great steeple to annoy the besiegers.'

✶✶✶✶✶✶

18th.— On the 18th I was obliged to give up the house I had at Lichfield, my landlord, Mr. Carey, having sold it. In consequence I was reduced to the necessity of purchasing an habitation, as there was not a house in Lichfield to be let. I bought from Mr. Parr the house in Tamworth Street that formerly belonged to Mrs. Porter, the daughter-in-law, (stepdaughter), of the celebrated Dr. Johnson.

✶✶✶✶✶✶

Samuel Johnson (1709-1784); son of a Lichfield bookseller; married Mrs. Porter 1735; the famous controversialist and lexicographer.

★★★★★★

As my new purchase was unfurnished and required some alterations, we removed all hands to Whittington, and resumed our former station in my poor old mother's house. The latter end of March we were honoured by an invitation to Shuckborough, and paid a visit for two days. I never witnessed more splendour or great hospitality than at Lord Anson's.

★★★★★★

Thomas Anson, Viscount Anson (1767-1818); married Anne, daughter of Thomas Coke of Holkham; created Viscount Anson and Baron Soberton 1806.

★★★★★★

We had delightful weather and a most gracious visit. The months of March and April the finest season ever remembered, and in consequence the earliest spring.

May 29.—On the 29th I went to Stafford to inspect the East regiment, under the command of Lieut.-Colonel Wilson; a miserable rainy day, and the men in the field standing over their shoes in water.

31st.—On the 31st I went to Wolverhampton to inspect the Western regiment under the command of Sir John Wrottesley. I received a very polite invitation from Sir John to go to Wrottesley, but declined and returned home to dinner.

June 4.—The Southern regiment had assembled at Lichfield on the 25th under the command of Sir Robert Lawly, and on the 4th June I had a gala parade in honour of the birthday of our gracious king. The corps assembled were the 7th Dragoon Guards, a squadron of the 14th Dragoons, six troops Staffordshire Yeomanry and the South Stafford local militia. The line assembled on Whittington Heath and made a very handsome appearance. The day was fine and collected a vast concourse of people. I gave a dinner to fifty at the Swan; my house not being finished at Lichfield I was still living at Whittington.

July.—Went to London to pay my respects to the Duke July of York, on his being reappointed to the command of the army.

★★★★★★

The Duke of York had been removed from the head of the army in 1809 in consequence of the conduct of his mistress, Mrs. Mary Anne Clarke, who was bribed to use her influence to obtain army promotions from the duke.

His Majesty King George III.

★★★★★★

2nd.—Attended His Royal Highness's *levée* the next day, and was in hopes to have had the honour of being at a *levée* of the prince regent's, but he had given up the intention of having any more *levées* for the present. I therefore made my excuse through Colonel Bloomfield for not having been in London before.

★★★★★★

Benjamin Bloomfield (1768-1846); chief equerry to the Prince of Wales c, 1806; major-general 1814; knighted 1815; minister plenipotentiary at Stockholm 1824; raised to the Irish peerage 1825.

★★★★★★

10th.—On the 10th September Lichfield races; I was one of the stewards with Sir Oswald Mosley. (Sir Oswald Mosley born 1785; succeeded his grandfather 1798; M.P. for the northern division of Staffordshire).

A good deal of company, and but little sport as to racing.

What a change in the appearance of the Heath, with respect to carriages, compared with the races five-and-twenty years ago, when there were generally ten coaches and six, and a dozen coaches and four; now the only set of horses was Lord Stafford's, and three or four coaches and four.

November 7th.—On the 7th I was ordered to Nottingham by a letter from the commander-in-chief's secretary in consequence of the alarming riots that existed in that town and neighbourhood. The stocking manufacturers had committed great outrages by breaking the stocking-frames of such of their employers as would not increase the price of wages.

★★★★★★

The Luddite rioters broke frames throughout Nottinghamshire, Derbyshire, and Leicestershire. The streets of Nottingham were placarded with notices offering rewards for the delivery of the mayor, dead or alive, to the Luddites. Finally, seven regiments had to be drafted into the district to keep order. Joseph Heathcoat, the inventor of a lace machine, left Loughborough in disgust after his machines were broken and set up at Tiverton.

★★★★★★

I remained at Nottingham until the 14th, having distributed the 15th Dragoons and Berkshire Militia in the several villages where disturbances had happened to keep the peace, and proceeded to Lough-borough to attend a meeting of magistrates of the county of Leicester, there having been some symptoms of discontent in that country; but the appearance of a military force prevented any repetition of outrage, and I returned to Lichfield on the 15th.

January, February, and March 1812.—Living quietly and comfortably at home, enjoying the delights of domestic life,.

April 1.—Set out with my wife Eleanor and Dick to London. Slept at Dunchurch and Brickhill, and reached town on the 3rd. Travelled with our own horses. We had apartments at Warner's Hotel in Con-duit Street, but when disengaged lived with our aunt and sister in Grosvenor Square.

15th.—On the 15th I attended the prince regent's *levée* at Carlton House and was graciously received. I wished to have paid my duty at Windsor, but did not know how far it might be proper in the lamen-table state of the king's health. (The death of Princess Amelia, in the autumn of 1810, upset the intellect of George III. for the last time).

I wrote to Colonel Taylor on the subject, (Sir Herbert Taylor—1775-1839; secretary to the Duke of York 1794, to George in. 1805, to Queen Charlotte and William IV.), and received a gracious message to say the queen would wish me to pay a visit, and which I proposed to have done, but was ordered down to Lichfield on the 30th April in consequence of the disturbance that still continued in the county. A system of dissatisfaction had seized the manufacturers generally, and had appeared in an alarming posture in Cheshire and Lancashire, which occasioned a considerable force to be collected at Manchester, as also at Nottingham and in parts of Yorkshire.

30th.—I left town on the 30th and reached Lichfield on the 2nd May with my children, having left Mrs. Dyott with her sister in Lon-don.

3rd.—Lieut.-General Maitland came to Lichfield on the May 3rd, having been sent to take the command of this and the north-west district and to fix his headquarters at Manchester. I was left by myself, as Mrs. Dyott did not return from London till the end of June. In con-sequence of the disturbed state of the country and the system of or-ganisation that was discovered amongst the manufacturers, a camp was ordered to be formed in the neighbourhood of Lichfield, and which took place on Sutton Coldfield near the village of Little Hay on the

11th June, consisting of a brigade of Royal Artillery, two squadrons 7th Dragoon Guards, the Sussex and the Edinburgh militias.

On the 1st June I went to Newcastle to inspect Colonel Wilson's regiment of local militia; returned by Stafford and saw Colonel Chetwynd's, and on the 3rd went to Wolverhampton to see Sir John Wrottesley's regiment. Very wet weather all the month of June.

October.—On the 13th October I went to Manchester to be president of a general court-martial which continued sitting until the 20th. Was much disappointed with the town of Manchester, which I had expected to have found much better built and more regular.

November 16.—On the 16th November self and wife set out for London, where we remained until the 27th; I went to Windsor on the 18th to pay my duty to the queen and princesses. It had a most melancholy appearance, when the deplorable situation of the good king was considered. Her Majesty was most gracious, and when I took my leave was pleased to say she was obliged to me for my visit, and should always be glad to see me at Windsor when I had nothing better to do.

★★★★★★

Editor's note: This point terminates General Dyott's associations with a military life and so the remainder of his diary has been excluded from this edition.

www.ingramcontent.com/pod-product-compliance
Lightning Source LLC
Chambersburg PA
CBHW032050080426
42733CB00006B/221